STORIES

FROM THE

DIRT

INDISCRETIONS OF
AN ADVENTURE JUNKIE

JOHN LONG

FALCON ®

Guilford, Connecticut

FALCON

An imprint of Globe Pequot
Falcon and FalconGuides are registered trademarks and Make Adventure Your Story is a
trademark of Rowman & Littlefield.

Distributed by NATIONAL BOOK NETWORK

Copyright © 2017 John Long

Cover design by Diana Nuhn
Front cover photo © iStock.com/vovik_mar; back cover photo by Dean Fidelman

British Library Cataloguing in Publication Information available

Library of Congress Cataloging-in-Publication Data available

ISBN 978-1-4930-3095-8 (paperback)
ISBN 978-1-4930-3096-5 (e-book)

♾™ The paper used in this publication meets the minimum requirements of American
National Standard for Information Sciences—Permanence of Paper for Printed Library
Materials, ANSI/NISO Z39.48-1992.

Printed in the United States of America

Contents

Author's Note

MOST OF these stories were written (over 3 decades) for magazines or journals, meaning they were all one-offs. They were never written to be "of a piece." With so many miscellaneous parts, it made sense to order them in some way. But instead of starting at the beginning, I've put most of the last ones I wrote up front. That way instead of getting tired and jaded, we get younger and more reckless as we go. *Andale, pues!*

Foreword

Swimming for It

By Jeff Jackson

J OHN LONG and Dwight Brooks were somewhere deep in the interior of Papua New Guinea talking to an official named Tsigayaptwektago Sorari who they'd found by reading the disciplinary reports in the Record Bureau in southwest Enga. As they plied him with questions, Sorari spun out a fantastic story ("Bikpela Hol," p. 130) about a huge cave that was home to a 1,000-foot serpent. The site was a 17-day march, Sorari explained, adding that the people along the way were possessed by evil bush spirits.

It was the mid-1980s and Long was working as a producer for the TV show *The Guinness Book of World Records*, dreaming up mad world-record stunts like the longest Tyrolean traverse, the highest BASE jump, longest rappel, etc. Not only did he concoct these exploits, but sometimes he pulled them off himself. This trip to the unexplored Gulf Province of Papua New Guinea was a scouting mission. So, propelled by his own gonzo-adventure ethic and . . . well . . . because it actually *was* his job, he and Brooks enlisted the help of two local boys and set out for the cave with the giant snake.

Fourteen days later, they hacked through the last bit of undergrowth and arrived at a limestone cliff ripped by a cavern. Undeterred by the proverbial snake, they waded down into the passage and followed it for six hours until it funneled into a pool of standing water that disappeared into a rock wall.

"We'll swim for it," Brooks said.

"Swim for what?"

WHEN IT comes to writing adventure-travel narrative nobody— and I mean nobody—can do it like John Long. For one thing, nobody got as far out there as Long. For a quarter century Largo (Long's nickname) charged hard, establishing the world's hardest rock climbs, exploring jungles, and even finding his way to the North Pole.

But it's not just his prowess as an adventurer that sets Long apart. He's a darn good writer, too, with a one-of-a-kind style— tight prose with spirited verbs and stories that seem to pick the reader up and transport her to someplace entirely other.

I had the pleasure of discovering Long's writing in the late 1970s and for a long time his book of collected stories, *Gorilla Monsoon*, was something of a hybrid writing manual cum Bible to me. I read and reread stories, underlined passages and stole from it all I could steal on my way to becoming a writer myself. You could say *Gorilla Monsoon* changed my life. Years passed and then, with the kismet of a John Long story, this book, *Stories from the Dirt*, an updated collection of Long's stories, landed in my hands to edit.

I glanced through the table of contents. Some of the stories were old favorites, some were brand new. There was only one thing to do. Like Brooks and Long in the mythical cave in New Guinea, I took a deep breath, and dove in—as should you.

Ripcord

YOSEMITE VALLEY. Dawn. Mike Lechlinski and I are just stirring in our hammocks, lashed high on the granite face of El Capitan, when we hear a whooshing sound, louder and closer, building to a roar. Rock fall. Falling right for us. We're dead.

Of course the upper wall is gently overhanging so any falling objects will harmlessly sail past. But I've heard that sound before, when Michael Blake's body plunged past me during my first attempt to climb The Captain. So I instinctively brace for impact and the end of the world as two BASE jumpers streak right over our heads at 120 miles per hour.

We scream, craning our heads from our hammocks, our eyes following the jumpers diving into the void, their arms dove-tailing back as they track away from the cliff, the pop of their chutes firing up the wall like shotgun blasts. They swoop over treetops and land 50 feet into the meadow. A beater station wagon rumbles up and screeches to a stop on the loop road as the jumpers bundle up their canopies, jog over, and quickly drive off. This last bit looks sped up, like a Keystone Cop caper, and we howl because we're still there, still alive. "I think I pissed myself," says Mike.

On a scale of one to a shitload, this 60-second lark is off the chart.

IN 1984 the adventure world—including this quite illegal BASE jump—was catching fire and anyone in that orbit was expected to blaze like hell. From our first sorties free climbing big walls to *jungleering* across Oceana, the mantra never changed: *Capture the fucking flag.* Our cousins in big wave surfing, kayaking, cave diving, and mountain biking were charging just as hard and we watched our group fever—a regular epidemic by 1980—trigger the X-treme adventure-sport craze. And the most visually dramatic show of them all was BASE jumping, the acronym for parachuting from a B: building, A: antenna, S: span (bridge), or E: earth (cliff).

Half a dozen years after my close encounter on El Cap, I needed something bold to gain traction in the TV business where I hoped to quickly score the trophy girls and crazy money. I was 2 months out of grad school, with a fistful of so-what degrees, tired of being poor and determined to leave Yosemite behind. But secretly I was not so much waving at the train as reaching for it, afraid of getting left behind.

David Paradine Television was a boutique production house with Sunset Boulevard offices, owned by the British talk-show maven and future Richard Nixon interviewer, David Frost. I hired on as an associate producer. The salary was moderate but my future shined. We had several hour-long *Guinness Book of World Records* specials that we needed to style out with electrifying content. The previous couple of episodes had featured a dull parade of magicians, carnivorous spiders, and an English mastiff named Claudius, said to be the world's largest dog. I was brought on to hose out the dog shit, so to speak, and boost the numbers.

I knew going in that staging world-class adventures for television was sketchy, but so what. I was handy with danger and eager to debut BASE jumping on primetime national television. The plan felt like money. The tricky bit was collaring someone to do the jumping.

My immediate boss, Ian, smooth, sardonic, and classically educated at Eton, was all for fielding exciting acts. BASE jumping was only one of several adventure pursuits, each riskier than the last, that I'd scribbled onto our dance card, and which the network, indemnified of responsibility, was eager to broadcast. Ratings were everything, of course, but in Jack Daniel's moments Ian sometimes asked, "We're not going to get anyone killed doing this, are we?"

"Not if I can help it," I said.

The stars aligned and in late June I flew to London and joined Carl Boenish and his wife, Jean. Carl, 43, later dubbed "the father of BASE jumping," was a free-fall cinematographer who in the 1970s had filmed the inaugural jumps from El Capitan, plus a host of jumps from high-rise buildings, antennas, and bridges. For sheer burn and ebullience, Carl was unique. Jean, 19 years Carl's junior, brainy, wholesome, and distant as polar ice, lived her life in a language I didn't understand.

From London, Carl, Jean, and I flew to Oslo. The Norwegian airlines were on strike, so we packed six duffel bags into a rental Volvo wagon and headed for the Troll Peaks in Romsdalen Valley, 8 hours north. The narrow road meandered through still green valleys, dark as tourmaline, laced with alpine streams and glinting under the midnight sun. When we stopped for beers at an inn (sodas for the Boenishes), I noticed the date, 1509, chiseled on the stone hearth.

Finally we crept into the sleepy town of Andalsnes, hedged on all sides by misty cliffs including the Trollveggen Wall, Europe's tallest vertical rock face—a brooding gneiss hulk featuring several notorious rock climbs, and the proposed site of our world-record BASE jump. Even in deep dusk I sensed the town was very small and very old. "Built when the mountain was built," I heard it said of Andalsnes.

I breakfasted on pickled cod, peanut butter, and black coffee, then we zigzagged up a steep road to the highest path and set out on a leg-busting trudge for Trollveggen's summit. We were joined by Fred Husoy, a young local and one of the finest adventure climbers in Europe. His intimate knowledge of the massif would figure large in locating our jump site.

We shouldered packs and started up shifty moraines toward a snowy col. Carl hiked so slowly that I finally took his pack, but halfway up he once more had fallen well behind. Fred pulled on his raincoat against the drizzle, insisting we pick it up or get blown off the mountain by afternoon storms. We slogged ankle-deep through a snowfield. When Carl caught up, wet clouds draped everything. No amount of coaxing could make him hike faster. Finally, a little stone hut 20 minutes shy of the summit ridge offered a welcome roof from the shower.

Carl limped in and collapsed. When he pulled up a pant leg, Fred and I stared. Just above the ankle, Carl's leg took a shocking jag, half an inch off plumb. I felt small and mean to have pushed him, wondering how he could hike at all with that leg.

"Jesus. When did that happen?" I asked.

His leg had snapped in a hang-gliding accident several years back, said Carl, laughing and clenching his way through a wonky exposition on natural healing.

"I don't know, Carl," I said. "An orthopod could surely fix that. It's hideous."

Carl swished the air with his hand. Who needed doctors when God Almighty would make things right? I watched his fingers tremble as he pulled up his sock, wondering if belief was the power that shaped his stubbornness. It felt incredible, and totally reckless, to stake my future on a man living off stardust and voodoo.

––––––––––

A WEEK before, we'd spent 5 days organizing at Carl's house in Hawthorne, a small suburb of L.A. From the moment I stepped through the door, Jean eyed me with steely reckoning, as though if she looked away I might pilfer the china. Her clothes, flawless though plain, and the house, so ordered and spotless, symbolized sobriety and decorum. Nothing admitted she and Carl dove off cliffs for a living.

As Carl raked through his garage full of gear, we'd talk—or rather he'd preach—about Baby Jesus, Coco Joe, or whoever. Suddenly Carl would dash to his piano and butcher some Brahms or Brubeck, then jump back into conversation, his drift ranging from electrical engineering to terra-cotta sculpture to trampolines and particle physics, galvanized by a screwy amalgam of mysticism and personal revelations. Often he would heave all this out in the same sprawling rant. Ian thought he was on LSD.

But Carl's laugh was so large and his fire so hot I found myself giddy by the inspired way he met the world. Every heart is all its own, but both of us were drawn to crazy shit. And in the brotherhood of adventurers, guys like Carl Boenish drove the bus.

Outside our little stone hut in the Troll Peaks, the shower slacked off and we continued up snowy slabs toward the summit ridge, a mile-long dinosaur back of sudden clefts, precarious boxcar blocks, and pinnacles digging into the sky. The whole ridge was so convoluted and multidimensional M. C. Escher couldn't have drawn it in his dreams.

Just off the ridge the wall dropped 6,000 feet to the Trondheim Valley. The rubbly slabs angled down behind us to a high glacial plateau where perpetual snow framed a tiny lake of aquamarine. Black and white clouds masked the ridge, cutting visibility to several hundred feet and making it hard to know where we were. Without Fred's knowledge of the labyrinthine summit backbone, I would have wandered blind.

The clouds parted for a moment and we lay belly-down and stuck our heads out over the vast, sucking drop. As the clouds converged, Carl rubbed his leg, laughed, grimaced, and laid out his requirements.

The wall beneath his launch must overhang for hundreds of feet, he said, long enough for a plunging BASE jumper to reach near-terminal velocity. Only at top speed, when the air became thick as water, could his lay-out positioning create enough horizontal draft to track—actually fly out and away from the wall to pop the chute, just as we had witnessed on El Capitan.

The new parachutes didn't simply drop vertically, but sported a three-to-one glide ratio—3 feet forward for every 1 foot down. Back then, it was not unheard of for twisted lines to deploy a chute backwards, wrenching the jumper around and into, not away from, the cliff.

"Here, that would be fatal," said Carl with raccoon eyes, peering back over the brink.

Just to our left, a striking, 200-foot-high spire canted off the lip like the Tower of Pisa. The most prominent spires along the ridgeline had long before been named after chess pieces. This one was called The Castle, later renamed Stabben Pinnacle, though I never learned why. An exit from the summit, hanging out over oblivion like that, had to be safer than leaping straight off the summit ridge, so it seemed an obvious feature to scout.

Carl hung back as Fred and I scrambled up the Stabben, running with water, to start rock tests. The top was a flat and shattered little parapet. We wobbled a trash-can-sized boulder over to the lip and shoved it off. Five, six . . . *Bam!*—a sound like mortar fire. Debris continued rattling down for ages.

"No good," said Carl, yelling up from the ridgeline. "Way too soon to impact."

We tried again. This time I leaned over the lip and watched the rock whiz downward, swallowed in fog 300 feet below. Three, four . . . *Bam!* My head snapped up. Had to be jutting ledges just below the fog line. We pushed off more rocks and kept hearing the quick, violent impact of stone on stone.

"Forget it," Carl yelled up. "Stabben will never do. It'd be crazy."

The flinty smell of shattered rock lofted up as Fred and I rappelled off the pinnacle and joined Carl. For another hour we continued with the rock tests, at successive points along the rubbly brink, and I could feel death watching, perhaps chuckling. That's what made it so heady to try to sort this out. But every rock we shouldered off dashed the wall after a few seconds. When lightning cracked all around, we ran for the valley. Carl hobbled slowly behind.

NORWEGIANS ARE a handsome people, normally demure, until you pull the cork on Friday afternoon and the *dritt* hits the *ventilere*. That night all the young people in town crammed into the pub in the downstairs part of my hotel where we drank Frydenlund like mad, chased it with beer, and danced to The Who. Several pitchers in, a tall brunette grabbed a handful of my shirt. She looked right through me, more curious than courageous, and unable to find the words. So I trotted out the only Norwegian phrase I had memorized from a handbook in my room: "*Hvorkan-jegkjøpe en vikinghjelm?*" (Where can I purchase a Viking helmet?)

"Are you a Viking?" she asked in flawless English.

I said I'd try to be one for her, and she said, "You are going to marry me."

That night I saw eternity and it looked like this: A girl and a boy dancing in a crowd on an unswept floor in a bar on a 1,000-year-old street.

Aud was her name and she was working some dreary retail job in Andalsnes during summer break from nursing school. We spent all of our free time together, and I learned there are moments where nothing is so grim as being alone. I was always basically alone, because I'd always been a shark who could only live in motion. Then Aud drew the restlessness out of me like a thorn, and I saw light leaking through a soul cracked open. Over the next month, as we got the jump site dialed in and waited for good weather, when I wasn't with Aud I usually was thinking about her.

The next day as Carl recovered in his hotel room, Fred and I humped back up to the summit ridge for the first of many recons, trying to locate a viable launch point. The existing world's longest BASE jump, first established 3 years before, exited the ridge well east and some 400 feet lower than Stabben Pinnacle. That left us to scour the quarter-mile-long serpentine ridge between Stabben and the old site—a confusing task for sure.

Over the following weeks, when we weren't kicking around the cloudy ramparts of Trollveggen, Fred and I would snag Aud and go bouldering on huge, mossy erratics, or hike up the back side of spectacular peaks or along jagged ridges snaking through the sky. I was 26; Fred and Aud were in their early 20s, all of us charter adults, carving out our place in the world. But for a suspended moment, we shared an enchantment.

Twice more Fred and I explored the summit ridge, ever dashed by hailstorms. Meanwhile, Ian watched the rain wash our budget into the talus, and my inability to nail down a jump site was wearing us out. The urgency to jump and be finished was real because Norway was the end of the production schedule, and the crew looked toward Paris, the Greek Islands, or home. We had to get this done.

On the ninth scout, after a nasty piece of scrambling and several tension traverses on crappy rock, we located what we knew was the highest possible exit from the ridge—The Bishop, to use the old chess name. But again, we got weathered off before we could begin rock tests.

We returned early the next day and lucky for us the sky was all blue distance, the entire ridge fantastically visible and spilling down on both sides for thousands of feet. After wandering about up there in the fog all those weeks it felt like getting paroled to finally see the whole rambling cordillera unmasked like that. We definitely were on the apex, walking unroped on a made-to-order, 10-by-50-foot ledge terminating in an abyss as sudden and arresting as the lip of the Grand Canyon.

Lashed taut to two separate lines, I bent over the drop and started lobbing off bowling-ball-sized rocks while Fred timed the free fall. The rocks whizzed and accelerated ferociously and dropped clean from sight. Twelve, 13 . . . I looked over at Fred and smiled. This could be it. Seventeen, 18 . . . *BANG!* I had to squint to see the puff of white smoke thousands of feet below.

That rock had just free-fallen farther than Half Dome is high. No question, The Bishop was our record site. Fred pointed out the original launch spot (or *exit site*), still far left and 300-something feet below. I chucked another rock and we watched it shrink to a pea and burst like a sneeze near the base, the echo volleying up from the amphitheater. I tried to imagine strapping on a chute and plunging off, but couldn't. And I couldn't yet imagine ever climbing this towering heap.

From a distance, Trollveggen was a colossus, a 2,000-foot-high talus slope topped by a 3,600-foot rock wall. At its steepest, the summit ridge overhung the base of the cliff by 160 feet. Up close, however, the greatest rock wall in Europe was all fractured statuary, a vertical rubble pile top to bottom. We ascended our fixed rope, reversed the traverse, and just as the first raindrops fell we hoofed for the valley with the good news.

For the next five days Aud, Fred, and I stayed glued to the Oslo news channel, glancing up through thundershowers for some telling blue patch and milling around the production HQ in the bottom of the hotel, living off chocolate scones and coffee. Helicopters were on standby, film cameras loaded, every angle reckoned, all logistics figured to the minute. Meanwhile, journalists throughout Scandinavia streamed into Andalsnes. The local paper started running full-page spreads in a town where the breaking news usually concerned someone hooking a record lunker in a local creek.

Approached and pried, Carl would laugh, then let fly with his exotic babbling as journalists feigned understanding but never took notes. Then Jean answered in two sentences of cold facts and figures. A celebrated Oslo stringer, a steel-eyed blonde with a tongue like a carving knife, worked a different line, citing previous jumping tragedies and questioning something that had every authority on edge. As hordes of admirers lined up to touch Carl's jumpsuit, she held, without ever saying, that the emperor had no clothes.

We slunk around. Rain fell in sheets. Tension mounted. With all the media hoopla, all the delays, emerging details raised the story's sails sky high. Norwegian television ran nightly updates. The big Oslo station sent a video truck. With a week's momentum the production took on the pomp and blather of Hollywood—precisely what I'd hoped to avoid. Several journalists took to quoting Carl directly. Quite naturally, the translation to Norwegian was problematic ("like Ted Hughes on peyote," Ian suggested), but the waiting game was somewhat relieved by trying to guess what the hell Carl was talking about.

All of Scandinavia stood by. Every day in limbo meant thousands of dollars lost to feed and liquor and house the crew and keep the circus in town. Suddenly there was an impatience for what required the most steadfast deliberation. Throughout, the Boenishes were ready to go. At 8 p.m., July 5, 1984, the weather finally broke.

We started scrambling, desperate to shoot something, even in bad light. In 2 hours, cameramen were choppered into position. Then the helicopter dumped Carl, Jean, Fred, and me into a small notch only 40 feet from the launch site on The Bishop. This avoided having to wheedle the Boenishes across the traverses that had given Fred and me fits.

Carl pulled on his flaming red jumpsuit and gamboled around with enough energy to charge a power plant. Jean began assiduous study of the launch site. I pitched off a rock that whistled into the night. Others followed to verify my estimates, but disclosed another hazard.

"Sure, they drop forever," laughed Carl, "and that's a good thing. But they're never more than 10 feet from the wall."

That left no margin for error. If they couldn't stick the perfect, horizontal free-fall position, if they carved the air even slightly back tilted—head higher than feet—they could possibly track backwards. Carl explained with his hands, one hand as the wall, the other for the jumper. When his hands smacked together, Fred and I cringed. Jean, cool as the Ramsdahl Fjord, seemed confident but rolled more stones toward the lip.

The light faded to a gray pall. Far below, the great stone amphitheater swallowed the night. Suddenly, the radio coughed out: "Come on, Long, let's get on with it!" The crew was freezing and the director of photography had declared it almost too dark to film.

"Hey," said Carl, suddenly lucid, "I can't be rushed to jump off this cliff, screaming past those ledges at midnight!"

I quoted this word for word into the radio, and the crew backed off. Rather than try a tandem jump—Jean first, followed closely by Carl—Carl decided to make a practice jump while the cameramen previewed and assessed the angles. The midnight sun was too low for full glory but a run-through was useful to dial in the details. The sky, though darkening, was clear and flawless, so with some little fortune we would enjoy another 12 hours of clear weather. After Carl's trial jump, we'd resume in a few hours, when full light returned.

Carl strapped on his parachute and I tried to capture his kinetic energy on film. But it was too dark to pull a focus. I packed away the Ariflex, grabbed a still camera, and turned to the drama before the jump.

"Ten minutes," said Carl, bug-eyed, jaw working, hands fidgety.

Jean helped Carl with the last straps. Cued by a week of front-page spreads, the road below was jammed with cars and people, headlights winking in 1 a.m. gloom.

"Five minutes," said Carl.

He pulled some streamers from his pack. Leaning off the ropes, I lobbed them off. No wind. They fell straight down, shrinking to a blur. Everything was *go*.

"One minute," said Carl, his voice high and tight.

He cinched his helmet and slid twitching fingers into white gloves. I pitched off a final rock and Carl tracked it, visualizing his line.

"Fifteen seconds."

He unclipped the rope and stepped up to the lip. Horns sounded below. I was tied off to several ropes, feet on the edge, with a panoramic view of it all. Carl's shoes tapped like a rhythm machine, eyes unfocused. He started his countdown, which Fred mimicked into the radio: "Four, three, two, one!"

And he was off.

Seeing someone jump straight off a cliff like this is so counter to a climber's instincts that Carl might as well have jumped into the next world. The void swallowed him alive and the sight of him streaking down the wall was more easily imagined than described. The air felt ripped from my chest.

After a few seconds Carl's arms went out to stabilize, his legs bending and straightening while his jumpsuit whipped like a flag. With roaring acceleration Carl passed several ledges with 10 feet to spare, body whooshing, ripping the air with a violent report. After 1,000 feet his arms snapped to his sides and he started flying horizontally away from the wall, tracking 50, 100, 150 feet, at 120 miles per hour, a swooping red dot. Thirteen seconds, 14, 15 . . .

Pop! His yellow chute unfurled big as a circus tent and he glided down to the meadow. The picture-perfect jump.

Fred and I crabbed back from the lip, looked at each other, and started laughing. Old Man Gravity had hurled Carl with such velocity and violence it sounded as though he was ripping the sky in half with his bare hands. Then at the zero hour as the ground rushed up, a swath of nylon and several yards of kite string cheated Old Man Gravity of certain death. We had to see it to believe it and then check with each other to make sure.

Back at the hotel at 3:30 a.m., it was chaos among the news crews, gnashing producers, frantic journalists, film loaders, battery chargers, pilots, and hangers-on, all guzzling espresso (club soda for the Boenishes) and ducking out to check for clouds. Everyone was anxious to get back to the Troll Wall, film the jump, and clear out. A chartered jet was gassed and awaited the crew once the filming was over, hopefully by noon.

At four o'clock I laid down with Aud for a short nap, but I was so charged with coffee and apprehension that it was impossible to even lie still.

At 6 a.m., two helicopters ground up through Persian blue skies and deposited us on The Bishop. Half an hour later, after some rock tests, and rechecking everything humanly possible, Jean tiptoed to the lip, Carl just behind her. I was 5 feet away, lashed to a rope, toes curled over the brink, shouldering a 16-mm film camera. A hundred feet straight out in space the helicopter yawed and hovered like a dragonfly. Fred gave the order to roll cameras and the Boenishes stepped off the lip and dropped into the void.

Jean later wrote: "Eyes fixed on the horizon, I raise my arms into a good exit position. Then from behind, 'Three! Two! One!' For an instant my eyes dart down to reaffirm one solid step before the open air. Go! One lunging step forward and I'm off, Carl right on my heels. Freedom! Silence accelerates into the rushing sound as my body rolls forward. I quickly realize that the last downward glance has been an indulgence now taking its toll, for I roll past the prone into a head-down dive which takes me too close to the wall. The first ledge is rushing towards me as I strain to keep from flipping over onto my back."

Through the viewfinder I saw Jean divebombing and start to cant over onto her back. I panicked and ripped away the camera to see her screaming down, missing the first ledge by a hair.

"Holy shit!" Fred yelled.

Jean somehow arched back to prone, her hands came back, and the duo swooped away from the wall, shrinking to colorful specks, still flying, 200 feet out, still free falling.

"Pull the chute!" I screamed.

Sixteen seconds, 17: *POP! POP!* It was history. A world record, no injuries.

Cameramen raved over the radios. Newsmen and bystanders swarmed the Boenishes after their pin-point landing. The world toppled off our shoulders. Fred and I were done, and drained.

It was all smiles, chocolate strawberries, and champagne back at the hotel (mint tea for Jean and Carl). Ian and I both thought we had a shot at an Emmy with this one and my career in television glowed. Aside from the delays, the show had gone without a hitch, but the crew was scrambling to pack and leave on the charter. Ian was so concerned about an accident that he hurried to clear out lest something happen retroactively. That afternoon the charter jetted for London and those left behind, including half the kids in Andalsnes, moved to the bar in the bottom of the hotel, where several storylines began to converge. I could never have guessed that the plot was just starting to thicken.

A NORWEGIAN named Stein Erik Gabrielsen and his fellow countryman Eric (last name unknown) had arrived in Andalsnes only hours before. When I met them in the bar, I figured they were two more Euro BASE jumpers drawn there by the big news, now splashed across Europe. In fact, while Fred, Carl, and I had been scouting Trollveggen's summit ridge, Stein and Eric (both working in America, and unaware of our plans) had purchased one-way tickets to Norway to attempt the world record jump off the Troll Wall, something they'd been planning for 3 years. They would have gotten the record, too, except they'd gone on a 10-day bender the moment they hooked up with friends in Oslo. Then a girl showed Stein the newspaper story about how Carl and Jean were already in Andalsnes, waiting for the clouds to lift.

Stein later wrote how he and Eric straightaway bolted for Andalsnes and arrived in late evening. With the midnight sun they walked to the base of the Troll Wall, anxious to scope out their record site. That's where they met "a drunk old Norwegian dude pointing at the cliffs in their ominous dark presence and saying, 'That is the Devil's mountain.'"

They walked back to town and spent their last *kroner* on beer at the pub where several dozen of us were just finishing our wrap party, a Hollywood tradition. I was the final holdover from the American production crew, there to settle accounts and hang with Aud. Stein and Eric, now flat broke, joined the bash only to learn the Boenishes had scooped them by a few hours. At best they could only repeat the record, the adventure-sports version of an asphalt cigar. Their consolation was sharing the $500 of production money I had left to spend on booze.

Stein and Eric found Carl, congratulated him, and asked about his launch site. Carl said he jumped from The Bishop. Stein had surveyed the ridge and felt The Castle (Stabben Pinnacle) looked higher. Carl said to check a chess set. The Bishop is always taller than The Castle. When Eric said that, regardless, he and Eric were going to jump The Castle the next day, "Carl became visibly nervous," Stein later wrote, "and suggested we all meet at their hotel for breakfast next morning around 10 a.m. Then they could go jump together." Pleased by the prospect of a free meal, Stein and Eric agreed. We closed down the bar and half-mashed on Aquavit, Aud and I staggered to her apartment and I passed out for 12 hours.

The following morning Stein and Eric met Jean at the hotel. Jean said Carl was in town, arranging their travel back to the States, and invited them to sit down to breakfast. An hour passed and still no Carl. Jean kept glancing at her watch, then out at the driveway, then back at the map of Trollveggen hanging on the wall. Finally Jean said she was sorry. She'd deceived them, but Carl had been afraid they would usurp his record so he'd left at sunrise to go jump The Castle. Jean figured he had already jumped and was probably at the landing field, waiting for a ride. Why didn't Stein and Eric take the rental Volvo and go pick him up, then head back up the mountain for round two? Jean needed to pack.

Stein and Eric drove to the landing zone in the big meadow around the time I started sorting gear and racking the bare minimum for a racehorse, 1-day ascent of the Troll Wall. I'd changed my mind a hundred times and finally I just couldn't blow off Europe's biggest cliff when it was right down the road.

I heard a quick rap on Aud's door, then in rushed Fred.

"Carl's been in an accident," he said, "and it looks bad."

A car accident? When I heard that Carl had supposedly hiked up at dawn, and had jumped from Stabben Pinnacle, I figured Jean was bluffing. After the last 2 days of humping around, Carl would be resting his bum leg for sure.

Our production had caused such a stir that for going on a week, jumpers like Stein and Eric had been streaming in from Sweden, Iceland, Denmark, and beyond; any accident had been theirs, I said, not Carl's. Fred shook his head. Carl had enlisted two teenage brothers, both local climbers, to hike him up. One of the boys, Arnstein Myskja, had witnessed Carl's accident and was there with Fred, trembling in his boots.

Ten minutes later I was dashing across peat bogs toward a vantage point with a clear view of the Troll Wall. I frantically glassed the lower face, nearly a mile away. Carl's body had to be somewhere on the lower slabs, but I examined every inch and saw nothing. Then I spotted his red parachute, unfurled and breeze blown on a shaded terrace. For 10 minutes the binoculars were frozen in my hands as I waited for some movement, a twitch.

"Goddamn it, Carl. Get up . . . signal . . ."

The red canopy billowed gently from the updraft.

"Carl!"

Fred drove up and put a hand on my shoulder. I followed him to a grassy field surrounding the grand manor of an expatriate British lord. A pall tumbled from gray clouds as the media streamed in, occasionally stealing glances our way. My center could not hold much longer; I was starting to fly apart. The police chief arrived and I told him what I'd seen. The part about no movement ended our conversation. I didn't have the courage to call Jean, but the chief did. Barely. Tears flowed from his eyes even though his voice remained stoic, calm, and sober. I will never forget his face as he talked with Jean.

"I . . . regret to inform you that your husband has been in an accident, and it doesn't look good."

This last detail was the bare truth and took enormous bravery to admit. I went outside and pulled on my harness. Nobody knew if Carl was dead, or even seriously injured, and I told everyone as much, confronting some with the news, yelling it. They nodded slowly and shrank away, huddling under trees, waiting.

The *whop*, *whop* of the giant rescue chopper ricocheted up the valley. It landed in a clearing, arching trees, buckling photographers, scaring all with its powerful thumping. Fred went and I stayed behind, shivering in a T-shirt and glaring straight up into the rain. Aud came over but I couldn't look at her. I thought about nothing, vaguely aware of the chopper's hammering pitch in the distance. When it returned the crew filed out, looking at the ground. Fred walked over. His face was terrible. Under the lenses of six photographers, we fled back to the lord's house.

"Stabben?!" I yelled. As a free citizen Carl could do as he pleased, but Stabben Pinnacle? Carl himself had called the site crazy.

The doctor, little more than 30 years old, requested that I go aboard to identify the body.

"For what?" I begged.

The doctor looked away, and I knew the ordeal was far from over, and that nobody was spared.

We walked through wet, knee-high grass toward the ship. Amber light glinted off new puddles. The day felt strange and fantastic.

We moved into the hold of the huge chopper and back to Carl's body, looking like he'd just laid down to get some weight off that bum leg. Regret was nowhere on his face and the young doctor and I stood there, mourning a life cut in half, gazing from death as if unhurt. But he'd screamed a music too high to scale, and the mountain got him. I was not so selfish to believe it was my doing, but the distance Carl had tracked away from us made me wonder.

I joined the crowd gathering on the grassy field, all of us looking blankly at each other—someone had to know why and how come. We watched the coroner and two policemen heft Carl's black-bagged body into a white van and roll off into the mist. It felt all wrong to leave it at that; but Carl could not die again. That was all. The end.

Fred and I silently drove to Aud's place and I wandered in a traceless land. Even Aud couldn't help me now. Why had Carl jumped from Stabben? I'd never felt such helpless confusion, and could have killed Carl a second time. That evening I went and found Arnstein, the oldest of the two teenage brothers who had guided Carl that morning.

It had taken them nearly 5 hours to basically short-rope Carl up the backside trail and up to the summit of Stabben Pinnacle. Carl conducted rock tests and in seconds, as before, they smashed off outcroppings jutting directly into the flight path. But Carl was hell-bent on going.

As Arnstein described to me and others, Carl was dead the moment he launched off the lip, or tried to. On his last exit step he stumbled and, unable to push off and get some little separation from the wall, he frantically tossed out his pilot chute.

With so little airspeed, it lazily fluttered up, slowly pulling his main chute out of the pack. One side of the chute's chambers filled with air and flew forward. With one side totally deflated, the inflated side wrenched the canopy sharply, whipping Carl around and into the cliff.

He continued tumbling down, said Arnstein, his lines and the canopy spooling around him like a cocoon. Five thousand feet later, Carl's tightly wound body impacted the lower slab "and bounced 30 feet in the air like a basketball."

Arnstein was so sickened by what he'd just seen—and shot on his Nikon—that he yanked the film from the roll so the images of Carl's last moments were lost forever.

A few days later, Jean hired several local climbers to hike her up to Stabben Pinnacle where she checked the site firsthand and did what a wife does where her husband has just died. Then she traversed the ridge to the original, 1981 launch site, jumped off and—I was told—touched down for a perfect meadow landing. Years later I read that she actually landed downwind, slammed on her face, and was dragged for over 50 yards. Other reports probably give a different account. The facts depend on who you talk to, and like a "real life" war story, nothing is absolutely true.

I found myself circling around Aud's room. For several weeks I'd agonized over leaving Norway without her—a puzzling concern for a nomad like me. But things were shifting. TV work stretched off like a cargo cult runway, inviting a rich future to appear. Then Carl crash-landed and it felt likely that I was one-and-done with production work.

Staring at the white stucco walls in Aud's tiny apartment, I couldn't see any future at all. I don't remember saying goodbye to Aud and Fred, but I must have. I only remember driving through the dark dawn shadow of the Troll Wall, heading for the airport in Molde. The giant cliff dominated the landscape, but thankfully it had weathered back in and I couldn't see the wall for all the clouds and rain.

OVER THE years, Carl and Jean's Norway jump became a seminal event in the short history of BASE jumping. I wasn't surprised when a producer called saying they were making a feature-length documentary on Carl, and could I come over to Andalsnes and do an interview? A paid trip to Europe sounded excellent and I found myself back in Norway soon after.

Everything about the Trondheim Valley, and that towering junker Trollveggen, was more impressive than what I remembered—which wasn't much. Andalsnes had modernized but still resembled a burg out of a Harry Potter novel. But my *feel* for the place was gone. Thirty years can blunt the sharpest memories. Mix in drink, work, a failed marriage and it's a wonder I remember anything.

Then I met back up with Fred and we went bouldering at the old haunts—the mushy fields and cow pies, the scabby orange lichen on the rock, staring up at the monstrous Troll Wall, talking and "doing the joking" as we got hosed on problems we'd once hiked in old Spanish Fire shoes—and the memories stirred. I talked to Aud on the phone and her voice pulled me back. But I still felt lost.

The next day I met the film crew at a grassy campground directly beneath Trollveggen, rearing up a mile beyond us. The director was a jocular young woman from Los Angeles, with loads of passionate intensity. The director of photography was a sloe-eyed Swede who'd tuck an entire tin of *snoose* behind his lower lip, then pace, mulling the next shot and spewing pools of brown juice like the spoor of a wounded elk.

The two went back and forth about the lighting, arguing like they meant it, so I didn't sit down for the interview till around noon, and by then it was raining.

They'd paid handsomely to get me there so I felt obliged to drop into deep thoughts and important feelings. But I couldn't elbow past my tough-guy noir. The director bore in. As I recounted the details, and Carl's eccentric stoke and fearlessness, the top layer didn't so much wear thin and translucent as things underneath started bubbling up. Yet I spoke without color owing to the gray way the past came back to me. Then the questions moved onto Stabben Pinnacle, and the rescue chopper, and standing in a drizzle and glaring straight up, and I slammed through the looking glass. For several minutes I said nothing, sinking lower in my chair. The rain beat down and we stopped filming. I didn't move.

The director pulled a blanket over my shoulders. For an instant I could see my life with jarring clarity as it ran from that July day in Andalsnes all those years before, and how my native love for cinematic narratives never made it off that rescue chopper. The part of me that can actually write was wedged like an iron strut between then and now, even as I continued to muddle along in productions I didn't believe in, without passion or inspiration, an also-ran in an industry made for me. This was a selfish take on "The Jump," as they were calling it, but to me, just then, Carl's death was the Godzilla that ruled my unconscious, setting me on my screwy course in life.

The next half-hour passed in a kind of hallucination. I'm not certain what I said, only that I meant every word of it, and it was mostly news to me. I normally measure my words, but I'd waited all these years to empty myself, never suspecting as much, so almost without choice I let it rip.

I came back to myself when the director asked why I thought Carl had risked a jump that he'd previously deemed fatal. This question had for years lingered over The Jump, adding texture and intrigue to the strangeness of Carl's last words.

As Arnstein had later told Stein Erik Gabrielsen, just as Carl stepped toward the edge of Stabben Pinnacle, he suddenly paused and asked, "Do you boys know the Bible?" Wide-eyed and breathless, they said, "Yes, of course."

"Remember when the Devil takes Jesus high up onto the Temple roof," asked Carl, "and tempts him to cast himself off, for surely the angels will rescue him?"

"Yes," Arnstein had said. He knew the story.

Carl reached one hand over the other shoulder, patted his parachute, and said, "I don't need angels."

Then he turned, took two steps toward the edge, and on the third step, he stumbled.

That night I sat alone in my room, trying to read. For years I'd stepped on the gas and whoosh—I was on the far side of life. But a slipstream lingered. Like perfume on a pillow. Like Aud.

We'd spoken several times and thought it best not to meet in person. But when I called and asked her to reconsider, she was in the lobby 10 minutes later. The woman had barely changed. Same stylish bob and crushing tenderness.

We stared at each other, stunned to remember that once we'd been young together. I could have ridden that feeling into the ground. Instead I powered up my laptop and showed Aud photos of my two daughters, Marjohny, with all the freckles, and Marianne, recently an MD, both stunners because they take after their mother. When Aud's daughter came to pick her up, I was staring at Aud herself, from way back when. It was crazy.

STEIN ERIK Gabrielsen and his friend Eric had barely arrived in Andalsnes when a local drunkard pointed to Trollveggen and said, "That is the Devil's mountain." Eight hours later, Carl died quoting the Devil tempting Jesus to fly. Stein quit drinking on the spot and hasn't jumped since. Eric, a wizard in the air, jumped the Troll Wall three times over the days following Carl's death. On his last jump, Eric logged a 30-second free fall with only a 2-second canopy ride before landing in the rocks, miraculously unhurt. He decided not to document the record free fall because the only way for someone to top it was to bounce. "Get me out of here before I die," he told Stein.

Eric is currently a healer in Berlin and skydives regularly.

Stein runs a small church (Saint Galileo) and teaches kite surfing in Miami. He still gets occasional flashes of Eric nearly going in during his astonishing, 30-second free fall.

"For now," he wrote in 2010, "I am content with the knowledge that I am a fool. Every day I thank my angels and pray for wisdom."

In the winter of 1989, Arnstein Myskja, the teenage guide who witnessed Carl's last jump, was killed by an avalanche while climbing the Mjelva Gully just above the Mjelva Boulder, the lichen-flecked stone where Fred and I climbed waiting for the clouds to part on Trollveggen.

Aud is a nurse's supervisor, has two gorgeous daughters, and is married to a fellow Norwegian who manages oil platforms in the North Sea.

Half a dozen years after The Jump, while parachuting onto the summit of a towering limestone Tepui in the Venezuelan rain forest, Jean Boenish compound-fractured her leg, greatly curtailing her BASE jumping career.

Fred Husoy went on to climb many new routes in the Trondheim Valley, then ventured to the Alps and Himalaya. He led the local rescue team for many years, and through innovative, often perilous efforts, saved dozens of climbers injured on the Troll Wall. He is married to a doctor and has two sons.

The film about Carl Boenish was called *Sunshine Superman*, and was critically acclaimed. Producers were disappointed that it didn't earn the Academy Award for live-action documentary. The director invited me to a private screening shortly after the premiere, with dozens of industry people, but I left early. It took me three times to finally watch it through.

A few months after returning from Norway I came tumbling down in a climbing gym, of all places. The first thing I saw when I rolled up was my tibia jutting out of a fist-sized hole in my shin. I spent the next 45 days in the hospital. One time in the wee hours when I couldn't sleep and the morphine carried me to the ethers, I gazed down and saw a girl and a boy dancing to The Who on an unswept floor in a bar on a 1,000-year-old street.

A popular saying in adventure circles is that BASE jumping has killed more people than malaria.

The Ride

WE PULLED into Del Rio at high noon, mummified by dry heat till another Talon fighter jet streaked in from nearby Laughlin Air Force Base and startled us back to life. We came for the annual George Paul Memorial Bull Riding challenge, "The Toughest Rough Stock Event in Tarnation," according to promotional flyers tacked around the Texas border town. The promo fliers, now collector's items, were Lone Star reboots of the *Return of Godzilla* movie poster, where the monster, with glassy eyes bugging and giant teeth barred, clawed air swarming with squadrons of Japanese fighter planes. The Del Rio flyer had swapped out the monster for a fire-breathing Brahma bull, with supersonic Talons jetting between its horns.

Many champions, past and present, were there in Del Rio, including the current points leader out of Henrietta, a five-time world all-around champ and the only man on the circuit to ride each rough stock event: bareback, saddle broncs, and bulls. But we'd come to shoot Jaime "Legs" Maldonado for *Telemundo*, a Spanish-language TV channel that I occasionally worked for in the late 1980s.

Back then, Legs was one of the few Mexican Americans on the pro rodeo circuit. Whenever a rodeo hit Texas, Arizona, or New Mexico, or wherever there were other Mexicans, they all turned out to watch Legs ride. Only 24, Legs labored to milk high scores out of pedestrian bulls. But on rank stock, where even the best hoped only to stay on board for 8 seconds (a qualified ride) and to escape without bleeding, Legs shone.

The long-forgotten *Telemundo* show was an early iteration of the Bulls Only rodeos that, 3 decades later, would pack venues from Madison Square Garden to the T-Mobile Arena in Las Vegas. Shortly after the Del Rio event, twenty-one cowboys gathered in a hotel room in Scottsdale, Arizona, and threw $1,000 each into a collective kitty to fund the start of a pro bull riding circuit. If you were one of the original investors in Professional Bull Riders, Inc., your seed money is now worth over $4 million in a sport broadcast into more than half a billion households in fifty nations and territories worldwide. But this was 30 years ago, when the overall winner took home a silver buckle and $2,500 cash money, and when bull riding clips were used as filler on late night cable, between cooking shows and *Bonanza* reruns.

As the writer on a proposed documentary on Legs (which never came off), I had zero qualifications, having never seen a rodeo. My grade-school friend, director Ruben Amaro, gave me a 3-hour crash course on Legs, Del Rio, and bull riding—"the world's most dangerous organized sport"—during the flight down from L.A. Brazilian riders were climbing up the world standings, said Ruben, complaining that the sport was getting outsourced. But what I saw was "rawhide" (American) all the way.

———————————

MOST OF the crowd had spent the day just over the border, in Ciudad Acuña, and many had a load on by the time the rodeo kicked off. When the stadium lights clicked on, the sun guttered on the horizon like an open wound. It was dusty and heat waves rippled off the blind above the bleachers. A water truck rolled through the arena and dampened the dirt, then made a second pass with one hose turned on the stands where men stood bare-chested with brown reservoir water gushing over them and into their open mouths and blowing the hats off their heads. Then the announcer, who went by the stage name of Ferris Irons, shuffled around the arena with a wireless microphone, and over a John Philip Sousa march blaring out of the P.A., in a drawl thick as linseed oil, gave a speech about "these great U-nited States."

Miss Del Rio—a corn-fed Nefertiti with valiant, torpedo breasts and most of a string bikini—cantered into the arena on a haughty palomino and half the crowd leaped up whistling and punching the air. As Miss Del Rio circled, cargo bounding and clutching a wooden flagpole as Ol' Glory rippled overhead, the national anthem sounded over the PA and everybody took off their hats and held them over their hearts and sang. Then Ferris Irons eased us into prayer, and everyone bowed their heads as he consecrated the riders, the stock, the fans, Yankee Doodle, Old Mexico, and all of creation.

I glanced behind the corrals, where the cowboys were limbering up and rosining their gear. Each of them had taken a knee, their hats off, eyes closed, faces set like Rodin's *Thinker* as Irons, with the solemnity of last rites, finished bargaining with Lord Jesus Christ about "being on the square" with the cowboys, and "protecting Our Father's champions," and a bunch of other blasphemies in this high kitsch theater.

Irons said, "Ah-Men," heavy-metal rock burst over the PA, and the crowd exploded.

Telemundo threw little money at these one-off shows, so we didn't have a remote video truck with real-time displays, meaning the two cameramen were shooting "iso." Once he got the cameras into position, there wasn't much for Ruben to direct till the interviews after the show, so the two of us climbed up onto the catwalk just above the chute, where the bulls were herded into a stall as the cowboys mounted and were released through a swinging gate into the arena. We were perched over the last partition and could peer down at the first cowboy, straddling the steel fence poles beside the first bull.

The stall was just big enough for the colossal, slobbering Brahma bull, which snorted and pitched as the cowboy shimmied around on its bare back, trying to find the sweet spot. The bull hated being mounted and clearly saw it as an act of domination, made worse by several men cinching a braided rope around its torso, just behind the big hump on its neck. On top of this rope was a thong handle for the cowboy's gloved hand, gummy with rosin, around which the tail of the rope was lashed tight as the rider could bear. Then they cinched a second, bucking rope around the bull's belly, close to its furry, pendulous balls. And they didn't merely cinch it. Three men heaved till the bull started jumping and jackhammering the stall with its rear hooves, its horned head rearing back to gore the rider on its back, savage eyes red as the sun.

"Coming out with Travis Pettibone on Skoal Psycho!"

The guy working the P.A. cranked up the rock track. Travis Pettibone shoved down his hat, gritted his teeth, and nodded. Then the gate flew open and a ferocious chunk of snorting, bucking, chuck roast from hell exploded from the chute, spun left, kicking its back legs so high it almost did a handstand, snapping its massive head straight back. The bull was all violent kicks and front-end drops, and so fast that the whole works looked sped up. This was no farm animal, but a highly tuned athlete in its own right. Travis was all flying limbs but hung on somehow and the crowd went off.

Then Skoal Psycho spun right and yawed into the fence, slamming Travis into a sheet-metal sign for Manuel's Steakhouse. The bull whirred away and Travis dropped limp to the ground. The clowns, called "bullfighters," raced up and lured the animal toward a guy on a tall black horse, who hazed it toward a gate that opened to the back corral. The bull shot through the breach knowing another guy was waiting back there to ease the rope cinched round its belly.

The second the arena cleared, paramedics raced in with a gurney, loaded Travis up, and wheeled him off. An ambulance with its tailgate open was already backed up to the rear of the arena. When they got the gurney there, Travis sat up and tried to get off, but a clown gently pushed him back down. They loaded Travis up, the ambulance sped off, and another, lights flashing, backed up in its place.

I ran back along the narrow catwalk to see the next ride, my sneakers sloshing through pools of inky "tabacca" juice that crooked old rodeo hands kept spewing onto the slats. Jimi Hendrix's "Astroman" blared over the P.A., and Irons yelled, "And it's Cody Lambert on Cajun Moon!"

The gate flew open, and Cajun Moon rumbled out and jumped completely off the ground, sunfishing—kicking all fours, twisting and rolling—then landed like a runaway train, dug its hooves, snapped its haunches almost vertical and Cody Lambert shot off into the night, landing in a welter of elbows, knees, and trampled soot. He must have wrenched something, but he crabbed to his feet, then sprinted to the fence and clawed up it as the big black Brahma bull rumbled after. Cody was safe enough, clinging 15 feet up the chain link, but Cajun Moon kept snorting and bucking beneath him, trying to loosen the rope that was strangling his gut. Then the clowns decoyed Cajun Moon around and the man on the black horse drove it back into the corral.

The clowns were if anything more athletic than the riders. One wore football pads and the other a knee brace and soccer cleats. Each time a cowboy ate dirt, and they did most every ride, the clowns would jump straight between the bull and the rider, diverting the furious animal from close range, feinting, circling and sidestepping with their bare hands palming off the Brahma's horned head. Often they got grazed or kicked and when Cody Flynn took a dive on the fourth bull out, one clown was launched rag-dolling through the air when the rearing bull's head got under him. That any clown made it through an entire rodeo was a wonderful thing, and the riders showed their gratitude after every ride with back slaps and fist bumps all around.

"And give a big Del Rio welcome to D. J. Mulroon, on Black Ratchet!"

The star of this match was not Mulroon—still futzing with his rope—but the bull, whose name brought cheers from the crowd and whose career Irons described with corny flair, ending with his buck-off rate: 96 percent over the last 3 years. Outside the stadium, several vendors were selling T-shirts with silkscreen images of bulls. One of them was Black Ratchet.

"The bulls are the cowboys' dance partners for the night," said Ruben.

Black Ratchet vaulted out and hobby-horsed wildly in front of the gate, went airborne, and "broke in two," uncoupling in the middle, hooves kicking, slammed to earth and spun like a cyclone, but D. J. hung on for 4, 5 seconds, and the crowd went off again. Then Black Ratchet juked to one side and D. J. skidded off center and slipped forward. The bull's rearing head slammed into D. J.'s chest and bashed him back to meet the monster's rearing flank, which drove him into the ground like a railroad spike—one hell of a one-two punch. The clowns swooped in and drew the bull away, but D. J. Mulroon didn't move. He was bleeding from his mouth and one ear. The image of the cowboy lying in the dirt like that, limbs all akimbo and not moving, reminded me of bodies piled at the base of a cliff after a climbing accident, and scared me down deep.

"That guy's dead," I mumbled to Ruben.

"*No se*," said Ruben, who broke into Spanish whenever he got excited. "These guys are *duro*, John. Give him a chance to get his wind back."

The paramedics stormed in. After a few minutes, D. J. came to, but he wasn't going anywhere on his own. Irons likened bull riders to gladiators, slipping in Disraeli's words about courage being fire and Jeremiah's promise that the lord would restoreth. Then the paramedics fitted D. J. with a cervical collar and loaded him up on the gurney. D.J. waved a limp hand to the restless applause. Then they wheeled him off and into the ambulance, which roared away as another backed into the hot spot.

In the next 15 minutes I saw two more cowboys body-slammed to the ground and another pitched into the fence and knocked cold. I saw a Brazilian cowboy from Dos Santos get kicked in the groin and another fracture his arm after an electrifying cartwheel exit off a bull called Hum Dinger, who got a standing ovation from the crowd as it rumbled around the arena. Two other riders—the Fawcett brothers, who both looked about 19—went one after the other. Both got rudely chucked off but not hurt. They gathered their gear, stumbled to the dirt lot behind the arena, and we watched them slump into a rusty old pickup and sputter off.

Only top riders could afford to fly to rodeos, said Ruben, which during the season averaged several a week in cities that might be thousands of miles apart. The top thirty or so guys made their money from sponsorship deals, mostly with beer, chewing tobacco, and apparel companies. Champion-caliber riders often owned planes and would sometimes hit two rodeos in the same day, picking and choosing high-profile contests with full purses. But most riders lived closer to the bone, forming partnerships with other wannabe pros and following the circuit in old pickups like the Fawcetts'. Win or lose, it was right back into the truck for another all-nighter to another rodeo in Tuscaloosa or Dodge or Tuba City.

If their vehicle didn't break down, they'd arrive soon enough to eat and rest, and maybe get a bum elbow rubbed down and taped up as they psyched to do battle. But often the journeyman rider would wheel in—road-warped, hungry and sore—and with little or no warmup would jump straight onto a bull. They'd hang around if they made it through the first go-around, maybe one out of three or four outings. Otherwise it was down the road in the old pickup, one passed out while the other drove, chasing a dream wherever the bulls were bucking. It was a tough go, but they weren't asking for sympathy and they wouldn't get any.

BUDDY DOLLARHIDE, from Checotah, Oklahoma, was the fifteenth rider out, and like most of the others went at about 5'8", was lariat thin and wound tighter than a hair in a biscuit. We watched him swagger up to the gate, a bantam rooster in embroidered chaps. He was only the fourth to ride 8 seconds to the horn, but he couldn't get off clean, landed with his legs crossed, flopped on his side and one of the bull's hooves mashed his left ankle. The clowns got the bull's attention and Buddy Dollarhide hobbled off, but I could see the jagged white bone jutting through a hole in his boot.

They'd run out of ambulances, so Buddy slouched back on the stairs below the judge's booth off to our left, yelling, "Goddamnit! Goddamnit to hell!"

A couple other cowboys rubbed his shoulders, and a man with a face like a saddlebag pulled a half pint from his hip, twisted off the top, and handed it to Buddy. He gulped, hauled up his pant leg and poured the rest into the top of his boot, screaming, "Son of a fucking bitch!" as the amber liquor streamed out pink through the hole in his boot and over the jutting bone. Buddy chucked the empty bottle against a horse trailer, then another ambulance wheeled up and took Buddy away.

The moment Skoal Psycho first burst from the gate a tsunami of adrenaline tore through me that ride after ride felt as if it would carry me outside my body. I'd spent nearly 20 years risking the farm but here, when things went south, there was a malevolent, 2,000-pound antagonist who wanted nothing more than to stomp your brains out, and that felt like a whole different thing. I couldn't believe any of this was legal.

"Coming out with Waco's own Bobby Reeves on A-Bomb!"

I glanced down at several cowboys limbering up on deck. One glanced back and straight through me, eyes fixed on the oldest drama on earth: man against beast. Jumping onto that beast's back was a direct deed hotter than Godzilla's fire, a fictional bugaboo made frivolous by mounting a stack of critical whoop ass, prefaced by hayseed salvation and jingoism, then enacted gruesomely to a rabid crowd and a feckless few thousand surfing late night cable TV. Raunchy? You bet your ass. But when a bull and a cowboy thundered out of that gate it was real and it was thrilling and the effect was like hauling a magic lantern into the cavern of our lives.

After about three turns, A-Bomb chucked off Bobby Reeves and a clown helped him stumble away to "shake off the bad." Reeves sank to one knee and pawed at his back.

"Getting a few *golpes* is part of the fun for these guys," said Ruben, but this went beyond fun by a country mile.

Ruben clasped the railing, peered over and said, "*Mira*, John. Here's our *paisano*."

We shuffled till we were directly above the gate, where we had a straight shot of Legs easing onto a big tawny bull. Legs couldn't have been more than 5'6", but thick-necked and ripped. A couple boys yanked on the rope running across the palm of Legs's gloved hand till he muttered, "Yup," in that edging into Cajun twang you hear around Stevensville. Legs fiddled with the lash around his hand, folded his fingers, and thumped them with his fist for purchase.

"Boy's got sand," said Ruben, referring to the self-contained grit cowboys so prize.

Legs slid forward so his rope hand was right at his crotch, nodded quickly, and was gone. When the horn sounded, Legs reached down and loosened the lash, and using the bull's bucking action, let himself be thrown, landing on his feet in a sprint—a nimble, trademark move that earned Legs his handle.

Legs rode differently than the others. He was a little stronger, a little more confident, had a little better balance. And when the tawny bull jumped straight up, twisting and rolling and kicking Legs's center of gravity across the arena, he snatched it back with his free hand, cutting the air for balance, his rope hand clenched to the braided line, a meager filament holding the two together.

All the Mexicans, including about fifty Mexican nationals, were sitting together on a bleacher off to the side, and they all whistled and clapped and shook each other's hands.

Legs's score wasn't huge, a 74, I think, because his bull wasn't as homicidal as some of the others, so required less moxie to ride. But when a cowboy lasted till the horn, and if he got away unscathed, that man won, and no person who actually saw it could believe otherwise.

After about half an hour the first round was over, and the arena cleared as the judges made the draw for the championship round. Of the thirty-two riders, only nine had ridden to the horn. Ruben and I climbed down off the catwalk and made our way over to the Mexicans, where Ruben had several friends.

It was a wide mix of people we met in that crowd, from Humberto Juarez, a multi-millionaire who owned a shoe factory, to rustic *frijoleros* who had snuck in through a hole in the fence. In Mexico, men like Juarez wouldn't be caught at a funeral with most of us, but in the arena they all kept together because they were Mexicans who had come to see Legs ride. I couldn't join the conversation because I didn't know rodeo talk. Plus it was hard to follow their rapid-fire Spanish.

Shortly the draw was announced and 3,000 "Ooooos" sounded from the crowd: Ferris Irons said Legs had drawn Vulcan. In the other bleachers, people were nodding their heads and shaking their hands in the air and whistling louder than when Miss Del Rio bounced through the arena on her big paint.

"Hell and devils!" cursed a man beside me, pulling at the corners of his moustache. "Vulcan!"

"Who brought that bastard here?" Ruben asked.

"He'll kill our boy just like he killed that gringo kid," said Humberto Juarez, extending his fists toward the others. The man was sincerely mad. And scared.

"You think Legs will even try Vulcan?" someone asked.

"Sheeeeet yes, he'll try," Ruben said in English.

The Mexicans started talking fast, arguing over each other, not sure if Ruben's forecast was the best or worst news they'd ever heard. Vulcan was a killer. Later, on the ride home, Ruben told me that only three bulls in history had ever been more than 5 years on the circuit and never ridden to the horn. The other two were in the Rodeo Hall of Fame. In the past 3 years, Vulcan had killed one cowboy outright, and had maimed a dozen others. One cowboy had a plate in his head courtesy of Vulcan, and felt he got off lucky. During the previous season riders often came down with groin pulls or bum elbows after drawing Vulcan. But this season nobody bothered feigning injuries; they just refused to get anywhere near the bull. So when word got out that Legs was actually going to ride Vulcan, or try to, the mood grew ominous.

During the short intermission, Ruben and I went down to the food stands and got a soda, and I learned how the rider's score was accrued from both the bull's and the rider's performance, each having a possible max score of 50 points. As I'd seen in the first go-around, the rankest bulls earned their riders high scores, but also concussions, broken bones, and buck offs. "Thinning the herd," as Ruben called it.

As the crowd pooled around the beer vendors, I found a quiet bench out by the tack house and started scribbling ideas in my notebook, searching out an angle for the documentary we never made. They called it sport, but I needed some figurative theme to push Legs and bull riding into a larger context. Problem was I didn't really know what I was seeing because it didn't feel *like* anything else. But what if this Bulls Only rodeo was a hayseed twist on a passion play, where cowboy messiahs faced life and death in the dirt? Jesus fought the devil and was completed. The cowboys battled the cosmically evil bull, who had to be defeated—if only for 8 seconds—stomping, goring, maiming the foredoomed sub-heroes in their loco do-si-do. I closed my notebook and smiled. When Ferris Irons announced that the bulls were running in 15 minutes, I hustled back to the arena, hoping I'd sorted out bull riding.

The catwalk overflowed with photographers and a video crew from ESPN, plus a couple local news stations. The rock soundtrack kicked back in and when Irons yelled, "Are we ready to rodeo?" the crowd went off again.

"Hide the jewels, it's Shoat Tremble on Doctor Gizmo!" And life was a blur once more, all streaking limbs and thundering hooves. A crash and burn, a perfect ride to the horn, another rider mashed into the fence, and the shrill wailing of the ambulance siren. But no stopping now. The ESPN video crew flicked on some lights, and the cameraman bent over the guardrail, an assistant holding onto his waist. ZZ Top's "Legs" came over the P.A., and the crowd erupted.

"Dad-burned right," said Irons. "We're talkin'bout *Señor* Legs on that son of a biscuit Vulcan, rankest beeve since the Forest Bull. So leash the dog and hide the kinfolk 'cause here comes Legs!"

I heard the gate fly open and the rowdy crowd roar, but the catwalk was too jammed to see anything for several seconds. Then the bull snapped into view like a giant eel fighting a riptide, writhing flanks, head and legs all convulsing in different directions and with the violence of an electrocution, now corkscrewing in midair, now hooves slamming into the dirt, pancaking Legs into the bull's back. And Legs stayed onboard. Then Vulcan bolted to the center of the arena and whirred into a flat spin. The beast was chocolate brown streaked with black, a grim and rippling hunk of heart meat.

After about 5 seconds, the crowd noise drowned out the music. Vulcan vaulted and reared his head, scalding bolts of snot firing from his nose. Legs seemed nailed to the back of the creature. Once, both his legs flew up over his head, then his torso doubled over to one side so far that the bull's flank knocked his hat off. But Legs was still there, still over his rope hand, the bull and the cowboy melded together like a Minotaur. The horn sounded—but the ride was just getting started for Legs.

Vulcan broke into a bucking sprint. And Legs's rope hand was hung up. He tried loosing the lash with his free hand, clawing at the cinched rope between bounds, his boots trawling furrows in the dirt. But it was no good. Twice they circled the arena, Legs flopping wildly, clawing at his hand, lashed in tight. Then Vulcan dug in and plowed to a stop. Legs flew over the horns, somersaulted and landed about 30 feet away, his limbs splayed awkwardly. One of the clowns dashed up, and Vulcan turned and chased him up the backstop fence (the arena doubled as a baseball park). The bull wheeled and rumbled after the other clown, who dove into a big red barrel just before Vulcan's lowered head crashed into it; and I swear that barrel sailed 20 feet before hitting well up the fence and thunking back to the dirt.

The guy on the black horse dashed in. Seeing Vulcan charging straight down the pike at it, the horse ground into a turn and galloped away for its life, sailed over the retaining wall at the far end of the arena and, unable to veer or completely stop, caromed off the Pepsi-Cola stand. Vulcan pawed the dirt, shimmied, tossed its head, and finally hobbled off and slipped through the open gate into the back corral.

Legs lay face down and didn't move. They cut the music. Everyone held their breath as the clowns raced over to Legs. Then, holding his side, and with a clown on each arm, Legs teetered upright and stared up into the sky, his mouth open and sucking air. Half the crowd clamored up the screen and hung by their fingers, screaming and rocking back and forth, nearly pulling the whole works down as the Mexicans stampeded over the rails and into the arena.

Someone put a sombrero on Legs's head and they started parading him around on shoulders to the strains of "Legs" cranked so loud people could have heard it in the Yucatan. Then the other cowboys came into the arena and hoisted Legs up in the air as well, and he tried to force a smile, though he mostly grimaced.

It took Irons 10 minutes to clear the arena. They prodded Vulcan back inside, where despite favoring a leg, he hissed and feigned charges at the crowd, his savage breath mixing with the steam welling off his body. Every man, woman, and child pressed up against the screen or the fence and gave the great bull a standing ovation. The cowboys were what the bulls made them, and Vulcan had just made Legs a champion.

I noticed one of the other riders, standing alone. He was big and lanky with a loud orange shirt, and we all watched Legs hobble over and embrace him. According to an old-timer there on the catwalk, the guy used to be traveling partners with the rider who'd died on Vulcan several years before. We watched him stretch one of Legs's arms over his shoulder and walk him back to the trainer's tent. Then Miss Del Rio, who'd changed into gold lamé hot pants with matching bustier, rode through the arena once more for good measure as the crowd, purged of a great tension, stood and clapped. Irons dropped his MC persona and said in plain English that he and everyone else had just witnessed history.

But they hadn't witnessed a passion play, or man against beast, any of the other inflated ideas I'd cooked up while riding a wave of adrenaline in Del Rio, when the crowd was small and the purse modest and the half a billion viewers of the future had never heard of the George Paul Memorial Bull Riding challenge, or anything like it. It was blood sport, no question, but also a ritualized chance to flout the taboos and let it rip, full fucking throttle. Miss Del Rio and baby Jesus, the great Devil bulls and stone cold crazy riders, blood on the dirt and twenty beers in your gut, lust, violence, melodrama, shameless sentimentality—all those passions that can move us to shudders and tears, yet strangely leave us feeling not shaken but reassured that someone, somewhere is not merely waxing genteel, but embracing the whole divine catastrophe, for the length of a hot Texan night.

A couple weeks later, back in L.A., Ruben told me that when Legs was flopping around on Vulcan he'd broken some vertebrae and would never ride bulls again. Vulcan was through as well. He'd torn the big tendon in his hind leg.

"They retired each other," Ruben said.

That was my last gig for *Telemundo*, and I never went to another rodeo.

FOR YEARS the Bulls-Only Rodeo in Del Rio dozed in my mind like a fevered dream. Every time I brushed against it the events seemed more starry till I wondered if time and distance hadn't worked the fantastic on an ordinary day at the rodeo. As the Pro Bull Riding circuit slowly blew up in the popular media, and even was sketched Talese-style in the *New Yorker*, I occasionally watched clips on YouTube of events so glitzed and so packaged they little resembled the unvarnished article I'd experienced in Del Rio.

Then work took me to Odessa, Texas, a rodeo town from the ground up. During a lunch break I strolled through Gentry's Western Gallery.

Many of the displays in Gentry's featured archive material— crackled leather and tarnished silver tack, a pictorial exhibit of a three-time saddle bronc champion from the 60s, and some charcoal sketches of World War Two–era roper J. Seth Granger, to mention a few. The rest of the space was given over to stars of the current Built Ford Tough, thirty-city event series, the "major league" tour of Professional Bull Riders competitions. Leading riders, each a well-deserved millionaire, were present in life-sized cardboard cutouts as a video monitor played a highlight reel of spectacular modern rides and dreadful wrecks in football stadiums and convention centers with six-figure crowds. The action was intense as a hanging, but gone, it seemed, was the illicit thrill of archetypal gratification, of every passion running amok and the cornpone nostalgia that gave the show such heart. Or so it seemed.

Just past the display was a small rotunda floored with cushioned mats and a dozen young kids yelling and taking turns riding a big mechanical bull, with "Vulcan" emblazoned on the side. On the far wall of the rotunda hung a 4-by-5-foot special edition lithograph, with the number 793 next to the tidy signature. The mural showed a muscular, swarthy cowboy aboard a brown- and black-streaked bull at the George Paul Memorial Bull Riding challenge in Del Rio, Texas—from way back when. The great bull was corkscrewed in the air, his massive head rearing back, blind rage in his red eyes, and steam blasting from flaring nostrils. The muscles and veins bulged in the cowboy's rope arm. His jaw was fixed like granite, his free arm crooked above his head.

At the bottom of the mural a small brass insignia read, "The Ride."

When Icarus Falls

MY PHONE chirps. It's a text from C. A., an American alpinist whom I admire as a friend and a climber.

John Long! My bros Kyle and Scott are over-due in Pakistan. I'm hanging with Kyle's mom in Salt Lake and my partner Jewell, Kyle's girlfriend. Keeping fingers crossed for improving weather.

Huh? How can C. A. tell me two of America's best alpinists have gone missing, then short me on the details? Can't blame her though, biting her nails with mom and the girlfriend. I log onto the web and skim a dispatch from Kyle's gear sponsor.

A week ago, Kyle Dempster and Scott Adamson started up the unclimbed North Face of Ogre II, in the Karakoram range in Pakistan. Their headlamps were spotted halfway up the face at the end of their first day on the mountain. Then a storm rolled in and nobody's seen them since. With the clock ticking and the storm raging on, family and friends set up a GoFundMe site to help finance a search.

Have to text C. A. back and say *something*. Just not what I'm thinking—that it's 6,800 miles to Kyle and Scott but they might as well be on the moon.

Whatever food and fuel they had is long gone. Searching with binoculars is pointless in a storm. Maybe you check likely descent routes if the boys topped out and got stranded getting down. Doubtful, but I kill the thought, not wanting to jinx them. A rescue team might traverse the base in case the climbers got blown off the wall by rocks or avalanche. You can have that job. And a helicopter (if there's one for hire) can't go anywhere near the mountain. Nobody can. Not in a storm, and not on a beast like Ogre II.

But just maybe . . . Who can forget the photos of Doug Scott crawling off Ogre I (just west of Ogre II) in heavy weather?

Doug Scott. Make that *Sir* Doug Scott, now that he's been knighted. I was a reckless teenager when I first met Doug in Yosemite, and we tried to cross the Merced to climb the Rostrum. Except the river ran like the Ganges in flood and we couldn't clear the current, hopping rock to rock, like I'd promised. Finally I said, "Fuck it. I'm roping up and swimming across." Doug laughed and said, "Forget it. You'll drown." Doug was older and looked like Moses with his beard, plus he'd just bagged a new route on Everest and had that clout. So I forgot it and we hitched over to The Cookie and climbed *Meat Grinder*.

I surf around the Internet looking for updates, backstories, a link to Google Earth. But there's nothing more about Kyle and Scott so I dig out an old *Mountain Magazine* with Doug's end-all survival story, "A Crawl Down the Ogre."

A photo of Ogre II shows the wall soaring off the Choktoi Glacier, stabbing the skyline like an ice-encrusted arrowhead. The North Face, says the caption, covers 4,600 feet of rock and ice. Tops out at 23,000 feet. "Futuristic." Then an editor calls from Nat Geo, asking about Kyle and Scott.

A week, I agree, is forever. But what else can I add? Never been to the Karakoram. Never climbed a real mountain. Never laid eyes on the boys. Came close to meeting Kyle last May, at an American Alpine Club awards dinner organized in part to honor Kyle and Hayden Kennedy's first ascents on K7 and Ogre I. Only Kyle showed up, in a gray shirt he must have slept in, jeans and sunglasses, looking amused to get a plaque the size of a STOP sign for climbs he'd bagged four seasons earlier.

Kyle read his acceptance speech off the head of a pin: "Thank you very much." Then he stood there in wrinkled glory till a crowd gathered round and herded him offstage, to hear all about it. By the time I made my way over, Kyle had left the building.

———————

THAT NIGHT I text C. A. back.

I sent a hundred bucks to help with the search. Wishing them the best.

Hey. Thanks so much, she wrote back. *It's kind of a logistical nightmare trying to get a helicopter in there with search capabilities. But these guys are real good and real lucky so I like their chances.*

She forwards a trip report about Kyle and Scott's first attempt on Ogre II, a year ago. A good story gets gripping just below the summit, where Scott took a 100-foot fall and fractured his leg. How weird is that? Forty years ago another Scott fractured *both* legs, descending off the top of the next peak over.

Kyle and Scott started roping down, the story continues. A few rappels from the base they ripped an anchor and tobogganed 300 feet onto the glacier, escaping further injury. Damn! That's more than lucky. That's like the rope breaking when they're hanging you.

A brush fire of updates burns through the night, which is morning over in Pakistan. Army helicopters have joined the search but weather keeps them grounded in Skardu. Porters are heading up the Biafo Glacier to the backside of Ogre II, where Kyle and Scott might have descended. No word yet from the porters.

Thomas Huber, a legendary German climber, is an hour down the glacier with an Austrian team prepping for an attempt on Latok 1, and they're anxious to help. But they can't get near the wall due to storm and avalanche danger. A report out of Karachi says the storm might pass tonight. Or at least by noon tomorrow.

In the time it takes to eat breakfast, the weather report has 7,300 shares. The GoFundMe site shows $97,734 raised from 1,934 donors.

We're 24 hours in and the crisis is gathering random pieces of a human jigsaw puzzle and arranging them into a community rarely seen during slack times. The hope is that Kyle and Scott will return and take their places in the puzzle, once the pieces settle. I picture 2,000 candles across the planet, lit for two Americans lost in a storm. In a moment that calls for decisive action, there's little else to do but watch the candles burn.

THEY CALL it *kill time*, waiting for news from people gone missing. Like when my high school friend and climbing partner Tobin Sorenson was overdue returning from Mount Alberta. Got a phone call from the rangers, then didn't hear back for 3 days. Or when my buddy Marty Navarro paddled into a canyon in Uruguay and I heard nothing for a month. Or the time my Yosemite pal, Alan Rouse, charged for the summit of K2 and vanished in the clouds. I doubt these guys ever met each other, but they all loved a sharp edge, disappeared, and left us hanging in kill time. None of them ever came back.

The GoFundMe kitty has $123,000, plenty to launch a search mission. C. A. e-mails me an update. A Global Rescue helicopter has joined the hunt, though low clouds on the mountain leave the aerial search team pacing in Skardu. But the barometric pressure is rising and Pakistani military choppers are ready to fly as soon as the weather clears. Porters have trekked up the Biafo Glacier from Askole to the backside of Ogre II. *We hope they can see something by daybreak,* C. A. writes.

I scroll down the GoFundMe site to a live chatroom, where hundreds chime in.

You still owe me a quad-shot Americano, Kyle, writes a friend from Colorado. *Get home soon!*

Below the text is a cell phone pic of Higher Ground, Kyle's coffee shop in Salt Lake City.

This is not mountaineering. It's selfishness, writes another, call him Bart, who feels it criminal to crowdshare something that they could have easily prevented.

The comment feels out of line, but everyone has a voice nowadays because everyone's given a platform. So we get the story in the round—the frenzied, schizophrenic jigsaw puzzle, not just the gaudiest pieces. Fair enough. But what kind of shitheel rags on Kyle and Scott, who either are dead or wishing they were. And it's ignorant to call them merely selfish, or damaged souls chasing a death wish. Such caricatures of adventure have been recycled by tyros and hacks in everything from the *New York Times Magazine* to *Men's Journal* and it pisses me off.

Nobody climbs an Ogre II for bragging rights, which can't get you over the first overhang, when your fingers freeze and the anchors are bunk and the way overhead looks hopeless. The Kyles and Tobins push on anyhow, not chasing death, rather life with the volume cranked, climbing for themselves but also for the rest of us slogging the low road, content with our neutered insight and vicarious thrills: waxing wise on art and justice; watching porn stars having sex on black-sand beaches—or Kyle and Scott defying the Ogre. There's always been a coliseum of a kind, and the bold win the laurel crown. Without gladiators, we have little but our fear. So fuck you, Bart.

Another update comes around noon: no break in the weather.

I'm boarding a plane in a couple hours, to cover an ultramarathon in Aspen, Colorado. I jam stuff into a day pack and start waxing clever—another ruse for kill time—wondering if Bart's fear of risk is his fear of being wrong. *Sure, being wrong is different than being creative,* I think. *But the fear of being wrong means you'll never do anything original. Will never cash out the big dream.*

But I'm making my stomach turn reciting half the story. The shiny half with the bones left out. Like that woman I broke the news to at the take-out in Gore Canyon. "I'm sorry, but your husband drowned." I didn't cover up when she started flailing her arms. What did "hero" mean to her when pallbearers lowered the coffin?

When we set down in Aspen, I check my phone for updates. A confirmed weather window is opening tomorrow morning, the first break in the 10 days since Kyle and Scott were last seen. Two Pakistani military helicopters will start searching in the morning. The next 24 hours are critical.

I roll out of Aspen and drive half an hour past Basalt and El Jebel to a bar-food restaurant in Carbondale where I meet *Rock and Ice* publisher Duane Raleigh. Another Yosemite refugee. We order some food and a text arrives from C. A.

Weather is clear at base camp. Hopeful for the search to start at first light.

Duane's staff is posting updates about Ogre II on their website fast as word comes in.

"You know Kyle was supposed to be a student in the last symposium," says Duane. I had no idea. For the past 3 years we've hosted a writer's symposium there in town. Finished the last one just 3 weeks before.

Kyle had plenty to write about. He'd won the *Piolet d'Or* and multiple Golden Piton awards for pioneering climbs all over the world. He'd looked forward to honing his writing skills at the symposium, but all ten slots were filled, says Duane, who arranges the production. So he had to tell Kyle, "next year."

"Then a student fell out," Duane adds, "so I called Kyle back and said, 'You're in.'" But Kyle had already made plans to return to Ogre II, so it'd have to be "next year" after all.

Yet again I'd come that close to meeting Kyle Dempster. As it happened, when that tenth slot opened up, Duane gave it to a girl, call her Wendy, who was also up against it.

Halfway through my burger, another text from C. A.

Helicopter finally took off. Good weather and they just landed in base camp to pick up Thomas Huber. I'll keep you posted.

I ask Duane what chance he gives the boys and he says, "Not much on such a technical face. But remember *Minus 148 . . .*"

Minus 148 chronicles the unlikely survival of author Art David son and seven others during the first winter ascent of Denali, back in 1967. The team survived 6 days in a cramped snow cave when temperatures dropped to almost minus 150 and winds howled at 150 miles per hour. Suddenly, Kyle and Scott seem all but saved.

"Davidson lives around here," says Duane, "and he just had a barbecue to celebrate the fiftieth anniversary of the climb. I was there and we talked about Kyle and Scott."

The far-flung pieces are filling in the jigsaw puzzle. People I haven't thought about in ages and faces known and unknown are racking into focus, all eyes trained on Ogre II.

Later that night, at a dumpy motel in Glenwood Springs, I brew coffee and start trolling the Internet for more of Kyle's writing, waiting for word from C. A. The coffee's bad. The bathroom has no towels. A baby's screaming next door and the bed feels like Chickenhead Ledge. I know nothing about the ultra-marathon I'm there to cover tomorrow morning, and I couldn't care less about any of it.

"I dreamed of a solitary adventure on a remote Karakoram peak," wrote Kyle in *Alpinist* magazine, "as a way to siphon off distractions and to answer the question of how much I was willing to give to the mountains."

Another text from C. A. *First flight around the mountain . . . no sign of them.*

That's dire, and I drown it out by returning to Kyle's story about another climb, Tahu Rutum, 7 years ago.

"After running out of food, I spent four days rappelling the wall and hiking back to base camp. Each time I fell, I had to find another memory with enough power to return me to my feet: The faces of family and friends. The sounds of their laughter. . . ."

I read every word I can find by Kyle and pass out when the coffee wears off. The next text from C. A. comes in the wee hours, when the chirp on my phone wakes me up.

Fuck, man. No bueno. No sign of the boys. One more fly-by after refuel.

I fumble to punch the letters on my phone.

Good they're sticking with the search. You never know.

My alarm goes off at 6 a.m. and another text is waiting from C. A.

No sign. But Huber feels confident in the search so don't let Duane publish anything in the magazine.

I sit up on the bed, vividly awake, clinging to the lives of people I've never met, in a place I've never seen. *What gives here?* Every feeling tone seems off key, except a disquieting chord of shame—that the crisis in Pakistan is a summons to all of us who once set stakes in no-man's-land.

Come on. Why so dramatic? You never thought like this or questioned anything when you were thrutching through that cave in the Solomons. It all felt direct and honest and all that mattered was seeing it through. Now you're the one who's through, getting your fix through proxy. Using these people. Pathetic . . .

I pound down some toast and watery oatmeal at the breakfast spread in the hotel office, then motor toward Aspen Mountain and hit another unsettling chord. The thoughts are quick and ruthless:

Who is the Ogre, really? Some verglassed cerro in Pakistan? Or a force inside that kindles risk and excess? Maybe the Ogre is the hero himself, strip-mining life for the stuff called adventure? But what of the crowds at a NASCAR track, jolted awake when the lead car flips and burns? Or the thousands following a search in Asia, all of us desperate to feel something. And the big feelings hit when Icarus falls. In the macabre spectacle of risk sports, that's the hero's promise, even his duty: to die. To gift us an emotional reboot. A catharsis to blow out all the crap and insincerity. "We're terribly sorry," and that right there is the vital feeling, the ritual conclusion that tells us we're alive. Money, sex and beautiful thoughts are small beer for people with dangerous appetites. Even God is wanting. We need a cannibal. We need an Ogre.

That might sound crazy but it doesn't feel dishonest.

I wheel into the grassy park below Aspen Mountain and start shooting 156 ultra-runners attempting the Icebreaker Grand Traverse, a 42-mile run along the mountainous ridge stretching from Crested Butte to Aspen. It starts raining around noon and the park is a swirling mud hole. The runners are crushed. Several fall face down in the muck as they slosh across the finish. Some weep and laugh at the same time, as if their greatest joy might be running themselves to death. The winning time is just over 6 hours. Half the field take 10 hours or more.

My phone has died so I can't check updates. When the last runner stumbles home at dusk, I race back to the motel, shower off the mud, power up my laptop, and read how late this morning, two Pakistani military copters made a close-proximity search of the north face of Ogre II, flying to within 100 feet of the wall. They also searched the entire northeast ridge, where Kyle and Scott planned to descend. And scoured the glacier between Ogres I and II.

No trace of the climbers was found.

C. A.'s text is respectfully short: *They called off the search.*

Nearly 2 weeks have passed since the team was last spotted on the mountain. Further aerial sweeps, dangerous at such altitude, hold out little hope.

I lay back on the lumpy bed and listen to the baby crying through the pasteboard walls, wishing for a second that I hadn't stopped drinking. The whole adventure racket feels demented.

Condolences float across cyberspace as pieces of the jigsaw crash to the ground, describing a new order, a new picture. Kyle and Scott are not on it. But C. A. is and so am I, and I haven't thanked her for keeping me in the loop. I try cooking up some fitting words but can't. So I blurt with my fingers, jabbing at the letters on my phone.

I'm sorry for Jewel and Kyle's mom and you and all of Kyle's friends and the same for Scott. But I'm proud of you for seeing your people through this.

Seconds later C. A. texts me back.

Thanks John Long. It's been some wicked heavy times, but there is a ton of support. Kyle was so obsessed with the Ogre II and obsessed with being in the mountains. Since it happened, it's kind of beautiful to think that he is now part of that landscape forever. Watching his mom has been tough, she just lost her husband 1 year ago. It crushes me to watch Jewell too, but they will be ok.

Then this on the GoFundMe site, from Robert L, I'm guessing from New Zealand.

I smash a pile of pikelets with strawberry jam and cream when these events happen—it's bitter sweet. Then try to do something nice for a stranger; to feel a little better about how tragic, beautiful and forgiving life can still be.

There it is. The labyrinth of the human heart, allied with a handful of words. But none of it's true when the Ogre's left out. And it's never really over.

BACK IN L.A., as a kind of eulogy to unknown soldiers, I log onto the GoFundMe site. They've raised $198,885 from 4,980 donors, a chunk of it after the search was abandoned. Wordsworth quotes, rants, and small talk stream in as people rattle out of kill time, writing the chapter that never gets told, the prickly part.

In a right-hand column is a roll call of names and numbers. A running timeline listing who's donated, and how much.

I toggle down, studying the names of people who might never have heard of Kyle and Scott till they read how the pair were in trouble. I stop at a name that I do know: "Wendy," the girl from the writers' workshop. She donated $150.

Wendy started climbing 2 years ago and found her people in the "fellowship of fools," whom she swore had saved her life. Then she made her way to our writing symposium, dragging along her craziness and runaway addictions that she'd recently reined in. Somewhere during the seminar she had a boundary experience, returned home, and got a job. Working in a restaurant. Little money, but that didn't stop her, a few days ago, from signing over her entire paycheck. Hoping to save two members of her tribe who were fighting for their lives.

I'VE BEEN scavenging for a grace note, something to restore the shine to the adventure game ever since Kyle and Scott were given up for dead. Wendy just gave it to me. But I'll have to spin it just so to clear the bodies.

I grab my pen and notebook. It always feels more authentic when I write by hand, though I can barely read my own writing.

She couldn't save Kyle and Scott, but through her act of giving, she managed to save herself, reclaiming the humanity stolen during the soul-murder of her early years.

That's treacle, but so what.

So she took her rightful position, perhaps for the first time, on the jigsaw puzzle of life, taking the place of Kyle and Scott, lost to the storm in Pakistan.

Jesus, what schlock. And NASCAR-gawker cheap. Cheap as wringing honey from a snuff film. I have no shame and no taste. And there is no resolution. *Quit using these people. Forget it.*

Then I remembered the video I've saved on my desktop, when Kyle "took off alone on his bike across Kyrgyzstan with a couple mostly-accurate maps, a trailer full of climbing gear, and a vocabulary of 10 Kyrgyz words." The title card shows a panorama of snowy mountains. In the foreground, bearded, in a tattered puffy and wool beanie, Kyle stands tall on some mountaintop, holding a handwritten sign: "I <u>LOVE</u> You!"

Love. As usual, I take it only when it serves me. Like now. I picture Kyle, peering down from the mountain at Wendy, finally back with the living, and him saying, "That's what I'm talking about!"

Not great, but the curse has lifted—till Wendy starts sending me messages, at screwy hours, full of run-ons and babble. Then she calls, bawling. She doesn't want to die but she's deep into a run on speedballs. Shooting coke and heroin. A week later she's in jail. My paean to love and heroes has been eaten alive by Wendy's Ogre, who always wants one thing: It wants *more.*

I wonder about Sir Doug, who after our encounter in Yosemite forged on to Kanchenjunga, Nuptse, and a dozen other peaks. How did he survive all that? He must have had better sense. Or maybe he knew that an Ogre unchained was a cannibal, and also knew that I didn't. So he said, "Forget it. You'll drown." Maybe *that* was love. How would I know? But it makes me want to fly over to England and ask the knight who saved my ass, and later crawled off the Ogre on two broken legs.

Several weeks later I got a text from Kathy D., former cover girl for *Climbing* magazine who after her marriage went bust, moved back to her hometown near the Florida Keys, and started cave diving, one of the most frightening, and dangerous, adventure sports going.

Out here in the woods, she wrote, *sitting here—cave divers are overdue. But don't say a word to anyone. They tried a long push, are 10 hours into the dive. No sign of them. Fingers crossed it's just a delay . . .*

Last Place on No Map

BLACK SMOKE spewed through holes in the ship's open deck, so gouged and rusted and darned with pig-iron patches that if a single spot-weld ever let go the entire quaking heap would crush itself and sink. The pilot was all leather skin and bones and his gaze had the set changelessness that comes from years of silence and solitude. He rarely spoke, though when the engine started clanking he'd grunt to his Caboclo assistant, maybe 13 years old, who'd duck below. Hammering would sound out. Once the engine hit its clunky rhythm, the boy would crawl back on deck, hacking from the smoke, smeared with grease and reeking of bilge and benzene. Otherwise, he worked a hand-cranked bailer every waking minute. He had a long lick of shiny black hair and strips of tire thonged to his feet. We hadn't seen him eat a thing during our 3 days on the barge.

The deck overflowed with 55-gallon fuel drums, cases of Pepsi-Cola, canned foods, rebuilt outboard motors, rolls of Visqueen and sheet metal, even a plastic Christmas tree dusted with snow—things ordered by the dwindling outposts, plantations, and native settlements upriver. The human cargo had thinned to the pilot, the boy, D. B., and me. This was my eleventh trip to the wild places with D. B., who I'd grown up with in Southern California, who would go anywhere at any time and was fine with discovering, somewhere along the way, why we had gone in the first place. Our last few adventures had been the best of them all because we started out knowing so little, drawn to an obscure river because of a sepia photograph in an old book written in Dutch, or by a curious-sounding village or tribe that nobody knew much about.

Late that afternoon, as the barge took on more fuel, we trudged through the mud, heading for the mine we'd read about in *Época*, a popular weekly we'd filched from the bar at the Sao Paulo International Airport, when we'd flown from Maracaibo, Venezuela, to Brazil the previous week. The pilot and kid stayed on board, doing small repairs. They'd already seen plenty of the mine, since the kid had spent more than a year down there before the pilot pulled him out. And anyway, their business was upstream. We had an hour before the barge hammered on.

The jungle was razed for 5 square miles, the fringe a splintered dam of logs crackling with flames and hissing in the downpour. The stench of sewage clashed with the ripe smell of worked earth as we approached a seething hive of ex-cons, ex-barbers, ex-doctors, even ex-priests, swimming in mud. The racket swelled and the smoke thickened as we trudged closer to the massive open pit and peered inside.

Two hundred feet below were an estimated 40,000 itinerant prospectors—*garimpeiros*—nearly naked, glazed in sweat and muck and rain, a thunderous livid mud hole of flashing shovels and writhing backs attacking a sloppy grid of claims averaging 20 foot square. A dozen men, hip to hip and ass to ass, worked each tiered plot.

I saw men slither into holes while others were dragged out by their ankles, bags of dirt clutched in their hands as all around men shoveled and swung axes and mauls and levered huge stones with pry bars. I watched a man turn to piss and get a pickax through his foot and the men fought and the one opened up the other's forehead to the bone as a dozen others piled on but the surrounding throng hardly noticed and never stopped.

A train of maybe 5,000 men trudged through the mud in an endless loop, humping enormous bags of soppy dirt up a steep slope, legs shin deep and churning, finally stumbling to the summit of a mountain of tailings and dropping their bags and collapsing as if dead except for their heaving ribs. Others, also by the thousands, as if standing on each other's shoulders, hunched under the huge wet sacks, teetered up a web of creaky bamboo ladders, some 50 feet high, linked via crumbling terraces.

Up top we watched the bags dumped and sluiced and panned by 10,000 other men while the carriers, sheathed in muck, rose wearily and joined the loop for another load from the wallowing sump, every task done by hand, the toil and wretchedness heightened by taskmasters screaming at the workers, who had little chance of getting rich and less chance of getting paid—40,000 muddy men, effectively slaves, gripped by gold fever, sustained by jungle tubers and coconut juice and the handful of millionaires strutting around the mud. One of them, featured in *Época*, was Guilhermino Caixeta, the 23-year-old son of subsistence farmers from Cuiaba. He'd dug out a nugget big as an attaché case and had bought a rancho in Borba with 12,000 head of cattle. Even gave his folks a job. As peons. I figured Guilhermino was still down in the mud owing to a virus known as *febre do ouro*, gold fever in English, a demonic soul sickness where healthy people stream in from the four corners hoping to catch it.

The mining operation and everyone in it was fueled by cocaine. Jacked by the drug, men could work longer, eat less, make more. Narcos controlled the trade until the military took over the mine the previous Easter. Now it was open war between the two, the brass looking to cash in either by strong-arming their cut or simply confiscating the blow and having junior officers peddle it directly to the miners. Freelancers trying to deal the generals out of their vig were given two options: a bullet to the head, or start dealing for the generals. But no matter, said *Época* in a lurid cover story. The blow would keep flowing over the Bolivian divide and up the river so long as there was a *cruzeiro* to buy it and gold to be had.

I paced along the calving mud perimeter, peering back into the mine, my eyes searching out Guilhermino Caixeta, the peon miner and multi-millionaire. He had to be down there somewhere, laughing, colossal nuggets in both hands. But all the faces swam together into a mirror image of my own dislocation.

Out beyond the swamp and the blazing shoal of trees, D. B. shuttered a photo of a spoonbill perched in a solitary jacaranda tree, peering down at a wilderness that no conscience, no soul, no God could endure. Only the *garimpeiros* could. Somewhere down there was their redemption. Somewhere down there was gold.

We forded back to the barge, trailing a string of young refugees—homesick and heartbroken—escaping from the mine, and pushed on upriver, hour by hour offloading our cargo of Caboclo and Indian kids. Prodded downstream by poverty, curiosity, or even indentured as the result of a father's dice game with the miners, the kids were thrown into the pit, surrounded by strangers and a strange language, fed strange food, made to work like animals. They sickened, collapsed, were sometimes beaten, and eventually clawed back upstream worse off than they were when they arrived and rarely one *cruzeiro* richer. They'd get off the boat at the vaguest shoals, find the footpath, and stumble into the fastness, never looking back.

Two days above the mine we passed the last boat scouring the riverbed for gold. Another day and we were past the last miner and the final logging camp and into primary terrain. The forest reared higher, the river narrowed, the current quickened, the boat slowed.

We hugged the bank against the current and plied through curtains of green light slanting down from the trees. The Caboclos called it *la salon verde,* the green room. Gnarled ropes looped down dangling in midair, flecked with black orchids and strangler figs. Bullfrogs croaked from fetid streams emptying into the river, and twice we passed coves of mangrove and the mad chorus of howler monkeys.

Every few hours we'd pass a small settlement marked by the sparse, meager homes of the Caboclos (the mixed-race river people of the lower Arce), whose thatched hovels, set high on piles, overlooked the river from above the monsoon line. Now and again the pilot would veer around islets of rushes in river shallows, his hands slow dancing with the giant ship's wheel.

I milled around the stern, smoking Brazilian cigarettes and staring into the trees. I started getting the feeling back at the mine that this might be my last sortie into the wild places, at least into the beating heart of it. But this time I couldn't turn away till I stopped clinging to my fatal uniqueness and holding off the world. Nothing out there had ever closed the distance, but we had no timetable so I'd stay till I found that hoped-for place where I'd molt out of myself and fly.

Suddenly the engine started clanking like hell, as if flying apart with each piston stroke. The pilot shut down to quarter power and the boy hurried below. Hammer blows rang out but the racket got louder so the pilot, fighting the current, pulled over at a small, abandoned settlement half a mile upstream, and tied off to a cannonball tree at the waterline. Several tattered, oblong huts stood on palm pylons in the small clearing.

The pilot and the boy worked below while we panted in the bow, then got forced off the boat when every inch of open deck was covered by the top end of a grimy diesel engine. The pilot came over and mumbled a few sentences, motioned toward the huts, handed me a sledgehammer, and went back below to the hammering. Portuguese was close enough to Spanish that I could usually catch the gist.

"He says the sun's going down and they need a fire to work by," I told D. B. "He's got to make Raul by Thursday and can't waste a day on repairs. We can get the wood off those shacks."

"What about the people?"

I glanced toward the huts. "The pilot said they all died last year. Measles."

We climbed up a notched log and into the first hut, haunted by the wooden basin intricately braided into the reed wall, a carved stool, a manioc grater leaning in the corner, as if carelessly left there yesterday. Then we went back outside and laid into the hut with the sledgehammer. In an hour we had a large pile of bamboo, reeds, and hardwood joisting and a fire licking 30 feet into the air.

The sky was dark and starless and all night the pilot and the boy tinkered with the engine, and all night D. B. and I worked the fire to keep the light high enough to slant into the boat, our shadows dancing over the somber screen of trees. Every so often my eyes were drawn to the prow of the barge where a big brass nautical figurehead, one of Neptune's angels, was welded in place, her profile standing out in relief but her features so gouged by collisions and deep green rust that she couldn't see a thing. But I kept checking to be sure because I felt like a grave robber, bashing down that hut.

The wood gave out in the wee hours, and D. B. and I took turns sledgehammering the palm pylons until they worked loose and we could draw them from the clayey soil and roll them down to the fire. Just past dawn, the engine fired over and the pilot waved us back aboard.

Behind us, a mountain of coals smoked and crackled. In a week the rising current would claim the cinders and the jungle would creep over the small clearing. Rain and wind would salt the ruin and in a matter of a few months there would be nothing but a solitary pylon to tell a traveler that people had lived and died here.

Rain beat down from one black cloud, the blood-red sun beside it. Steam welled off the moving water—dull, hanging, and so thick I could taste my own hot breath. Thunder clapped down the green corridor followed by sheets of blistering rain. The river would surge up a foot in 10 minutes, and 10 minutes later the sun burned alone and filled half the sky.

The barge forged on, the pilot's face pouring sweat and fixed upriver, like a man stalked from behind. Everything here was stalked from behind, from downriver.

The forest grew close and immense and the slender aisles between trees darkened. Late that afternoon the sky caught fire between rags of clouds and the river, flat and still, shined like liquid gold. An Indian paddled by, a huge manatee in the floor of his dugout. The Indian's chin was smeared red with annatto and on both sides of his face a tattooed streak ran from the corner of his mouth to his temple. He neither ignored nor acknowledged us, just slowly rode the current downstream, the tail of the huge mammal twitching and flashing in the light. We walked along the barge all the way to the stern and we kept watching the Indian till far in the distance he fused with the flaming water. It went like that for hours. I'd scribble in my journal, fold it shut in mid-sentence, and stare into the forest gliding by.

FOR MOST of a decade, since fleeing "The Ditch" (Yosemite Valley), my journal described a succession of exotic beatdowns consequent to chasing some feat or discovery: a first traverse, a first contact, an unexplored cave or uncrossed jungle or (fill in the blank). We didn't go to the wilds to just kick around and snap a few hero-shots. We had to *accomplish* something. Then on our way to a cave in Biak, in Irian Jaya, we met a shaman, and our trips changed course. Here was a man who conversed with crocodiles, a man, it seemed, from a planet different than our own. Except he wasn't. Nor were the native porters in Irian Jay who schlepped your bags wearing penis gourds, or the former headhunters in the middle of Borneo, or the Inuit in the Canadian Arctic who lived in a land of ice. We all were born and sang away, however we could, our private aloneness till our songs ran out of words. Nobody was spared and nobody was really different. Including me.

We gained the outpost at Quajos early the next day. Another small, grimy barge onloaded empty fuel drums and was heading downstream. D. B. and I helped the boy roll off most of their cargo, then the pilot steered the barge back into the current. The deck lay bare except for several fuel drums, three pallets of various foodstuffs, and the plastic Christmas tree. We watched the little settlement recede. A bend in the river, and everything behind us disappeared.

Three miles upstream the river pinched and steepened into a gutter of spume, roiling holes and small standing waves, and we drove straight into the teeth of the creaming tide, veering around sandbars and shoals, grating over river shallows as water-logged trees torpedoed the prow. In two weeks, the returning monsoon would raise the waterline 5 feet or more, but now, in low water, we butted river boulders and battled swirling eddies to swerve back into a precarious course.

Then the prop got entangled in a hydra of roots and lianas, and the pilot throttled down before the seizing engine blew us all to kingdom come. As the current plowed the barge downstream and out of control, the pilot dashed forward and threw off a huge rusty anchor, which dragged and skipped along the river bottom and finally caught with a lurch, the straining chain nearly tearing the strut off the deck. If a rusty link had let go, the recoil could have taken someone's head off.

The pilot lashed a rope around the boy's waist and D. B. and I braced to belay him from the helm, our legs stemmed out between crates on the iron deck. The boy drew a chest-full of air and dove underwater, machete in hand. We could hear the ticking on the prop followed by a mass of black vines floating to the surface. Finally, the boy's head burst through the foam and he gulped down half the sky in panicked mouthfuls before the current pulled him back under and we pulled harder still to reel him back into the boat. The anchor suddenly gave way and the boy disappeared underwater as the barge broached to the current, water gushing over the deck. D. B. and I scrambled back to the stern and hauled the boy in. He collapsed on deck like a big brown fish bound in roots and creepers, hacking and wheezing with water streaming from his nose. D. B. beat on his back until he heaved and hacked some more and started breathing right.

The pilot slammed the old barge into gear and battled to gain an upriver line as I returned to the bow and cranked the anchor back onboard.

On we moved, careening off rocks, grinding through snags, D. B. beside me at the bow, scouting and yelling out obstacles, pointing this way and that. The moment the boy caught his breath, he dashed below, hammering his brains out as the old pilot coaxed the rust bucket upstream, and it went on like that the entire day.

Toward sunset the river leveled off, and on both sides the green hedgerow ran straight ahead, a long hushed foyer tapering into the night. Far up in the highlands, outlined one against the other, the crests of a high cordillera were shuffled like a deck of stony cards— brusque peaks, bluish draws, jutting arêtes swaying and rising and falling in the harsh light, more inaccessible as we motored on.

The pilot maneuvered to the middle of the sleeping river, now 100 feet across. D. B. lowered the anchor. A mile ahead were more cataracts, said the pilot, and the 3 hours between us and the next settlement were the trickiest yet. He'd need all the daylight to navigate this stretch. We moored for the night.

Then the whole sky came down all at once. Through the gray pane of rain the land looked void and dark. The deck swirled shin-deep. Stripped to shorts, we stood in the bow, the hot rain streaming over us, staring at the pocked water, then at the buffeting limbs of the plastic Christmas tree, lashed to the deck. The pilot took great care with the tree, never brushing its snowy limbs when offloading drums and crates, and several times a day checking its lashings.

The new moon burned off the inky water. An electric silence fell around us and below it was the feeling of pure duration. The pilot gestured toward the left shore and said, "Urupa." As the two forms came into focus, we saw that these ghostly shapes were living things, squatting on their heels, their faces cast in irrefutable sneers. Somewhere in the bush around them lurked their clansmen, the dusky, bleeding sacrifices of an industrial juggernaut that added nothing to the beauty of their land or the life of their souls. In a few years, everything around us might be gone forever.

I asked D. B. how much farther he wanted to go. He looked upriver and said maybe we'd know when we got there, to the last place on no map, to utopia, which means, "there is no such place."

Under a pattern of stars, the pilot broke into a pallet and opened two canned hams. As we ate thick slices offered us on the tip of the pilot's stiletto, we watched the boy devour the entire second ham with his bare hands, jellied fat streaming from the corners of his mouth. Then the pilot found some beer and we drank two cans apiece and fell asleep where we lay.

Dr. Brown

N INTERN found the scratchy, 16-inch 33⅓
rpm Vitaphone soundtrack disc in the bottom
of a steamer trunk that for 70 years had gathered dust in the basement of the Malibu City
Library, which has one of the finest collections
of mountaineering texts in the United States. Back in the 1930s,
most radio shows used the Vitaphone discs, which run 15 minutes a side. The narrator on the Malibu article (possibly Damon
Runyon), striking the melodramatic tone common to radio back
then, recounts the life of a doctor and amateur mountain climber
named Nathan Brown. The disc was laid off to an MP4 file shortly
after its discovery, but if you want the full effect you can sit in a
booth in the AV department and listen to the recording on an old
RCA Victor "High Fidelity" record player a patron donated for
that purpose. A synopsis of the story runs like this:

Nathan Brown's ancestors arrived on the *Mayflower*. By 1850
they grew more Virginian tobacco than anyone and had four family members in public office. During the Great Depression, while
Nathan's stepfather served in the US embassy in Mexico, the family relocated to Mexico City. Here, young Nathan learned Spanish
and on weekends joined several young embassy staff for "climbing
expeditions" on Popocatepetl and Iztaccihuatl, the towering volca-
noes north of the capital. Nathan also favored bullfighting, mescal,
and girlfriends lured from the untouchable peon class. All of this

reflected poorly on the ambassador and at 18, Nathan was shipped back to Virginia for college.

Nathan had virtually grown up on the *volcanes* and in the piquant underbelly of Mexico City, and he missed both terribly. He excelled in school, but his private life still showed a weakness for women, drink, cards, and the ponies. There were several incidents. Nothing criminal, but family patriarchs condemned Nathan's weak character. Nevertheless, Nathan finished medical school and was immediately found in bed with the daughter of the pathology professor, a fierce man who launched a crusade against Nathan when the woman was found pregnant.

Records document a court order for the young doctor to cease and desist all contact with the woman—nicknamed "Ginger" for her long red hair—and Nathan Brown's arrest by federal marshals when the couple tried to elope. Nathan later spent 21 days in county jail for assaulting the professor after he shipped his daughter off to relatives in an undisclosed city. Nathan's stepfather, recently returned from Mexico City, gave him $300 and showed him the door. If Nathan was at all honorable, he would leave—forever.

Nathan went into the study and threw a dart at a map of the United States. The first toss stuck in Pennsylvania. He removed the dart and threw it again. This time it stuck in Arizona. Nathan scanned the map, saw 12,600-foot Humphrey's Peak, and he was on the next train heading west. Nine days later, standing on top of the peak, he gazed out over the plains. These mountains, and this broad and empty land, would have to do.

He made his way to Flagstaff, then just a wide spot in the road, where he let a room above a dry-goods store and opened up shop. One of his first patients, a woodworker who'd lost a finger in a lathe, made him a little wooden sign that he tacked to the bottom of the staircase: "Doctor Brown—Office Upstairs."

Town managers thought he should work out of the local clinic. But Dr. Brown didn't like the formalities, or making the poor sell their possessions to pay for treatment, so he continued seeing patients in his little room above the store. Decent citizens disapproved. But the many Mexican immigrants living in the dusty barrios just outside of town had no problem with Dr. Brown or his office. Here was a doctor who spoke their language, and he didn't even require cash money. *Frijoles, sopa de albondigas*, chickens—anything would do and no one was turned away. Day and night the infirm could be found sitting on the stairs of Dr. Brown's "office."

In time, owing to his habit of making for the mountains as soon as the staircase emptied, the woodworker fashioned the doctor a second sign that he would hang on his door: "Gone Climbing."

Then the daughter of a local merchant fell in love with Dr. Brown and the two were to be married. An engagement banquet was arranged. Important people were invited from Prescott, even Phoenix. Here was the chance to draw the good doctor back into society, where his talents could be appreciated and rewarded. But on the morning of the banquet, Dr. Brown was called away by a Navajo man who said his daughter was ill. The fiancée begged Nathan not to go, even arranged for an intern, newly arrived from Yuma, to take the case. But Doctor Brown couldn't have a young stranger handling his business with a man and a family he had known since he first arrived in Arizona. Since Dr. Brown had no car, they rode on the Indian's horse. It was a long ride. The girl had dysentery and over the next few days the doctor nearly lost her several times. When he returned to town, his fiancée's father met him on the stairs with a Colt .45, and the doctor was made to beg for his life.

Dr. Brown fled to his mountains. Instead of thinking about life, he'd simply lived it, and this always left people angry and disappointed. And the people he treasured so often went away, which was no one's fault but his own. All the way down the mountain Dr. Brown vowed to become someone earnest and upright, an influential man. But the idea died on the stairs of his office above the dry-goods store, where half a dozen patients were waiting.

And so Dr. Nathan Brown carried on, never quite sure if he was ducking life, bravely facing his fate, or trying neither and doing both. His mountains were a balm. After the broken engagement, townsfolk turned their backs on the man who had spurned them in favor of "wetbacks and Injuns." Rumors hinted that doctors at the local clinic would sometimes anesthetize a patient, then secretly fetch Dr. Brown to perform the surgery to which the patient was never made the wiser and the doctor was never paid or acknowledged. The rumors were denied by town managers, who demonized the doctor for his cheap and shameless conduct.

The doctor was too busy to reply, and anyway, most of the charges were true: Dr. Brown liked playing cards and drinking tequila with undesirables. Dr. Brown and his Mexican house cleaner were known to share the same bed. Dr. Brown stole medicines from the clinic and sold them to the poor—which was only half true. He gave the medicine away. And Dr. Brown was irresponsible because he risked his life every week in the mountains. The park ranger himself called Dr. Brown rash and reckless. He'd climbed every surrounding mountain a hundred different ways, usually alone, never using any safety equipment. Dr. Brown, they said, cared little for his life.

Years passed. The little town grew into a small city, with all the things you'd expect to find, including a town hall and a real hospital. But Dr. Brown stayed above the dry-goods store, and the audience on his staircase only grew.

Then one winter the doctor was visited by an elegant woman with long red hair, and a teenage girl, also a redhead. Nobody ever heard the doctor speak of family or relations, so the arrival of these visitors surprised everyone, none more than Doctor Brown. The trio were seen in the diner by the railroad depot, and later in the doctor's home office, leafing through a photo album the woman had brought along. His housekeeper had never seen the doctor, known for his easy conversation, look so low and speak so little. But the housekeeper didn't speak English and could provide friends no details except for the girl's quiet beauty and the woman's considerable diamond ring. Nor could she say why the red-haired woman and the girl left on the afternoon train. For the first time in memory, the doctor deserted patients waiting on his staircase and went to a Mexican saloon in the barrio north of town, and was thrown out for *borrachera y pelea*—drunkenness and fighting. He left for the mountains that night.

Two days later a storm hit Humphrey's Peak, just as the doctor reached the summit—or so the rangers figured. On his way down he apparently ran into a three-man party in bad shape. They were stranded, and were unprepared for the storm. Evidence suggested that the doctor tried to get the three down the mountain in the snowstorm, which lasted 2 days and 2 nights. The youngest victim, a boy of 14, was wearing the doctor's hat and parka when they found the four bodies, frozen into the slope. Doctor Nathan Brown was 42 years old.

The sheriff discovered that the doctor barely had enough money in the bank to buy a pine coffin and pay two men to dig a hole on the flanks of the cemetery. The newspaper made no mention of the death. No minister gave a eulogy and no businesspeople or city council members paid their respects. And yet over 500 people came to say goodbye to the doctor.

Most had walked there, some from great distances. A few had ridden horses or burros. The woodworker, an old Navajo man, and two Mexicans lowered the coffin into the ground with a rope. Several women lit votive candles and set them on the hard ground around the grave. Then one by one people came up and dropped mementos into the hole: locks of braided hair, poems, novenas and supplications, marriage certificates, baby photos and baby shoes, garlands of saguaro cactus blossoms, and whittled effigies of Jesus Cristo.

The people watched silently as the woodworker shoveled cold, rubbly earth onto the coffin, and planted a wooden cross. Then all the people wandered off for home. All but the old Navajo man. He sat down and stared at the grave.

One morning, years before, he and Dr. Brown had ridden a horse a long way. During the following 2 days, the doctor treated his daughter and never mentioned a fiancée or a banquet. For a man like Dr. Brown, a fancy marble headstone was not quite right. And who could afford one, anyway? But two scraps of two-by-four nailed into a cross wouldn't do either. The old Navajo man thought for a long time. Then he set off for the doctor's office above the dry-goods store.

For many years afterwards, if anyone walked out to the rocky edge of the cemetery, they'd come across a grave marked by a simple wooden cross upon which hung two little wooden signs: "Gone Climbing," and "Dr. Brown—Office Upstairs."

Gravity

THE SOUND hit me like a punch. My head jerked right and way over on the skyline I saw a human body pinwheeling from the bridge of the *Nose* all the way to the toe of the South Buttress, some 3,000 feet down. Then, silence.

The body came and went in no time, but I didn't move for an age, slumping at the anchor, frozen by the violence of a human meteor punching a hole through the sky.

The rock around me slowly came back into focus. The haul bag was still half a rope length below. The pulley, racks, and neatly stacked cords—all of this gear, and me standing there, on top of the Half Dollar, 800 feet up the *Salathé Wall* on El Capitan, suddenly felt criminal. I glanced down at my partner, Ed Barry, ratcheting up on ascenders and cleaning the pitch.

"Did you *see* that?!"

"No, but I sure the fuck *heard* it."

I finished hauling the bag and when Ed pulled onto the ledge we sucked back against the wall and started chain-smoking.

This was my first full summer in the Valley after graduating high school a month earlier. My mentor, Jim Bridwell, the biggest cheese in Yosemite climbing at the time, said I had to get up on El Cap while I still was green and could find an epic. Now I hated Bridwell. And climbing. Next morning we rapped off and I hitch-hiked back to Southern California. It was June 8, 1973.

I kicked around my folks' place for a few days, doing yard work and sleeping like a wild animal, on and off or not at all. The *Los Angeles Times* reported that Michael Blake, 19, of Santa Monica, California, had fallen from the "last rope" of the *Nose* route on El Capitan. For reasons under investigation by park rangers, the rope had severed and Blake had died. I must have seen Blake out at Joshua Tree, or up at Tahquitz Rock, the favored practice climbing areas in those days. Back then few Southern California teenagers were scaling El Cap, but I couldn't put a face to his name.

Though only 18 myself, my life didn't flow, it spun and churned. But once I locked sights on Yosemite, the currents raced in one direction. Now every hour and sometimes more often, Michael Blake surged through my mind like a riptide. It took the rest of that summer and many winter weekends out at Joshua Tree before the ferocious downfall of Michael Blake ebbed away.

I returned to Camp 4 the following May, the moment school let out. Straight off I ran into Beverly Johnson. The previous autumn she'd made the first all-female ascent of El Cap, with Sibylle Hechtel, and I wanted to hear all about it. But Michael Blake jumped in from the shadows, and Bev turned gray.

"I just got to the belay at the end of the Great Roof (1,800 feet up the *Nose)*," she said, "when I heard what sounded like a rocket lifting off." She looked up and saw, and nearly got cleaned right off the face by Michael Blake tumbling past.

Bev wasn't climbing much just then, she said. A couple of summers later she soloed the *Dihedral Wall,* also on El Cap, and I always wondered if that's what it took to purge Michael Blake from her life. (Bev was nails like that, until she later died in a helicopter crash.) I kept going to Yosemite, climbing walls for another decade until I finally got enough during a heat wave on Mount Watkins, gasping up a first ascent with Bridwell.

FAST-FORWARD FOUR decades and change. I'd written so much about climbing in Yosemite that even I couldn't face another John Long story about back-in-the-day. Then Dean Fidelman wrangled a deal to publish a large-format art book on Yosemite climbing in the 1950s, and he asked me to write the text. It took a year of haggling and revising before we finally finished *Yosemite in the Fifties: The Iron Age*.

Shortly after the book launch at Patagonia's shop in Santa Monica, I got a call from Jerry Volger, a stranger to me but a local Venice, California, man. A nephew had gifted him a copy of our new book. There was magic in the 50s, said Jerry. He knew because he'd been there, and when he cracked open our book it all came rushing back. He wanted to meet in person, though he never said why. I had too much going on to swap climbing stories with a hometown duffer, but for nameless reasons I felt compelled to go.

I met Jerry for breakfast a few days later, at a deli down in Marina del Rey. He had a collared shirt, a face thrown wide open and the eyes of a kid full of beans. Adventure people often have those eyes. The fascination is how most of us die without ever growing old.

"I'm ancient," said Jerry, now pushing 80, "but there was a time. . . ." And we both flew back to the Valley. Much as I had, Jerry came to climbing through athletics.

"I was a great surfer," he said. "I did all the sports."

Jerry had partnered with many of the Californians who I'd idolized and frequently saw during my high school days out at Joshua Tree and Tahquitz, where the old guard used to hang. But by 1973, and well into his 30s, Jerry still hadn't managed an ascent of El Capitan, the pot of gold for all California climbers.

"Then I met a young man bouldering out at Stoney Point," said Jerry. "An up-an-comer named Michael Blake."

My hands gripped the table and I stared at Jerry, unsure which surprised me more: my recoil at hearing Blake's name, or that through some cold-blooded fluke I was eating breakfast with Blake's last partner. I had largely forgotten Blake for going on 20 years, though at random moments a kind of lunatic film clip of his fall would flash through my mind, shoved back into shadows soon as the clip rolled out.

"I was there," I said. "Over on the *Salathé.* I saw Blake falling down the *Nose.*"

Jerry's wrinkled hands reached for his coffee cup.

"When I decided to call," he said, "I looked up your name in the white pages and there were over 50 John Longs. But I was ready to ring them all to try and find you, to thank you for doing the book. The first number I tried, was you."

I must have scowled. From the darkest cranny in my mind, where I'd stuffed all the other junk, the ghost of Michael Blake sprang out like a jack-in-the-box, and was standing on the table with his hands around our throats.

"What happened up there?" I finally asked. "I know the rope broke but I never heard how."

I wasn't worried about asking awful questions and rattling an old man, and wasn't amused that unseen forces had shoved us together. Blake was back and we had to deal.

"I was hanging from the bolts at the last belay," he said—then he stopped.

I'd visited that belay numerous times, at the top of the final headwall, with continents of air sucking at my feet, the trees and river, and tiny cars creeping along the loop road feeling more like a mirage than anything real. Just above this last anchor the wall rolls back abruptly after a few body lengths of easy fifth-class friction.

"Mike was coming up the last bolts," said Jerry, "which, if you remember, run a little sideways. I'd just hauled up the bag and tied it off when he yells up for me to look down. Mike was clipping up the bolts with aid slings, pushing one jumar up the rope as a backup. He wanted to stop at this great spot and take a photo."

Jerry sounded unsure about what followed, so the details are soft. Apparently, Blake stopped just below Jerry's belay, standing on a tattered sling threaded through an original Warren Harding bolt, and started framing the pic as Jerry, looking straight down, leaned back from the anchor for a hero-shot.

The only written report I found was from "Off the Wall: Death in Yosemite," co-written by then park ranger Butch Farabee Jr. The summit bolt ladder was 16 years old, the write-up reminded, and when Blake put his full weight on one of the final bolts, "it gave way, yanking out of the wall."

The moment the bolt pulled, Blake must have wrenched onto his one jumar (a dodgy technique that betrayed his inexperience) clamped at an angle on the taut lead rope. The oblique loading torqued the ascender off the rope. Because Blake hadn't tied in short, Volger watched him free-fall to the end of the line, "which severed against some unknown salient on the face," wrote Farabee. "Literally within feet of finishing a Grade VI route, Blake fell 3,000 feet off El Capitan all the way to the base of the Dawn Wall." And Jerry Volger watched him go the whole way. I only caught the ending.

"What happened next?" I asked.

"I don't know," said Jerry. He looked old and vacant. "Next thing I remember was meeting some hikers on the Falls Trail, 5 or 6 miles away."

We sat silently, sipping our coffee. Rilke wrote that a ghost's greatest fear is aloneness, and I wondered if Blake was still holding Jerry hostage. The thought didn't feel strange because the whole encounter ran like a hallucination. I shifted focus to those final moments on the bolt ladder, scrambling for solid ground.

Shortly after the accident, rangers and several climbers from the rescue site had hiked up to the summit, roped down and inspected the last belay. The haul bag, I was told, still hung off the bolts as did Jerry's gear, including a ragged end of lead rope dangling in the void.

"You must have untied and soloed to the top," I said.

After just watching Blake go the distance, those last friction moves must have felt lethal in lug-soled Robbins boots.

"It's all a blank," said Jerry, staring at nothing. Part of him was still hanging on that bolt ladder, the part he couldn't remember.

"After the accident, I struggled," he said. "Finally a friend told me I'd had a shock and had to rest."

Jerry never climbed again.

I kept talking but I've no idea for how long, and whatever Jerry said is lost to me now. The same gravity that had pulled two strangers together had hurled a teenage climber to the ground, merciless fallout from a force so weak that scientists can barely measure it. Yet it took all of our words and silences to finally get the measure of our experience, and the ghost of Michael Blake, no longer alone through our remembering. Slowly, without us noticing, Jerry and I became just a couple of people talking to each other.

When the bill came, I asked the waitress to take a picture of us with my cell phone. Later, at home, when I studied the photo, nothing in either of our faces suggested the climb that took 43 years to finally be over.

El Tiburon

CARLITOS RETURNED from the *licoria* with enough Lager Polar to put out the Great Fire of London. We took our time loading the giant ice chest and pouring three bags of ice over the glistening brown bottles.

"You're probably thinking the ice cools down the beer," said Carlitos, "but really, the ice sucks the heat out of the bottles. It's called convection."

"You're just making that shit up," I said.

"Give me the keys," said Marisol. Carlitos went to complain and she cut him off. "If you *gafos* are drinking your way across the *sabana*, I'm driving."

Carlitos handed Marisol the keys and we piled into the panel van, rolled out of El Tigre and across the *gran sabana*, heading for the coast. The sweet musk of mint thicket and *flor de Mayos* swirled in through the windows we kept rolled down to kill the heat. It was 1992, and if you needed a solid dose of tropical exotica with a side order of beauty queens (I married one) and fried plantains, you couldn't do better than Venezuela. But it takes some getting used to.

Life in Venezuela, for the common Juan like me, defies the rules of proper narrative, with a beginning, middle and end, an actual plotline, however vague, and discrete scenes with transitions, logically connected, that a casual reader can follow.

Instead, life lurches and stalls like a picaresque novel with the chapters randomly shuffled, the characters driven not by love nor money, but by whatsoever shines, amazes, smells good, has magical powers, is big and fancy, is fat, scary, or very small, is very noble, or stinks to high heaven—all compelling reasons to jag sideways and see where it takes you. A person with a one-track mind can make a fortune down here, but he'll have few friends and no fun. An excellent Venezuelan story wanders on whim, never arrives, and the path never straightens till the church bells ring. And everyone talks shit the whole time. This might be a better characterization of myself than anyone in South America, but you get the picture.

Marisol and my wife, Teresa, took turns driving and swerving around potholes 3 feet across and veering onto the dirt shoulder when the asphalt vanished or the road trundled through a bog. Every 6 years a new governor promised to fix the roads. No one was sure where the money went but it never went into the highway, which stretched off arrow-straight across vast pastureland veined by lazy streams, all blues and greens heaped upon an unbroken horizon. Far in the distance a lone horseman led a few cattle. The cowboy could walk for days, but there'll always be more *sabana*. Always the *sabana*.

"CAN A man get some music back here?" asked Carlitos.

The old tape player was lashed to the dash with wire and duct tape and it cannibalized everything from *Gaita* harp music to proto-*merengue* tunes with enough quick horn play to raise the dead. The only cassette to survive was a homemade tape of balladeer Julio Jaramillo, whose heart was so broken we couldn't stand it, so we sang along. It was Christmas Eve. None of us were religious but the yuletide in Venezuela—bound up with Catholic voodoo, food to die for, and a monsoon of booze—is like found money. And we were out to spend it all.

Late that night, Marisol pulled into the queue at the Conferry docks in Puerto La Cruz, where an armada of ferries looped to and from Isla Margarita, the "Pearl of the Caribbean." Many of Teresa's extended family were *Margariteños* who had moved off the island but still had homes there or had relatives with homes and who'd always return for the holidays. So we'd head over for Christmas and New Years and continued this tradition so long as my two daughters were growing up.

Around midnight we joined the crowd rolling onto the ferry, climbing a steep metal staircase to the upper decks, above the jalopies and big rigs stowed below. The moment the women and children lay down on mats and dozed off, Carlitos said, "Let's go," and we joined the men crowding the open space near the prow, drinking and watching the stars.

"It's only 49 miles to Margarita," said Carlitos, "but the ferries are old and one just like this capsized in the Philippines a few years before and killed 600 people."

Carlitos was always hopping up the facts like that, thinking he could make the person, thing, or story "more better." But he couldn't improve the night, drinking beer under a canopy of stars onboard the MS *Rosa Eugenia*, which managed the trip across the water in less than 5 hours, landing just after daybreak.

Ropes were strung from high places on the ship over to great rusty thwarts on the docks. Skinny kids, dark as burl, walked the steep ropes bare-footed and dove like thunderbolts after coins we threw into the water, sometimes far below. Many tried tricking the kids, throwing nuts and bolts and sparkly bits of whatever they could scavenge off the ferry. But the kids only dived for real money. "I don't know how they know the difference," said Carlitos, "but they always do."

We were staying with Teresa's childhood friend, Luz, a Margarita native who had moved to Caracas after college. Early on she'd tangled with men and now she ate them alive, though I managed to stay out of that mostly. Her folks, Don Julio and

Doña Rosalva, rarely left the island and had a two-story place in La Asunción, several blocks from Cathedral Nuestra Señora de La Asunción, the oldest church in Venezuela. Doña Rosalva was a retired grade school teacher and Don Julio, also retired, had played valve trombone in the state orchestra and local salsa groups and he drank the powerful native caña like water.

Don Julio's son, Chico, was also no stranger to liquor bottles. Back then, many on the island were accomplished drinkers. Locals had appropriately rechristened then Governor Fucho Tovar (Fucho = diminutive for Rafael), Mucho Tomar, or big drinker. That's how people rolled before the Venezuelan currency tanked 2 decades later, when populist president Hugo Chavez ("*El Eterno*") and his Castro-inspired *socialismo* ran the country into the shitter and bankers and professors had to kill their pets for food. But the Bolivar was strong for the moment, so for this trip and many that followed, we drank.

The hacienda had half a dozen rooms and two stories. A big open square in the middle had the roof cut away. Afternoon showers fell in a torrent, filling plastic paint buckets, old truck tires, and other makeshift flowerpots overflowing with hibiscus and oleander. In that redolent pause after the rain stopped, moths and butterflies swarmed the blooms, including a deep blue *mariposa* that floated flower to flower like a piece of living sky.

Milagros del Valle Marcano Paz, Luz's grandmother, sat in unhinged majesty, propped up in a plastic lawn chair pulled back clear of the rain.

"She's well over a hundred years old," said Carlitos when we first saw her sitting there in the front room space. "People have been saying so for 10 years, easy, and that makes things true in Margarita."

Over in the corner, brother Chico swung in a hammock, watching English League *futbol* on a black and white TV and working on a bronze liter bottle of Old Par. Margarita was a duty-free island so good booze was cheap, a fact that killed more locals than old age, heart disease, and cancer combined. Chico used the bottle cap as a shot glass—a chintzy way to drink, I thought, except he'd tilt the bottle every 5 minutes so it drained quickly enough.

Once we got the kids settled, we drove over to visit Kin Ting—that's the phonetic spelling, and I've no idea where the Siamese-sounding name came from since the man was Creole head to toe. Kin Ting was a fisherman and one of Don José's childhood friends. Margarita roughly describes an hourglass on its side, and most residents live on the more developed eastern half of the island, near the duty free shopping in Porlamar, a favorite getaway for Dutch and Germans fleeing fierce Euro winters. Kin Ting lived and fished on the western, leeward side of the island, where he and Don Julio had grown up.

The single lane road passed through an isthmus, then slashed through jade hedgerow climbing right to a ridge, while plunging left straight into the ocean. Clouds skittered over the working sea, where turquoise winked to blue then silver, slate, and aquamarine.

"Agnostics never make it this far," said Carlitos, repeating the local phrase. "But Christopher Columbus did." The green mountain, said Carlitos, a mermaid sighting, and other miraculous things were all mentioned in Christopher's journal, which he presented to Spain's King Ferdinand in 1492.

Just past El Manglillo, "which has more dogs than people," according to locals, we followed a dirt road to a continent of sand drifts and terraced rock. A few dozen cinderblock houses were cobbled into stony hollows, reminiscent of the Anasazi dwellings at Mesa Verde. A tin-roofed A-frame, set back from the edge of the sea, covered a haystack of nets beavered over by teenage boys, all fishermen in training. We met Kin Ting, with handshakes all around, climbed onto a motorized skiff, and headed out over flat water.

Kin Ting was burned black and had that far-reaching gaze you sometimes see in cowboys and Bedouins who grew up in open spaces. He stayed up in the prow, mostly, pointing directions to his grandson, Felipe, who manned the tiller with both hands and whose eyes never left his grandfather. It was Christmas Day and Felipe wore his new red trunks and a baseball cap for his favorite team, the Caracas Lions. They had the day off but the sea was their life.

A certain kind of person, who fits in awkwardly most everywhere else, has always found sanctuary on the big water. It keeps them poor and exhausted, and is chancy when the wind picks up, so rational people don't normally work there. But they rarely have what the fishermen has: magic. Adrift in old rhythms. And drinking whiskey when they feel like it. Kin Ting had a fifth of Johnny Walker and he'd stop every few minutes to pass the bottle around the horn. Then we'd motor on to no place in particular, never dreaming of being somewhere else.

I'd been up for days, so next time we paused I dove into the water to clear my head. Currents I never saw swept me off toward Trinidad. I dog-paddled like mad but only drifted farther to sea till Kin Ting motored over and hauled me back in with a calloused paw. Forget about swimming in those waters, I said. I'd be right about that, said Kin Ting. "But El Tiburon—"

Don Julio stirred at mention of that name, which means shark in Spanish.

El Tiburon was a legend with local fishermen, and like everyone on this side of the island, Carlitos had heard the stories so many times he could scream. But Tiburon's name was heard less and less because he was going on 80 and had hung up his nets years before, though he still swam daily. And far, said Kin Ting.

In the days before motors, Kin Ting and friends would row the nets out to set their buoys. No one remembers when, but El Tiburon began swimming the nets out by way of a rope lashed round his waist. He could drag the nets for miles, sometimes towing the boats behind him, sometimes with a knife between his teeth—surely a poetic touch—sometimes getting separated from the flotilla and having to swim ashore from way out there. One time El Tiburon got snagged in evil currents that pulled him miles out to sea and his *familia* feared him dead till a day later when he washed up in Paraguachí, far down the coast. By then Johnny Walker was doing most of the talking, but Don Julio and Kin Ting kept nodding their heads saying, "*Es verdad*," as Carlitos related the old stories he had grown up with. They were wonderful stories, and I all but forgot them soon as we motored back across the isthmus.

Chico was drunk. And worried. "Officials," which mean many things in Venezuela, had chosen him to help carry the Virgin. An honor, said Chico, and we had to get to The Sanctuary, over in Margarita Valley, right now. Don Julio reminded us that nothing during Christmas season ever came off on time, so just relax. Virgins are an endangered species all across the Caribbean, and I wondered which one Chico had been chosen to carry, and why. I was still working slightly in the dark per Venezuela, having only been married 3 years.

Cars were parked bumper-to-bumper along every street surrounding The Sanctuary, a white shrine for La Virgin del Valle, Virgin of the Valley and patroness of eastern Venezuela. A life-size effigy of the child Virgin, with a pearl-encrusted cape and solid gold tiara, garlanded with white roses, was bolted to a wooden platform big as a billiard table. Red velvet curtains draped down over a dozen bearers hunkered underneath the platform, who inch-wormed the Virgin around the mob. You'd have to be born into old-school Margarita to feel the beating pulse of this fiesta. But here was a great event.

Aside from a few thousand of us pilgrims, a group of dignitaries, mostly priests and Venezuelan naval officers, turned out in garish ceremonial outfits, were seated up on a stage. The ritual borrowed somewhat of the Hajj, where a mob of Muslim faithful circle the sacred Kaaba stone. Except here, the Virgin was paraded around the dignitaries, who rose when She passed, crossing themselves and drawing sabers and saluting, while off to one side a girl in fashionably ripped jeans, heels, and mirrored sunglasses butchered Ave Maria on a megaphone.

The problem was liquor. And heat. Especially in the space under the Virgin's platform, where Chico was stooping and marching with friends. They'd all been drinking through the whole vacation. Fresh air could hardly penetrate the velvet curtains. The bearers were tiring fast and sweating buckets. After several laps around The Sanctuary, the Virgin herself was looking loopy as her platform rocked and pitched.

Then it happened. One of the bearers upchucked, fomenting a dire miasma that had no escape and triggered a chain reaction, and the holy procession was saved only because the mob grabbed the platform at the last second, before it went over and The Virgin took a dive.

For one suspended moment the whole raucous, high-gloss, holy-watered production tumbled into farce: The Virgin, kitschy custodian of chastity for every deflowered Juanita in eastern Venezuela; the bishops and generals up on the stage, a fêted band of blowhards play-acting in Halloween costumes; and all the adorable little girls in their colorful party dresses and shiny shoes and braided hair, their tiny lips painted red, like the Virgin herself, as if their hovering mothers sought to sugar and preserve them like fruit, that they should never age and do the nasty with jackoffs and rummies and never learn that every heart is broken and we all must die. Who wouldn't grope after God? And when that went bust we drank a little more—the drinking that made corpses. And the girl blaring into that megaphone sang a little louder. Anything to ease the death of miracles.

The rest of that visit is a blur. The booze and fatigue and New Year's chaos spun me into a vortex I didn't escape till leaving Margarita a week later and flying back to L.A.

THE FOLLOWING Christmas I found myself back in the house in La Asunción, watching rain fall through the hole in the roof as Chico, parked in his hammock, worked a bottle in the corner. In order to control our own drinking, Carlitos and I swore off daylight boozing and spent the time running, hiking, hitting the gym if it was open, and playing pick-up basketball. And we ate smart, too. None of that greasy fried crap. Rather fruit, vegetables and lean meats. Through this routine we spent the greater part of our day boosting health and sanity, which we believed limited the carnage when the sun went down and we started drinking like crazy.

During an afternoon jog down by Playa Varadero, we noticed several trucks emblazoned with logos for Cerveza National, a popular Venezuelan beer. Twenty day-hires and a *Chinito* (Chinese) boss in board shorts were erecting bleachers on the sand and inflating an arch that would serve as the finish and starting line for an open ocean swimming race. Triathletes and watermen, said *Chinito*, were arriving from all over to compete. An Olympic hopeful from the national team was favored to win, but local money was on a Cuban named Rubio. Governor Fucho Tovar would personally supervise the bikini contest. A big motor launch had dropped anchor a mile and a half off shore—the turnaround point for the out-and-back swim—and a tethered National blimp was hovering above it. National was donating fifty kegs of pilsner beer, so twenty-five might actually get there.

"So long as the beer lasts," said Carlitos, "Mucho Tomar will hang around and so will the crowd. This could be epic."

A long surf ski, basically a sit-on-top kayak, was offloaded from the National truck. Chinito said that as a promotional gimmick, a local waterman named El Tiburon was scheduled to perform a short demonstration swim before the official race kicked off. The kayak would follow the old fisherman in case he tired and needed something to hang onto. I reminded Carlitos about the yarns he'd recited about El Tiburon during our expedition on Kin Ting's boat—how he swam nets out with a knife between his teeth and treaded water all night long in a hurricane.

"And was born in the ocean to a mermaid," said Carlitos, and how he later was found clinging to the back of a snapping turtle, something even Don Julio said was *probablemente no es cierto*, was probably not true. And now this Creole Poseidon would swim a few strokes for the crowd, who knew him by way of the classic stories, or not at all. It was a novel promotion and a great honor for El Tiburon, said Carlitos.

Back at the house in La Asunción, a handful of retired fisherman, all grade school friends of Don Julio's, had joined us to eat glistening loaves of *pan con jamon* (a smashing sweet bread and ham medley) and the traditional Christmas *hallaca*—marinated pork, raisins, capers, and olives wrapped in cornmeal dough, swaddled with plantain leaves, tied with twine and boiled like a tamale. Interlarded with strategic shots of rum and a running stream of cold lager, the yuletide carried us far.

Once the serious eating was over, the women drank sweet Uruguayan wine and sang carols and we men shambled into the front room to play checkers. Someone produced a bottle of a local rum called Cacique, which drained straight to the migraine corner of your brainpan and sloshed around there for days. The shade was stripped off the lamp, which cast dancing shadows on the whitewashed wall. We were just getting started.

Carlitos put on some Dominican salsa music and mentioned that their boy El Tiburon was scheduled for a demo swim at the comp the next afternoon. They must be excited to have one of their own representing at such a big event, he added. The fishermen hardly looked up from the checkerboard. I wondered if they weren't secretly frightened for their boy. I mentioned the rescue kayak, in case El Tiburon tired, and they chuckled. Carlitos wasn't so sure. Maybe it was reckless to have an old man out there battling those currents, kayak or not. Finally one of the fishermen spoke up. He was built like a rhino and had hands as calloused as a rawhide.

El Tiburon never missed afternoon mass, said the fisherman. Not since he retired years ago. And why would he screw around with a bunch of kids swimming in his ocean? If El Tiburon showed up at all, he'd swim the same race like everyone else. And he'll win going away.

The others grumbled, "*Claro*," and "*Por seguro*," and moved the red and black pieces around the boards.

"*Por favor*," said Carlitos. Like some waterlogged old carp, pushing 80 years old, could keep pace with Olympic-caliber distance swimmers and triathletes. I held up my hand to Carlitos—it wouldn't do to ridicule a couple, three fishermen who never got out of grade school and knew less about modern athletes than thermodynamics. One of the fishermen thrust the Cacique bottle at me and chuckled again.

"Go over to Playa Varadero tomorrow," he said. "If El Tiburon shows up, you can see for yourselves." The others weren't bothered to even talk. We were being suffered as fools, which felt quaint and wonderful.

Next afternoon, Carlitos and I jogged over to Playa Varadero and watched the crowd gather while a rock band from Trujillo threatened to blow out the sun. We all marveled at the beauties marching around a stage in bikinis. National brewery was good to their word about the fifty kegs. Dozens of hostesses trimmed out in blue satin National bikini tops brimmed tankards of beer just as quick as we could shove them under the tap.

An athlete's-only area near the start, below the inflatable National arch, filled with swimmers small-talking and psyching each other. With National giving real money to the first ten finishers, these guys meant business. There were several girls as well, including a giantess named Prima Doña, an alabaster beauty with close-cropped, bleach blonde hair and a wire-thin, creeping vine tattoo winding around her torso. Carlitos and I couldn't take our eyes off her. Rubio, the Cuban favorite, resembled a deep-fried James Dean. Even had the pout. With all this going on we hardly noticed the old man pushing a bike across the sand.

"That's gotta be him," said Carlitos, elbowing me in the ribs.

El Tiburon was taller than I had imagined, around 6 foot, was more golden than brown, with barnyard shoulders and a saint's face as rucked and seamed as the floor of Lago Maracaibo. He set his bike against the arch, padlocked it, and folded a ragged towel over the cross bar. Then he walked over to a spray unit set up to cool the racers and he stood there in the misty curtain like a triton in a fountain, staring out to sea. As the fisherman had promised, El Tiburon had come there to race, something so incidental to the proper competition it got only casual mention over the loud-speaker. We stood outside the roped-off area and had a clear view of the other athletes, who hardly noticed and didn't care about the wrinkled fishermen swimming in their race.

Three minutes and counting.

The competitors stripped down to trunks and started wind-milling their arms and jostling for position at the starting line, a short ways inland from the National arch. The crowd tightened at the edges. We elbowed around in order to keep staring at Prima Doña's granite ass. El Tiburon stood motionless at the back of the pack.

"*Cuatro, tres, dos, uno—*"

The gun sounded and the swimmers stormed across the sand and dove into the sea, surfacing in a flurry, their arms thrashing the water. All but El Tiburon, who walked toward the water on unsteady legs. Just to his right a young man dragged the rescue kayak, just in case. The main pack was well out in front when El Tiburon duck-dove under the shore break and took his first stroke, which brought a charity roar from the crowd. The kayaker flipped in the surf but quickly crawled back aboard and caught up. Carlitos and I got a beer and trudged up to a bluff overlook, where we could see the race unfold and where the bikini models were preening and signing T-shirts and slapping the traveling hands.

The pack quickly lengthened into a loose chain, churning past small breakers in the shallows and clearing a sea ledge where the ocean floor dropped off and the water went gray to Persian blue. In open ocean at last, swirling currents yanked the chain apart, sending the pack in all directions, like a stain spreading out on a blue tablecloth. An on-shore wind and low rolling swells doubled their trouble. A swimmer was lucky to pull a couple clean strokes before getting hauled sideways by the rip. The stronger swimmers held a ragged trajectory, but they were covering 15 or 20 feet to gain 10 on the motor launch and the turn-around, still better than a mile out there.

Far behind, El Tiburon swam at a casual but fluid clip. Once he pulled into open water he was little affected by the violent rip tides, and seemed to glide through hidden troughs, now hitchhiking onto the off-shore edge of whorls that thrust him out at speed, as if he and the currents were on speaking terms. Slowly he closed the distance with the stragglers in the main pack.

"Old fart might make that boat out there," said Carlitos.

The kayaker tired of fighting the currents and turned around. If El Tiburon couldn't gain the motor launch, we'd have a dead fishermen on our hands.

We watched the swimmers shrink to specks, then occasional white flashes. Then only a working sea stretched vacantly out to the motor launch and the tethered National blimp, two dots bobbing on the blue horizon. Time for another beer.

The crowd defied gravity and flowed uphill to the bluff overlook where the bikini girls were bumping and grinding on the back of a flatbed truck as the band played at 100 decibels. There was a dancing competition with all us guys ogling the models. A trophy and two judges lent the contest a veneer of respectability. Then the generator went down and we were all left standing there. It'd take a while for the swimmers to stroke back into view, so I headed over to the hot dog cart and ran into Governor Rafael "Fucho" Tovar.

Though I grew up with Spanish, they always know I speak "the English," and Fucho's wasn't half bad. He'd learned most of it listening to Frank Sinatra LPs and watching *I Love Lucy*, according to Carlitos. We both bought dogs and Fucho garnished his handsomely with mustard, onions, and croutons. I mentioned Prima Doña—not that the governor would have noticed—and I thought the man might cry. Whatever else one might say about the governor, he was right there with the rest of us common Jose's, sans bodyguard and fanfare, the gazillionaire owner of Conferry, who grew up selling empanadas off a cart in front of his house in nearby Juan Griego, who later left for Caracas and worked in banking, went to law school, fought his way into the Senate, the governor's office, then dropped by the swimming comp there at Playa Varadero, eye-balled a couple bikini babes, and bought himself a dog. The chances of sharing a frank with such a man in an American or European country were exactly zero. And it's this wholesale disregard for hierarchy that gives Latin America, for all of its blunders and hogwash, a leg up on every other culture on earth.

"Holy shit," said Carlitos, who'd begged a set of binoculars off a Dutch tourist and was glassing the open ocean. The swimmers were growing on the horizon and we moved in a crush over to the edge of the bluff, where one of the bikini girls tripped and took a nasty tumble down to the sand below and was helped back to her feet by fifty local boys.

Carlitos handed me the binos and I framed up the first three swimmers, roughly moving together, several hundred yards in front of the others. And El Tiburon was one of them.

The Dutch tourist snatched back his binos and Carlitos and I scrambled down to the beach. Word quickly spread and "El Tiburon" was repeated a thousand times in 30 seconds. The great fisherman was surely pushed by unseen hands; only a fellow Margariteño could swim so wonderfully; and according to the man screaming over the loudspeaker, we were witnessing a miracle.

El Tiburon could never keep pace with the other two in an Olympic pool. But out there in open ocean, on this squirrely-watered, windward side of the island, El Tiburon was nonpareil, not so much swimming as navigating the rips and whorls. Now the other two, Rubio the Cuban, and Prima Doña, were trying to track the old man's course, but lacking his feel for the currents, they could only compensate with furious strokes. Slowly they tired and fell back as El Tiburon, with the wind and swells behind him, squirted over the sea ledge, snagged a gentle comber, and body-surfed up onto the sand, soft as church music.

Police and lifeguards fought off cameramen and the mob to give El Tiburon a clear path up the beach, through the inflatable National arch and just beyond to the finish line. But El Tiburon hadn't run in 20 years, and as he shuffled toward the arch in no kind of hurry, Rubio and Prima Doña closed behind him.

The crowd jumped and shouted "*¡Ándale!*" and "*¡Ir!*" as if the force of their voices might blow the old man to victory. Instead we all watched El Tiburon stop at his bicycle near the arch, rinse himself off in the sprayer, then towel himself dry, watching curiously as Rubio and the giantess sprinted past.

Attention swung to the finish line, where Prima Doña out-leaned the Cuban by that much. The mob converged and Prima Doña was marched around—ten boys at each elbow—as the band played "Tush" up on the bluff. Carlitos and I jostled over to the arch, but El Tiburon was already gone. Probably to mass, said Carlitos.

Tirada los Tubos

WE PLANNED on an early start but Jimmy got waylaid by a *telenovela* (soap opera) marathon about a young lothario named Figaro (prodigal son of a cruel and filthy rich cattle rancher), who stumbled across a smashing nun named Milagros, who used to be Figaro's squeeze during grade school in Maracaibo. Then a fire broke out and the plot took off but we didn't, not leaving the "*esquisito*" Hotel Maravillas till going on midnight, when we rolled out of Caracas in a rusty Chevy Biscayne.

Early the next morning we sputtered into El Tigre, Anzoátegui state, a ghetto town on the upswing, sprawled across hot savannah broken here and there by mint scrub and bushy palms. This was a decade before Venezuela nationalized their petro industry, then largely managed by *Yanqui* engineers holed up in vast, hermetically sealed *campamentos*. The mercury sizzled at 95 in the shade—if you could find any.

The cinderblock house went wild when we arrived. Three-hundred-pound Grandmamma stopped kneading the *arepa*, quavered to her feet, and kissed Jimmy, her very nephew, on the lips while his arms went rigid and he bicycled his sneakers. Niece Pepina, 6'1" and thin as a cactus quill, dashed over with a tray of pig's feet *al carbon* as a dozen kids sprang from shady nooks. A home in Venezuela is rarely short on kids. The people pride themselves on getting married when they want, not when they should, and they quickly fashion a couple *niños* because they can. Three years before, I'd been the first gringo to enter their house, or their neighborhood, but so long as I was Jimmy's friend, and now Teresa's fiancé, the house, and everything in it, was mine.

We slept till dinnertime, when brother Luis Manuel rushed in from work, cowboy hat perched just above his dark eyes, a chrome starter's pistol in his hand. A thick, mustachioed 35-year-old with the face off a flyer in the post office, he worked 60-hour-a-week shifts at the petrochemical plant outside Anaco to preserve the dignity of the household.

He bolted past Jimmy and me into the *jardin* to fire three glorious rounds (blanks) into the sky. Then he laid down several Creole dance steps, booted a sleeping *perro*, cracked his bullwhip, fired a fourth blank at me, then slapped my back till I gasped. His black eyes narrowed: "*Matrimonio? Cuando?*"

When I mentioned a tentative date for the wedding, Luis Manuel kissed me, then Pepina, then Jimmy, then Grandmamma, then he broke back into his dancing, faster this time. My first time in El Tigre I swore Luis Manuel was acting for effect, like he was starring in bad TV. Only when I spied him all alone and acting the same way did I believe he was this uncorked. He once more made for his pistol but was halted by a bottle of Doña Bárbara (a low-grade rum that could strip the paint off a battleship) proffered in Grandmamma's plump hand. He swilled a tan inch before Pepina snatched it back for Grandmamma to lock in a chipped wooden cabinet to which there was only one key, the silver skeleton Grandmamma tucked into her black lace brassiere, a fallow acre no man sober or drunk would dare trespass.

We all sat down and feasted through flanks of *bistec*, fried plantains, *ensalada aguacate*, crunchy sheets of *casabe*, quarts of *jugo de tamarindo*, and various colorful tubers whose names I could never get my tongue around.

Later, Grandmamma got a headache. That required a trip to the *farmacia* for headache medication, an expedition of nearly 5 blocks.

Luis Manuel could have walked there and back in 10 minutes, but he took the pickup—because he had one, because it had a full tank, because he'd washed and waxed it on the weekend, and because it had straight pipes and when he gunned it, which he normally did, it roared like the cannons at Pampatar. All this made the man seem the more *magnífico* as he thundered down the street to the cheers of friends lounging in hammocks on their verandas.

Luis Manuel would not travel alone, because going to the farmacia in the pickup was an event, and an event in Venezuela, no matter how big or small, is always performed in numbers.

I wedged myself into the bed of the pickup among a dozen kids, several dogs, and Grandmamma, whom Luis Manuel, Jimmy, and I had conveyed there in an easy chair, and who would check the date on the medication to ensure it was *bueno*. As Luis Manuel gunned the truck down the road, frame sagging to the pavement, the great straight pipes belching 3-foot flames and whoops sounding from every open door we passed, I reentered the emphatic world of a people who lived like everybody would if they could ever stop worrying about life and just live it.

Back in the house, as I watched a red gecko creep across a peeling white wall, Luis Manuel laid out his plan. Or started to.

"*Guacala!* What now?" Jimmy moaned.

As I later learned, Luis Manuel's plans often ended in spectacular debacles, including bulldogging range donkeys, a stunt that cost Luis Manuel several teeth and a fractured collarbone; salsa dancing with the mayor's wife, resulting in jail time and a flogging for Jimmy; and paddling a canoe after the truculent Yajiros, the local Indians, into the darkest jungle and getting lost for 3 days.

"*Tirada los tubos*," said Luis Manuel.

"Shooting the tubes?" Jimmy asked.

"*Si, chamo.*" And Luis Manuel explained.

During construction of the nearly completed hydroelectric plant in Tascabana, 30 miles out of town, the Cariña Indians had discovered tube-shooting through a fortunate accident. The plant's cooling system required re-routing several surrounding rivers, this accomplished via 5-foot-diameter steel tubes that piped water along a twisting path to a central aqueduct, where it drained into the plant and exited to a river below. *Tirada los tubos* was to intentionally do what had accidentally happened to a young Indian boy, who while diving for crayfish, got drawn into one of the half-filled drainage tubes and became a human torpedo, tearing in black, downhill passage for several hundred feet before his free-fall exit into the open aqueduct.

To give us a clear picture, Luis Manuel—who'd punished a covert bottle of *anis* for several hours—assumed various dive-bomb positions on the cement floor until he spotted a terrific *cucaracha* on the wall, a 3-incher, black as sin. He sprang for his bullwhip, but Pepina thrust out her pool cue leg and tripped him. The roach zipped into a chink beyond the lunging boys and the roof nearly blew off for all the laughing, none louder than Grandmamma, who farted like a tent ripping, the key to the liquor cabinet clinking from her dress. Luis Manuel dove for the key, but got only a handful of Pepina's moccasin. Grandmamma repositioned the key back in no-man's-land, broke wind once more, and we all just cleared the hell out.

Luis Manuel fanned himself with his hat and spit earnestly, pining that tomorrow's tube-shooting would be the last of it. Engineers would weld grates over the tubes' entrances before the plant fired up on Monday. Since Teresa wasn't due in El Tigre till the following evening, tube-shooting was fine by me. The chickens were roosting and Doña Bárbara was all gone. Luis Manuel grabbed his bullwhip to look for cucarachas.

WE HEADED out for Tascabana and the tubes the next morning, rumbling through a scattering of drowsy pueblos. On the outskirts of San Jose de Guanipa, I saw an adobe shack topped by a peeling icon, gaudy as a circus bill, featuring a ravaged Jesus dragging the cross toward Golgotha. Several Roman soldiers were whipping Our Savior who, under a crown of thorns the size of a tractor tire, stumbled on, drenched in blood. A long line of people, mainly children and old women in mourning, were filing in one side of the shack and out the other.

"For 50 *bolivars,* you can get in line to see part of Jesus' genuine crown of thorns," said Jimmy.

"Is that a fact?" I said, craning my neck to study the grisly icon.

"But it's only a small part," Jimmy added. "Over in Falcon they got a whole one."

"*Verrrrrga!*" Jimmy yelled as Luis Manuel wheeled his pickup toward the sprawling mob at Tascabana. Easily 500 people were already there. Some had driven from as far away as Ciudad Bolivar. Others had ridden burros for hours across blazing plains to shoot the tubes, or to drink, or both. The city council and the National Guard had drummed up various safety procedures, all ignored, and a phalanx of soldiers was there to try to enforce them.

From atop two junkers parked on opposite banks of an Olympic pool–sized mud hole, the mayor of Tascabana (Don Armando Brito, renowned for reading nothing except Marvel Comics and the Bible) and one Lt. *Coronel* Juan Baltazar Negretti de Negron megaphoned commands, sounding like crazed hyenas, challenged as they were by the blaring stereos of 200 cars that girded the sump in a formation so tight that Luis Manuel, Jimmy, and I had to tread over trunks, roofs, and hoods to gain the aqueduct. At the waterline, Indian kids hawked pork rinds and bottled pop, and already the lagoon floated more trash than a World Cup soccer stadium.

Enriched by dollar-a-liter booze, the mob laughed, jeered, and shouted, anxious to go before their valor washed downstream. Bobbing pop cans, plastic wrappers, basketballs, a wiener dog, and dozens of humans rapidly drained down the twenty-odd tubes, continuously replaced by roof hoppers on the rebound, bruised and frightened but ready for more.

Luis Manuel gazed suspiciously at the layer of foam in the water, then grumbled something I couldn't understand.

"He wants to go to the highest launch," said Jimmy. "Faster tubes up there."

"Lead the way," I said.

Our bare feet made slurping sounds in the mud as we followed Luis Manuel a quarter mile to the higher pool. This one had a tenth the people, half the tubes, and five times the soldiers. I waded in and stroked for a tube, but—*Alto!* A young soldier would first have to take an official ride.

"*Por que?*" begged Luis Manuel.

"*El gordo. El gordisimo!*" said a private, knee-deep in the murky water and clutching an old rifle. Some fatty had apparently just taken off, so the scout would have to flush the tube for our safety.

Luis Manuel grabbed our arms and the three of us kicked over to another tube and slipped in, me clutching Luis Manuel's ankles, Jimmy, sheet-white and trembling, clinging on to mine. The logical choice was to go one at a time, but again, this was Venezuela, where anything worth doing is worth doing en masse. So we went all at once.

The turns were 5-degree welded elbows, so at turn one, the three of us were jolted apart, as were half of Luis Manuel's remaining teeth and most of my vertebrae. Heavy flow meant mossy tubes and in seconds we were vaulting down into blackness. We slammed through another turn. If I hit another bend, I'll dent the tube, I thought, trying to ignore the screams of careening bodies.

After a long minute and a few hundred yards, just as my nuts had shrunk to chickpeas, light showed far ahead. We rifled out and free-fell into the casual water of the aqueduct, flailing to avoid hitting each other. We swam to shore and started rubbing our barked hips and shoulders. Nobody could stop laughing and

Jimmy carried on as though he'd just slain the Hydra with his bare hands.

"It takes a set of *huevos* to take that ride, *primo*," he yelled.

We kicked back in the mud and watched for a while. I noticed that better than half of the tube-shooters were women and girls, but Jimmy kept on about his *huevos grandes*.

The uphill end of the aqueduct was dammed by a 50-foot cement wall festooned with a dozen pissing tubes, whose positions varied from below the waterline to near the top of the wall. So far as I understood, the tubes originated from various nearby rivers and *lagunas*. The tricky business of discovering if a tube ended here, or in Paraguay, was a question I asked about.

No one wanted to repeat the accidental feat of the young Indian boy, who got sucked into that first ride, so according to Luis Manuel, a National Guardsmen got the wise idea of chucking stray dogs into the tubes and finding out that way. The bit about feeding a black dog in one end and a white dog splashing down in the aqueduct—its coat blanched from fear—had to be bullshit. But Luis Manuel promised that all tubes had been vetted and ridden many times by now. And the exit was the best thing about it.

From tubes high and low on the 50-foot wall, screaming bodies came whistling forth, backward, upside down, landing on friends who had landed on friends. Everyone howled as the human bullets, stunned and dumbfounded, hobbled over to the bank, collapsed into the mud, and licked their wounds.

"*Cooooooño!*" shrieked Luis Manuel.

I caught sight of a girl, maybe 16, who came rocketing out at the 40-foot level. Her scream could have woken Simon Bolivar, and she pawed the air like a cat as everyone below dove for their lives. Whop! A 10-point belly-flop. Yet she quickly stroked to the bank and raced off.

"*Vamo, pue,*" said Luis Manuel, jumping to his feet.

"The bastard can't let a girl outdo us," Jimmy said to me, white and shaking again.

We scampered after the girl, but lost her in the crowd. That's when I noticed steady traffic staggering to and from a cordoned area surrounded by a dozen menacing soldiers.

"Oh, that?" said Jimmy, encouraged that we'd lost the girl. "Liquor is forbidden anywhere near the tubes. Much too dangerous. But anyone willing to walk to that huddle can drink themselves half dead and go right back to the pipes. You figure it out."

Back at the high mud hole, Luis Manuel spotted some footprints leading off and the three of us tracked them a quarter mile to a small rivulet, vacant save for the girl we'd just seen delivered high above the aqueduct. Luis Manuel beamed as the girl peered into five half submerged tubes.

"These babies look a little rusty," I said.

Luis Manuel scoffed, and with a casual flick of the hand said most of the pipes were old to begin with, and it didn't matter anyhow because all pipes led to Roma. Luis Manuel questioned the girl, who answered by slipping headfirst into the middle pipe.

"Oh, sheeeet," Jimmy said, as Luis Manuel waded over to the middle tube. "We better take this one feet first, *muchacho*. Better to have your feet take those bends than your freakin' *cabeza*."

Sage advice, since soon after the entrance, the tube angled down sharply, slammed round a bend and we shot into the darkness at speed. I tried to stay centered on the slime, clutching my gonads, praying I'd find no V-turns or sloppy welds. The girl's screams died off. Then the pipe vanished beneath me and I tumbled through the darkness 10 feet, 20, who knows how far to splash into some sort of tank. No sound from the girl. I thrashed for Jimmy and we clasped hands, treading and terrified, only to be whisked into a whirling eye like in a draining bathtub. We gasped what we reckoned were last breaths as the vortex sucked us down a thin, vertical shaft.

After the 2 longest seconds of my life we smacked into a pool, touched bottom and were gushed out into a larger pipe, known so only by the more gentle curvature beneath our speeding gams. Then we pitched down a ramp so steep our arms flew up and we started racing all over again, only slightly reassured by the stale air and Luis Manuel's distant screams. His shrieks shortly gave way to something sounding like a drumstick raked across a mile-long *charrasca*, a stuttering, wrenching racket we soon matched when we ground across a corrugated stretch that tweaked and pummeled every joint.

The aqueduct was way behind us now, and in total silence we whistled along for an age, regaining some wits, and a numbing terror. Finally I managed a scream, as did Jimmy, somewhere behind, and finally Luis Manuel and the girl, both well ahead. All we could do was course through the darkness. My mind raced with images of the pipe forking into two, slamming me into a V and cutting me in half, or getting extruded through a grate, or slamming into a steel wall, or getting spit out at the top of a 300-foot high dam.

Finally, we bruised off a final bend and shot for a pinhole of light. I breathed again, bashed across a final washboard, and only half felt my 10-foot freefall and landing into more mud than water.

No one could tell how long our ordeal had taken, only that the mud had dried before anyone could rise. I wobbled toward moving water to soak and check injuries. The girl had a strained neck and didn't know if she was dead or in Patagonia. Luis Manuel rubbed his collarbone and blood trickled from a gash on his chin. Jimmy hobbled around in circles, ranting about huevos grandes and some matador named Belmonte.

The distant sound of truck horns proclaimed the *autopista* several miles away. Not a great distance, but we'd be hoofing it naked since the tubes had stripped the suits off all four of us.

Meltdown

I

T TAKES 2 days and five different planes to fly from Los Angeles to Pangnirtung, near the southern toe of Baffin Island, well into the Canadian Arctic. I've come to scout the mile-high west face of Mount Thor for a film project in July, a likely story that should allow me plenty of time to take in Baffin's huge rock faces. For years I'd heard about these granite monoliths but have only seen a few photos in British magazines. That's all about to change.

Pangnirtung has one small guesthouse, Peyton Lodge, and the manager gets hold of her cousin, a burly young Inuit (Eskimo) named Tommy Kilibuk, who agrees to round up two snowmobiles and join me on the recon. He suggests tossing off the remaining coffee and heading out straightaway, yelling at another "cousin," not yet a man, to "get the machines warmed up." "Cousin?" I ask. "That's what we call our friends," he says drolly.

Like Native Americans and everyone else, back in the states, the Inuits—and everyone else in Canada—have for a million reasons always lived in a parallel culture, secluded in a homeland of ice. It's my job to adjust, not Tommy's, and the transition is apparently over. I haven't slept in 2 days. Tommy said he hasn't either. With perpetual light from the midnight sun, sleep is elusive. You just lay it down at some point and pass out. Maybe later.

We pull on layers of silks and polypropylene, huge duvets and animal hides, then trudge out into minus 5 stillness. It's mid-March, when even the Eskimos are shivering by the stove. Tommy has wrangled the fastest snowmobiles in town, rumbling orange beasts that blast us out over the frozen fjord.

Twenty minutes out we spot the Guardian's bold profile, half a mile high and sheer as Gibraltar. Tommy says a French team scaled the lower face, but bailed at the headwall. Another project. I have a thousand.

My original plan was to cruise around and develop some feel for the terrain, which is impossible owing to the speed I must carry to hang with Tommy, and because I've never been on a snowmobile and don't know what I'm doing. The farther we go the more granular the ice, which makes for squirrelly going at 60 miles an hour.

We enter Auyuittuq National Park, pierce the imaginary boundary of the Arctic Circle, and motor into the melting, sloppy falls, now a frozen staircase of 5-degree ice steps. After 3 hours we've hauled one 300-pound machine onto flat ice but are too tired to manhandle the second one. We pitch a tent, slide under 40 pounds of walrus hides, sip a short dog of Pappy Van Winkle I'd filched from the boss back at the office, and die for 10 hours.

Next morning we start laboring the other machine over the ice step. Tommy's sealskin boots paddle on the surface and my spine bows, absorbing the 300-pounder, unwieldy as a grand piano. Several times we lose it and watch the $5,000 monster slip and bounce back to the start of the falls. It's almost funny. Finally on level ground, we fire up the machines and glide toward Mount Thor. Distances deceive. Thor swells, while never drawing closer. We gain the last passage, 5 miles past the falls.

We motor through a roofless tunnel of ice. The frozen walls are gray. As the ice recedes, light floods in and the valley opens up. The snowfield is uniform and stretches into the horizon. Out left, a ridge of rugged peaks jags north; to our right, Mount Thor prevails. Backlit, its 6,000-foot shadow bisects the snow pack dead center. White and black. We pause at the edge of the shadow. The sky is blinding blue. There is no wind, no sound. We idle along the shadow's edge, skids straddling the line of light and darkness. Just left, melting snow glimmers. My right skid grates on the ice.

Again we stop to rest. Nothing moves; my ears hum.

We pass the next 2 days beneath gray granite walls awesome and fantastically couched. Mount Thor (called Thor Peak on the topographic map) looms 5,700 feet above the glacier. We work north and leisurely circle Mount Asgard, whose 3,000-foot east face hosted Rick Sylvester's ski-parachute descent that opened the James Bond thriller *For Your Eyes Only*. From certain angles Asgard resembles a giant smokestack, its summit lathed flat by the ages. While Yosemite climbers rake over the same old cliffs, ferreting out a precious few feet of new ground, nearly everything we see is unclimbed. Asgard alone has potential enough to exhaust a thousand dreams. Another project.

The weather holds. For hours, or seconds, or days—I can hardly tell which—we wander, putting about on impulse. The magnitude of our surroundings, and the penetrating stillness, roots us in a moment with no beginning. Here in the frozen heart of the Arctic, I feel the earth's great age and vast aloneness. We rarely eat or pause. A heat wave hits on the second day and we strip off a few layers, and only reluctantly turn around and start the long haul back to the lodge. The enchantment of the Arctic derives from the profound stillness found in the middle and around which all things turn, the vaguely sensed background in the fury of our days. I'm sorry to leave it so quickly.

Tommy guns it at the terminus of Thor Glacier and we rocket toward the falls where we slow and bang our way down. Then he dials on the speed and we blast across the white expanse.

We power-drift around an outcrop, Tommy bombing in the lead when he throws up a hand, locking his machine and skating sideways to the juncture of land pack and sea ice. Just beyond, the edge of the fjord is ringed in jumbled, icy blocks bobbing in a foot of slush. Glare ice looms half a mile out, but that too gleams with a veneer of meltwater. With the rising tide, the whole mass moans and crunches from the ocean's pulse. It hardly seems possible that 8 or 10 hours at 35 degrees has transformed a virtual concrete causeway into this sloppy tract of uncertainty. Tommy has never seen the sea ice soften up so much, so fast. We've got to go, before it gets worse.

Tommy promises that a ways out, toward the center of the fjord, the ice is diamond hard and yards thick. However the perimeter, especially during breakup, often has treacherous bubbles. Puncture one and you're in the brine—and frozen solid in minutes, says Tommy. Maybe a mile out over the sea pack we hear a thunderous cracking followed by a plume of seawater geysering up through the fracture. I wonder if it's not better to ditch the machines, write off our losses, and tromp a ridge 40 miles to Pangnirtung. Unnecessary, says Tommy, revving his engine. Velocity is safety, translating to less time spent on marginal ground. At speeds beyond 75, he claims, one can traverse on eggshells. There's only one rule: "Never, ever stop."

Tommy's eyes focus on that point of safe ice some ways out.

"Remember," said Tommy, "carry your speed. Full throttle." Then like a thunderbolt, he's off.

Tommy's brief instructions might have encouraged an expert but I'm still a novice on a snowmobile. I love the silence but hate the cold. I was born in Coachella Valley, in Southern California, which is all desert all of the time. But it's time to go.

A throaty two-stroke shatters the Arctic calm. A white rooster tail explodes behind, the belt chews in and all 750ccs vault me onto the pack ice. The chunky surface means a 75-horsepower bull ride, hard enough to just hang on. Gaining speed, the rig slips, slides, and crashes over floating blocks. As the surface slowly levels, it thins alarmingly. Meltwater settles in low spots, giving the illusion that the ice is paper-thin. I vault past 60 mph; firm ground is a mile behind. Thirty-nine to go.

The surface is still bumpy, but shortly after hitting 80 miles per, I enter a half-mile stretch smooth as an ice rink. Instantly the machine is skating, yawing sideways and un-steerable. The belt whines on the glare ice with no effect. Now backwards, at 60, skimming like a hockey puck, I chatter onto a mottled section. The belt digs in and the effect is like dropping the clutch—the engine dies without a sputter.

I slide to a full stop as the sound of breaking glass fills the air. I restart the engine and the belt carves an ever-deepening rut that quickly fills with water. And that snapping sound continues until my perimeter is as crack-laced as a Bingham vase. I furiously yank at the starter cord. And again. "Come on, you fuck!" Wafers of ice tilt in. I'm sinking. Every combination of throttle and choke brings no result. I get up on my toes to keep the water from pouring in my boots, fearing the rope will snap if I pull any harder or faster.

Then I hear Tommy's sloshing trot.

Winded and soaked, he wastes no words, just flips up the engine housing and cups a gloveless hand over the carburetor.

"Pull, John!"

With the first yank, the ice groans and we sink another four inches. I yank again. The engine hacks—it's flooded. Through gaping fissures belch the tide's basso notes, silenced by intermittent water gushing from the depths.

"Again!"

The engine coughs, farts, then revs to a shrill din. Good thing, because I've just yanked the starter cord off the sprocket. Water and ice shoot from the speeding belt. Our feet churn in deep slush and my hands are numb from heaving on the cord. I would have ditched it long ago, but now we've sunk so deep we need the machine's velocity to pull us out. In a 40-foot circle, the ice has sagged, like a coin on loose sheets. Tommy jumps into the driver's seat and barely feathers the throttle, but the belt gnaws deep into the ice. The ocean groans then geysers, a plume of water spraying behind. We've chewed through.

Backsliding, the nose rears. Tilted 45 degrees, I'm holding on behind Tommy looking into the icy black water as the belt catches on the hole's edge and we lurch forward. Under quarter throttle, the machine claws up over fractured plates, dragging us out of the slush, only to backslide, then lurch forward once more. I'm clutching the seat with my feet dragging behind as Tommy fights the bars. A last backslide and we finally shoot out onto level ice.

We both leap onto the seat and immediately enter another ice rink. As Tommy's machine nears, he goes side-saddle, then he jumps off at speed, sliding for 50 feet on his sealskin boots till he jack-knives up onto his machine, left running, but half sunk. He dials on the throttle and we're side by side, at 50, 60 miles per hour.

We rocket onto a 5-mile stretch of wafer-thin trash. Water flows beneath the marbled surface. After half a mile, we've ground a foot into the fluted skin. Oddly, we can maintain the crazy velocity with the trailing rut, much like a slipstream, affording some little stability. I can't tell if we are chewing farther into this trash, and it's a nervy guessing game as to where that last layer lies. This seems a likely place for that bubble; I'm just hanging on at 80 per.

In a mile we sail onto solid ice, the thrill of our escape fueling us well beyond. Only slowly do I realize our new and dire jam. I'm panting and my torso is frozen. Soaked, on a speeding snowmobile, I'm stone cold in no time. We are covered in so many layers of wool and hides that it is not so much frostbite as hypothermia that threatens. My hands are wooden, so the only way to steer is to drape equally wooden arms over the handlebar and pull the throttle lever with my shoulder.

My rig is plowing a ragged course and each bump jolts out more warmth. My legs are senseless from mid-thigh down; my stomach knotted, my face cast in iron. I'm getting kind of woozy.

With the lodge in view, we slip into stupors. Left on its own, my machine putts around in a drunken circle, then freezes to a stop. Tommy is hunched over, speechless. We're sticks in the snow. I feel myself falling toward a dark blue sea.

A few kids are out playing hockey on the glacier. They spot us and get several men who haul us to the lodge where the girls take over. I'm stripped and thrust into a tub of tepid water. I have no feeling anywhere; my eyes roll and an all-powerful drowse is arrested only by the slapping, screaming girls. One is really bearing down on me, shaking, smacking me back awake, talking in blasts of Inuktitut I can't understand. I can't focus so I can't tell what she looks like. As she bends my limbs I'm force-fed hot liquids. Minutes, sounds, hands all flow together. Everything begins to recede, but life comes back with my first sensation, a remote titillation that grows into a writhing, electric jabbing, 10,000 hat pins pricking my flesh, known to ice climbers as the "screaming barfies."

As nerves slowly come alive, I'm slowly dragged from that dark sea. Water churns from the tub as the girls keep rubbing and bending my arms and legs. When my eyes clear I discover a girl, clothed and waist deep in the tub, sitting on my chest and rubbing oils on my face. She smiles and I relax. Whack! She slaps me back awake. When the pain eases to a hot glow, she leads me over to the polar bear rug and starts kneading my flesh, palming blood into ever-warming limbs. Dreamless sleep.

Tommy kicks me in the ribs and says to put some clothes on. Several girls are still massaging my hands, arms, and feet. One, whose gorgeous round face might fill a hula-hoop, says I've been out for several hours and had talked all kinds of shit. I asked her what kind of shit and Tommy laughs, kicks me again, and says, "That's my sister, cuz."

Selama-Lamanya

WE TRAVELED up a river that had no name, heading for a green alp in the jungled highlands. The river curved into a shady vestibule where the hardwood trees came down to the waterline and the canopy nearly blocked out the sun. In a clearing on the left-hand bank, under a ramin tree arching over the river, a small, slat-sided hut perched on palm pylons. We motored down and glided onto a gravel bar. Our last sight of human life lay 3 days and two tributaries behind us.

An hour later, a young woman walked from the jungle leading a naked girl toddler with one hand and dragging a big ripe jackfruit in the other. Near sundown, the woman's husband pulled ashore in a hand-hewn, motorized dugout. He invited us inside the hut. Seamus dug out some shag tobacco and we smoked huge cigarettes rolled from pages of a Raymond Chandler paperback I had in my pack. One of our group spoke Bahasa, and we learned that for 5 years the man had panned gold from a network of creeks nearby. Recently he had tickled out fortune enough to move back to Bandung and do most anything he chose. Even buy a car. But he and his wife had no plans to leave. They would stay there on the riverside, *selama-lamanya* (forever), he said. And his wife nodded.

The woman fried some rice and we rustled up guavas and alligator pears. Then the man invited us to follow him, and for nearly

2 hours we walked upstream along the river, more feeling than seeing our way through blindingly thick jungle. The sky burned with stars, but there was no moon and the close jungle was dark and the lazy river black as ink. The man stopped and swam out into the river; we followed, and rolling onto our backs, let the delicate current carry us along. We floated through the night. Nobody said a word. On both sides the banyans rose in the black decor.

Back in the hut, as we prepared for sleep, the man tapped out his pipe and said that when the day came that he found himself old and tired, he would make amends to Allah and wait for night to fall. He would have a last meal of rice and durian fruit, and would say goodbye to his family. Then he would wade out into the river and drift with the current. He would not swim to shore. He would just keep on going. *Selama-lamanya.*

Improbable Marksman

N ONE OF the native Ibans could remember a longer drought. The air felt like fire in our mouths and all living things, withered into a state of great tension, cried out for relief. Twice we were startled by horrific cracking sounds and ran for cover as centuries-old hardwood trees exploded, fragments tearing through the canopy like falling skyscrapers. Rather than track the overgrown jungle trails, we followed the streambed, normally gushing and now cinder-dry, skating over river stones submerged for a thousand years.

We were miles into the Sarawak jungle, Malaysian Borneo, five people, led by Bilap (who resembled Sitting Bull in the old daguerrotype prints), a native Iban chief I put at about 50, though he could easily have been 60 or more. His torso was a tattooed cavalcade of deer and snakes and impossible animals. He'd never worn shoes and his feet were wide as fronds and so tough he could jog over river scree like it was beach sand. Two young Iban hunters carried our food in huge rattan packs. Like most Ibans, they continually chewed mouthfuls of betel nut and every so often let fly salvos of spit that stained the river stones bright red. And Hassam, a Malaysian soldier little older than the hunters, assigned to us because the government suspected all foreigners (me)—especially when they partnered with Ibans.

Since the early British colonial days, the Ibans had defied assimilation. During the 1950s, a good way for an Iban to turn up in a gully with a bullet in his head was to sound off to officials. But this was decades later and Hassam had the starry-eyed enthusiasm of a scout on his first camp-out. Always tripping over creepers and stumbling through streams, he somehow managed to shadow Bilap and keep his ancient single-shot Browning held across his chest. I rounded out our five-man crew. The plan was to film a documentary on the nomadic Punan Dyaks, the renowned kings of the jungle and source of countless tales, mostly exaggerated—so exaggerated, in fact, that the TV folks wanted proof that the Punans actually existed before committing six figures to a film project. I had 3 weeks and $1,500 to complete my scout.

We weren't an hour into the tall trees when Hassam started in with his stumbling, slowing our group to a crawl. Rather than trying to force him along, Bilap began schooling Hassam on just how to swing the machete, pointing out dire insects and critical plants. The young Ibans, addled by the nut, spat their mouthfuls and trudged on. I didn't have much of a pack, and kept pace okay.

We never saw sky through the tangled green canopy, but rain was so long overdue we expected and prayed for it. When rain still hadn't come by the 4th day, we rose early and fell in behind Bilap, who seemed to float along the intricate riverbank, Hassam always staggering an arm's length behind, but moving faster than before. The leeches were bad, drilling every inch of exposed flesh, which was most of us, stripped down as we were in the heat. Even Hassam was hiking in shorts, swatting all bloodsuckers.

The rain held out and I noticed everyone but Hassam glancing at the surrounding terrain, where black crags soared from stark lime bush. The return of the monsoon worried us, for the river could flood in minutes, forcing us into the spiked, squelchy hedgerow that climbed from the flat river passage.

In late afternoon we camped on a sandbar that hooked with the river's sharp bight. It took the young Ibans and me 30 minutes to clear the scrub and limbs washed there during high water. Meanwhile Bilap and Hassam, laughing and clowning, collected twigs for a fire in the lee of an ironwood trunk that we couldn't budge.

We spent an hour damming the river. But no fish ever came. The next morning it still hadn't rained so we broke camp at sunrise, eager to cover some dry miles and close the distance between us and the Punans. We could thrash out a roundabout route through the jungle, or follow the riverbed through a steep ravine. Bilap chose the riverbed. We'd have to move fast, for the march through the ravine would take 6 hours, and if it started to rain hard and fast, we might get flooded out. Once committed there was no escaping the ravine into the jungle—just too steep. Bilap held up a hand vertically and nodded, as if to say, "This steep." Hassam had found his jungle legs, but if things got tight I doubted he could put on some speed.

The year before I'd filmed an early raft descent of the upper Kapuas. A week into it the sky cut loose and we scrambled high onto a bordering crag where pounding rain pinned us down. An hour later and far below, a wall of muddy water and uprooted trees tore past, taking our rafts and a New Zealand boatman along with it. It took us 17 days to tramp out to Tanjung Sellor.

WE ENTERED the ravine after an hour. Overgrown walls rose sheer from the river. The streambed was easily a hundred feet across so I figured it would take even a deluge several hours to fill the canyon. But it could and often did, judging by all the splintered logs teetering atop 20-foot river boulders.

The first few miles passed quickly. On both sides, dripping red orchids spangled the vertical walls. Furry corkscrew vines spiraled down, looping and crossing the shallow river, then sweeping back up the opposite bank. Dawn vapors crept up the cliffs to form a steamy nimbus, broken in spots to expose the canopy's green weave far overhead. The air below was furnace hot, gummy, and still, and the river so low it barely made a sound. We stopped.

Bilap gave a short speech, his outstretched arm waving to one, then the other, canyon wall. He emphasized words I could not understand. Hassam nodded quickly, sweat pouring down his face. He twice checked the safety on his rifle, making sure it was off. Bilap resumed his march, his dark eyes traveling between the canyon walls, Hassam's eyes burning holes through his back.

Bilap barked and Hassam closed the distance between them to a rifle's length. On both sides, the young Ibans flanked out.

Suddenly Bilap stopped and raised his hand. The young Ibans froze, but Hassam jumped and for the first time moved the rifle away from his chest. His knees flexed. His face was twisted with fear and excitement.

Ever since he'd set boot into the jungle Hassam had shadowed Bilap with his silly rifle, and every couple miles Bilap would stop, turn around and instruct Hassam about something. Maybe chiding him about being so slow. Or fanning his fear about the Punans, who scare everyone and who some say ran Michael Rockefeller through with a spear, lopped off his head, then ate him (if this happened at all it was by Asmat tribesmen, across the border in Papua). More likely, Bilap was warning about sudden rain, so long overdue. Whatever his point, Bilap meant it, repeating words till Hassam nodded quickly and made some small adjustment with the way he wielded his rifle or the distance he kept behind the Iban. Then Bilap would light off again and Hassan would stumble behind just as before. Whatever this all meant was lost on me and was Hassam and Bilap's business. Curious as all of this was, I only wanted to get clear of the canyon.

Bilap dropped his gaze from high on the right-hand wall and marched on. Hassam brought the rifle back across his chest and fell into file.

The heat and humidity hung on us like a curse. I tramped on, staring at Hassam. A thin drizzle began bleeding through the canopy.

Bilap started hiking fast. In another hour, the vapors had burned off and shafts of blistering sunlight gleamed through holes in the canopy, intermittent with sheets of scalding rain.

Bilap's attention returned to the cliff-sides, which slowly eased in angle. I panned up the left wall—it looked like the same verdant brawl from waterline to sky. Meanwhile Bilap threaded silently from shadow to shadow. Off to each side, the young Ibans did the same. When Hassam stumbled, Bilap shot him a glance and Hassam nodded bashfully. His rifle shook in his hands. A copper taste hung on my tongue. The river had risen a foot and in spots covered most of the riverbed.

We moved through a cut of sunlight. Bilap treaded lightly along a spit of gravel, three creeping shadows playing across the moving water to our left. I froze. Punans! Fuck! But the shadows were our own. And we were there to *find* the Punans. The tension was rising with the river.

Bilap's gaze lingered high upon the right-hand wall. With a last step so slow it took some balance to perform, his hand came up; with his eyes still riveted up and right, he froze. Hassam froze. Spread out on both sides, the young Ibans froze. I froze, and could feel my heartbeat in my hands.

Bilap suddenly wheeled around. Hassam extended the rifle at arm's length, one hand clasping the middle of the barrel, the other, the butt of the stock. In one motion Bilap snatched the rifle, shouldered it, turned, and no sooner had the barrel settled on a spot high on the right-hand wall than a flash leaped from the muzzle as the report banged off the canyon walls, volleying up and out through holes in the thinning canopy. A dark object rolled down the wall, tumbling with greater speed till it plunged over a last, vegetated ceiling and splashed into a pool 50 feet away.

The Ibans were instantly on it, machetes drawn. But when I raced over I saw it didn't matter because Bilap was a deadeye: a gaping hole right through the deer's head. A brain shot. I'd read about Daniel Boone shooting eagles from the sky with a flintlock, but Boone had nothing on Bilap, who'd nailed that buck from 200 yards, easy. With the river rising fast the Iban hunters didn't pause to dress out the animal. The biggest one just threw it over his shoulder fireman's-carry style and marched on.

I turned toward Bilap but he had already wandered off downstream, his eyes probing high on the left wall. Hassam fumbled to thumb a new shell into the chamber, looking up to see how far ahead Bilap had gone. Gun loaded, safety off, Hassam stumbled after and took up his position, walking quietly and in step behind Bilap, the chief.

In 15 minutes the storm shot through the canopy like a blast from a fire hose, and we all began charging downstream, half jogging, half fording through the rising current. When the ravine opened up an hour later we'd been bodysurfing a waist-deep torrent for half an hour and were barked and bashed all over. Nothing dangerous, since the river was so wide, but the young Ibans had lost the deer and Hassam had lost his old Browning. And we never did find the Punans.

FIFTEEN YEARS later, while reading a magazine on a Singapore Airline flight to Kuala Lumpur, I ran across an article about the history of Sarawak during the Second World War.

In 1942, the article ran, the Japanese secured the island, the fifth largest on earth. A year later, owing to their harsh treatment of natives, the Japanese started losing significant numbers to native Iban sharpshooters. The situation confounded the Asian invaders, who were unaware that shortly after their invasion, Australian paratroopers had penetrated the jungled interior, hooked up with various nomadic tribes, and trained a handful of young males as snipers. By war's end, the article stated, many of these native riflemen had become "remarkable, if improbable, marksmen."

King Kong Comes
to Wabag

D. B. LOOKED amused as he pointed to a blurb headlined with: "Two Die in Enga Fight." He flipped me the newspaper and I skimmed the story. "Two men died of ax and arrow wounds on Friday after a fight broke out between Lyonai and Kundu tribesmen outside of Wabag, in Enga Province. Joseph Yalya, 38, of Pina Village, died of an ax wound to the neck, and Tumai Tupigi, also of Pina Village, died from an arrow through the chest. Police said about 800 men were involved in the fight. The brawl began when Lyonai tribesmen accused the Kundu clan of using sorcery to kill a Lyonai elder."

Two casualties seemed rather modest for an 800-man mêlée, but this was Papua New Guinea, which some say God made first, when his technique was uneven. Since every production resembles its creator, God is both crazy and brilliant, for everyone, natives and travelers as well, stumble around Papua in a sort of daze, half astonished, half bored. D. B. and I had gone there strictly for the hell of it, looking for novelty while licking wounds following a 9-week exploratory thrash down the Strickland Gorge. We'd had a rough go of it, but after 2 days kicking around Mount Hagan in the remote Highlands, we were jumpy for another epic. Our flight to Sydney and then on to California was leaving in 8 days, so it would have to be a quick one. Fact was we'd worked and scrimped and flown to the far side of the globe, hacked down that hateful gully all those weeks hoping to discover the Lost Tribe of Levi, or something equally focal, only to stumble out the ass end with little more than dysentery. But one look at that newspaper article and our prospects brightened.

We snagged a ride from Solomon Chang, a high-strung engineer of Chinese-Papuan parentage. Chang was driving to a reservoir project at the end of the road, 20-something miles past Wabag, and wasn't expected there till the following day. The road, known as the "Highland Direct," was straighter than the Oregon coastline, but rockier, and this gave Chang nearly 5 hours to ramble on about native "warfare."

"The buggers spill onto the road sometimes," said Chang, "but they'll usually stop for cars. Maybe bum a smoke or two. And I've never seen them fight through lunch neither."

So there were some histrionics to this combat, though according to Chang, someone eventually had to die "to keep the contest real."

We had a solid week to get into trouble. Chang only had that night but liked his chances. However, when we wheeled into Wabag we were disappointed not to duck a salvo of spears and arrows. Rather, the same old array of tumbledown grass huts and the shambling open air market, a regular ant farm of Kanakas dressed only in "ass grass," a patch of kunai grass in front and back secured with a leather belt, axes over their shoulder, feathers or boar tusks through their septums, and as always, every jowl bulging with betel nut and rancorous red spit. We were right back to swatting mosquitoes again, but our boredom was nothing compared to Chang's.

"Look," said Chang, "we ferret out some Chief, thrash his ass and make off with his daughters." He considered for a moment. "Better yet, his pigs. That'll get the machetes flashing."

D. B., citing our bunglings with the Uhundunis (when a native sorcerer got hold of DB's Walkman and thought we had crammed the spirits of his dead relatives into the tape deck) stressed the need to proceed cautiously with cultures we didn't fully appreciate, and Chang said, "Leave off with that travel guide bullshit. I was born here for Christ's sakes."

There was a long silence—not counting the truck bottoming out several times in potholes—and I could almost hear the gears grinding in Chang's head. "OK, it's Saturday. We'll swing by the bar, then hoof it over to the theater for *King Kong Meets Godzilla*."

"Followed by a little Schubert on bamboo instruments," said D. B. Wabag didn't even have a store, so I was with D. B. in doubting this talk about a theater.

"I'm on the square here," said Chang. "It's been Kong and Godzilla every Saturday night for 2 years. But it's not the flick that's the draw, but the Kanakas. Most of them think they're watching a documentary. I've seen them hike all the way in from the Gulf Province to see it. And that's fair dinkum."

We checked into the Wabag Lodge, an open-air dive with "running bath" (the river), then headed for the bar. No Hard Rock Café, this was a cage of double chain link, with a cashier and stock of South Pacific Lager inside. We paid first, then the bottles were slipped out through a little slot in the fencing. We drank a couple then made our way toward the theater, following a dark path to a small clearing in the otherwise impenetrable thicket.

The theater (the "Wabag Ritz," as Chang called it) was a converted cement garage used previously to store the province's three John Deere tractors. A noisy queue of Kanakas passed through the tiny entrance. Dressed exclusively in ass-grass, they were obliged to check in their axes and machetes, receiving a numbered bottle cap to reclaim them. Several men, apparent newcomers to the Ritz, were confused by this procedure, but were quickly pacified by an enormous native official at the front door. He, too, wore the ass-grass, but also a creased khaki shirt and a red beret on his billowing bouffant. He flashed a wide smile when he saw Chang.

"*Sainaman tru.*" This from the giant.

"*Strongpela tru,*" Chang came back. The two exchanged a five-move handshake, then Chang turned toward D. B. and me and said, "*Dis pelase mi prem bilong mi.* Americans."

"Oh, how ya doing?" the giant said fluidly. "You best grab a seat while you can."

We went in. Seventy-five natives were already pressed inside. Various benches were in place, but most Kanakas chose to squat in the oily dirt. The front wall was whitewashed. The ancient projector sat askance on a bamboo stand. The heat was withering, but the aroma could have turned the stomach of the Discus Thrower. The natives' diet is almost exclusively forest tubers and manifold shrubbery, and they continuously pass a crippling wind, unabashed and most sonorously. Blend that with knee-buckling body odor and the fetid stench of betel nut expectoration, then box it all in a vent-less concrete sarcophagus and you have the Wabag Ritz.

"Swank joint, eh?" Chang asked.

"Probably no worse than the atmosphere on Mercury," I said.

"*Pasim tok,*" the giant barked, and the crowd quieted. He flipped on the projector, which made a gnashing noise like someone feeding hubcaps into a wheat thresher. He compensated by turning the volume way up, which distorted the dialogue beyond anything human, but rendered King Kong that much more horrendous. As Kong stomped through Tokyo, swatting down skyscrapers and feasting on pedestrians, their legs flailing in his jagged teeth, the mob shrieked terribly and many Kanakas dove beneath the benches, cowering and trembling and babbling about the "*bikpela monki, em I kaikai saipan man.*"

During the scene when Godzilla and Kong had it out, a fight erupted in the corner. Just as a free-for-all looked a certainty, a torpedo-busted mother of six squealing kids swung her bilum bag of spuds upside a Kanaka's head, and all eyes returned to the wall. Then a courageous Kanaka stole up to the wall to "touch" Godzilla. He turned around, squinting into the light and was bombarded by sweet potatoes and betel nut husks. He screamed, the crowd howled, the giant howled, and the bushman bolted back to his bench.

The end credits rolled out and the wall went dark. A short silence was followed by shouts for more. The giant yelled, "No gat," but the crowd wouldn't hear a word of it, so to avoid a sure riot, he simply rolled the film back in reverse. As King Kong back-pedaled through Tokyo, withdrawing reconstituted pedestrians from his snapping jaws and placing them back on the sidewalk, D. B., Chang, and I were right there with the Kanakas, all up on our feet waving our arms, ducking spuds, screaming and cheering at the miraculous events dancing on the whitewashed wall.

Part One: Dream On, Irian Jaya

by Dwight Brooks (D. B.) and John Long

WIGHT: WE flew 1,000 miles past Jayapura, the capital of Irian Jaya, to Jakarta. Both of us (John Long, a historic crossing of Borneo behind him, and me, heading to remote Indonesian locales for the fourth time) were well aware of the bureaucracy involved in getting permission to enter the unexplored areas of Irian Jaya, Indonesia's most troubled province, and ethnologically the most primitive place on earth. If you don't have a Jakarta-issued rag of paper called a *Surat Jalan*, you can't even enter Irian, let alone catch a bush plane to Wamena, where mountain (as opposed to swamp) fun begins. While astronomical sums might part the bush for a full-scale expedition, there are no guarantees of free and easy access.

In 1984, for example, a large American film crew was deported on arrival, in spite of approval from Jakarta, due to expanded efforts by the Indonesian military, or ABRI (Angkatan Bersenjata Republik Indonesia), to "pacify" various reactive mountain tribes that were angered into battle after learning they were no longer Hirn-Yals, or Sibilers, but "Indonesians." We heard that rather than try to bribe every soldier we met, being polite, patient, and most importantly, fluent in Bahasa Indonesian were the most effective tools for covering ground. On the other hand, journalists had been shot at and smugglers shot, but most of those people acted clumsily, or foolishly, around soldiers, and by the time muzzles barked they knew why.

No matter what your Irian itinerary, you must enter through Jayapura, formerly Sukarnapura, Hollandia, and Kota Baru. It has degenerated shockingly since the Dutch were forced out in the early 60s, and this no thanks to a bungled ABRI para-drop which saw hundreds of soldiers dead from cannibals, disease, and starvation, and not one Dutch casualty.

This once-idyllic tropical nugget is now a floundering coastal outpost, where most civic amenities are defunct and decay is the rule. Migrants from other provinces funnel in, asserting a hereditary right to Melanesian West New Guinea, which stems from the marginal control exercised on its coasts by the Tidore Sultanate in the 17th century. Raw sewage flows in the streets, Manado prostitutes abound, buildings are either patched up with rusting tin or engulfed by jungle, and the military presence is strenuously pronounced.

With no reservations we left this sweltering commode for Wamena (Wam = pig, ena = I have: pigs are the paramount symbol of wealth in New Guinea), a scenic mountain village in the pastoral Baliem Valley, which has become increasingly accessible to tourists. Once-feared Ndani warriors, naked save for the penis gourd, or *koteka*, stare absently, ask for cigarettes, and gladly agree to porter loads for smokes or crumply red dime-value notes. Less than a generation ago they sat atop 40-foot bamboo watchtowers, scoped raiding parties, and met them in battle with 15-foot lances.

Warfare once defined power structures, and payback raids ensured economic stability. Today such activities are brutally suppressed by ABRI with bullets, burning of villages, and, reportedly, torture. Old ways persist in some areas, however, and the cordillera running through Irian Jaya features a staggering array of valleys, ravines, caves, sinkholes, and forests that far exceeds the administrative scope of the government.

In 1984, Stone-Age people still existed in certain parts of Irian Jaya, and there was a broad range of acculturation. Many had seen airplanes and electric goods and were quite accustomed to them. Others had seen these things but thought they were forms of magic. Still others had seen white men or Indonesians only occasionally and were unsure what or who they were. In a few torturously isolated places it was still possible to make a first contact. John and I were lucky in this regard because we applied rock climbing skills to jungle-shrouded limestone, giving us access to remote plateaus and sinkholes. These features, densely green from the air and too airy for foot patrols, were the best bet. We looked for hunter-gatherers who moved their villages frequently, and who were never seen unless they wanted to be. We reached some very primitive places and neither of us could say where, exactly, those places are located. We could guess within a map grid, but we felt it best to clam up, especially with the occasional soldier we encountered.

For weeks we traveled light and fast with hunters who meandered extravagantly through excruciating bush. We spent nights in many obscure places: caves, trees, and declivities where wide-eyed inhabitants occasionally regarded us as other-than-human. We had tremendous luck making friends with many people who weren't sure whether we were ancestors or ghosts. Maybe this ready friendship was because we opened the packs and gave things away: food, tobacco, medicine. My best guess is that they picked up immediately what a charge we got from seeing them in the first place. They liked that. All vibe. We were big; we could hike as fast as they could; we chewed plenty betel nut, and we laughed a lot, bossed no one around, and acted no better than anyone else. No big deal—most of the time.

Trekkers wander the Baliem and some go to Illaga to climb the Dolomitic Puncak Jayawijaya, aka Carstensz Pyramid, which at 16,023 feet is the highest mountain in Oceania. But few engage in systematic deviation from the maze of central foot tracks linking the various large villages of the massif. Traveling with the locals on their own circuitous routes, doing things their way, will position a person for discoveries. Most big villages have an Indonesian administrator who'll direct you along, as well as pointedly dissuade you from visiting certain hot areas. What worked for us was to go, discreetly, right to the most forbidden area and start from there.

If you are willing to take the time to confront the hazards involved, you may win the confidence of someone who will slash routes over dozens of 10,000-foot ridges, share bugs with you for food, pick a tenuous descent down a limestone face, slide down lianas into a sinkhole, and point out a hidden village. Usually, there is a sort of password for each region. You shout it out. If it is shouted back, you're in. If not, you push on. We did both. Grim things can happen, obviously, but it isn't likely, unless you chop down a papaya tree or kill a pig. The guys you're with will read the bush signs, maddeningly subtle ones that say, "Come on," or "Shove off."

OUR FIRST "first contact," 22 days out of Wamena, was with a group of Uhundunis, who had heard about white people but had never seen them. After each male had pinched our skin to ensure we were there, we watched them hack up a giant cassowary, a flightless bird whose talons are quite capable of disemboweling a man. In order to communicate with the various tribes, we had accumulated interpreters as we progressed. To greet an Uhunduni is not simple: Justinus, our Ndani (pronounced *Donny*) friend, could speak to Itthips, a Woogi. Itthips, a Yali, was conversant in Jinak, and so spoke a good deal more with Ekjinak (tribe unknown) than Justinus could ever dream of. Ekjinak however, spoke no Uhunduni, nor did Ombaipufugu, a Korowai tribesman who did indeed speak Jinak. Without the bilingual Ombaipufugu we wouldn't have been able to express our good intentions to the band of Uhundunis. As it went, they sacrificed the cassowary on our behalf, and proved hospitable, though guarded hosts. They didn't so much cook the stringy meat as draw it slowly over the fire. I was uncertain about this. Not so John, who hovered over Chief Kabatuwayaga and his minions as they apportioned servings.

A premature reach for the banana leaf on which his serving lay nearly cost him his hand, which was blocked by a swift stone axe stroke. They screamed and jumped about, getting very clearly across that he should hold his horses. Scarcely deterred because he was starving, John squatted back and looked on with determination. Then Chief Kabatuwayaga summoned his sorcerer, Tebegepkwekwe.

Tebegepkwekwe smiled at John benignly, and spoke to Ombaipufugu. Our four interpreters put their heads together and Justinus explained in Indonesian that Tebegepkwekwe wished to reassure John that he knew John hadn't intended to reach for the food. Surely he wouldn't have been so reckless. A *mogat*, or major bush spirit, had impelled his hand, and if it seized him again Tebegepkwekwe volunteered sterner measures to ensure it would leave him alone, so long as John didn't mind being suspended upside down with thick blue smoke purifying his head.

Tebegepkwekwe declared the mogat had probably been following us for days, and asked if we'd bathed in the bend of any river. Well, we had, actually. He rested his case. Then Tebegepkwekwe withdrew from a snakeskin sheath an 8-inch cassowary quill with a tiny white egret feather lashed to the tip. Feverishly he waved the quill over each serving. None of the Uhundunis could believe we didn't know what he was doing. Of course, it finally came through: lesser spirits, *sulumilewolebalabats* by name, must be carefully shooed away from the food before it would be safe to eat.

Instead of eating a second portion, as John did, I asked Justinus to find out where they got their axe heads, which were made
of a deep blue stone. Eventually it was explained that several
times a year they met Monis, with whom they traded women for
blades. The usual price was three for one, and I haven't the heart
to spell out which went for which. Apparently the axe heads were
obtained swimming among fish in a secret stream, whose location
was jealously guarded. We were fortunate that a Moni was then
among them. The terrible scars he had on his knees and ankles,
these from the adzes that had slipped his grasp, validated his claim
about swimming ax heads.

JOHN: AFTER adventuring nearly continuously for a decade,
things that once seemed unimaginable were now barely noticed
and rarely remembered. Then the Uhunduni sorcerer waved a
plume over the grub and it was like I'd never been out of Los
Angeles. I imagine few Uhundunis had strayed far from their
private grotto, and our persons, and the things we had brought,
seemed as novel to them as their arrow wounds, kotekas, and por-
cine financial structure seemed to us. We decided to hang out—
for a while anyway—with the Uhundunis, if only to rekindle the
old stoke that had started us adventuring in the first place. Two
days later, the old stoke burst into flames.

We'd spent the afternoon fishing in a deep lagoon, caught a
few, and watched curiously as an elder told fortunes by analyzing
a carp's entrails. Around sunset it started raining, so about twenty
of us packed into a squat little cooking shack. Elbow to elbow
we fooled away several hours chewing betel nut and smoking
cigarettes hand-rolled from green jungle tobacco strong enough
to gag Vulcan. As with most whose lives are hard and unforgiving, the Uhundunis were devotees of tomfoolery and wackiness,
a fact proven when, every so often, a tribesman would let fly a
shaft of betel nut spit into the wee fire. The tribesman would all

righteously curse and wail and make a great show of it all, smacking the perpetrator upside his bouffant as toxic fog welled off the coals. The grumbling would slowly die off and several minutes would pass in silence as we huffed our rank cigarettes, the tension building as all eyes stared expectantly at the flames. Shortly, the native who with sovereign dignity had just dressed down his neighbor would himself spit into the fire, then laugh himself to smithereens as we all screamed and smacked him around. It was a riot. I thought about some of the anthropologists I had read, and their artistic interpolations of tribal life. Then I thought about us slackers in that hut, squatting on our heels and spitting into the fire, and wondered what an expert might read into this.

D. B. rolled another smoke but couldn't get it stoked off the soggy coals. He rooted through his pockets, drew out a Bic lighter and lit up. You would have thought he'd pulled a flying pig from his hat for the reaction of the tribesmen. In turn they all snatched the magical lighter from one another and, marveling, made fire. The lighter eventually ended up in the hands of a senior elder, old as Aesop's granddad. A deft and passionate orator, he delivered a 5-minute homily on the lighter and concluded by pitching it into the fire. D. B. and I both dove and I fished out the melting article seconds before it blew us all over the Papuan border. We tried to explain by way of our various interpreters but before the message rounded the horn, the senior elder snatched back the lighter, harangued D. B. and me for another few minutes, then pitched the lighter into the fire again, and again D. B. had to roast his hands digging it back out. The tribesmen perceived this action as usurping the elder's authority. Or they perceived something grievous because the dwindling fire now seemed to burn in their eyes and they were all yelling at us.

We needed some diversion to diffuse this rhubarb, so I fished out my Walkman, pressed PLAY and, in a moment I'll regret forever, slipped the little headphones over the ears of the senior elder. He froze. His features screwed up, his eyes went out on stilts, and he fell into an absolute paroxysm. D. B. quickly nabbed the headphones.

"Christ, man. They're going to think we're practicing black magic on the old fart."

In a flash, one tribesman wrenched the tape deck from D. B.'s hands, slipped on the phones, and began pawing and slapping himself as though army-ants were marching all over him. Another donned the phones and broke into jungle scat singing. Twenty other warriors jumped about with uncontainable curiosity, anxious to get their turn. The senior elder continued ranting. The scene escalated. Eager tribesmen crowded around the listener as veterans all screamed about the experience to no one in particular.

Suddenly, a shriek, and half a dozen tribesmen dove for the exit, damn near bringing down the hut. The eyes of the current listener bulged like a rock cod, due in part to the volume having accidentally been cranked up to 10. The searing jazz fusion tape was chaos in musical form, and it totally mastered the listener. He droned and screamed, both hands clutching his adze, which he whirled wildly, splintering this, shattering that. (Several years later I would see a Vanuatu Islander wield a machete in much the same way when we were trying to yank one of his wisdom teeth with pliers.) Then he rose off his haunches, twirling his tool at speed, screaming, limbs flailing, his face seized with who knows what.

The remaining tribesmen didn't bother with the tiny horseshoe exit, now log-jammed with diving black bodies. They simply blasted headlong through the hut's thick grass siding. This decimated the shack's superstructure but did nothing to check the hatchet of the crazed Uhunduni. Fiendish howling poured from the hut as firelight seeped through the exits, outlining two-dozen jumpy tribesmen, whose glassy eyes alternated between the sacked hut, and us. We squirmed, our four interpreters rattling in terror, their heads lowered and shaking, lips quivering.

"I think we go now . . . I think we go now," volleyed about in four languages.

Suddenly, with the crack of adze to wood, the shack shifted wildly left and collapsed, the crazed tribesmen groping free just before the reed roof burst into flames. The resulting bonfire played across a crowd of glowering Uhunduni faces all staring at us.

"You know," D. B. said, "my dad hates jazz as well."

But the joke found no traction with our little group, especially with Justinus, who trembled horribly. The Uhundunis had been traditional enemies of his clan, and he stood on hatchet blades owing to our crimes: affronting a sorcerer by grabbing food prior to having the ghosts exorcised; spurning the senior elder by twice snatching the butane lighter from the flames; and now causing a native to lose his mind and destroy the communal cooking hut.

Several tribesmen prodded us into a hogan-like structure where once again we faced the senior elder, who fingered the bright yellow Walkman while his teary eyes burned holes through us. First, who was responsible for cramming all those people into the tape deck? Second, how did he know those imprisoned were not the souls of his dead relatives? Third—and this he voiced with gravity—who had tortured those souls enough to make their voices sound like trumpets and electronic guitars?

To be accused of torturing the souls of the big man's dead kin put us at a disadvantage. Aesop's granddad and our four interpreters carried on, always acquiescing to the thunderous elder. Once the old man's drift trickled down to Justinus, we had great difficulty understanding his pidgin Indonesian and Precambrian English. Justinus wisely capitalized on this, telling the elder it would take all night to explain the question and decipher an answer. The elder wouldn't give us all night but he would wait until the moon was overhead. With a flick of his hand, he ordered us to our assigned hut to work on some answers. We quickly exited past thirty savage eyes. One hundred yards away lay our hut, luckily isolated.

"Think we can talk our way out of this one?" I asked D. B.

"Nope."

"You want to try?"

"Nope."

We quickly sorted through our packs, pitched non-essentials, and cinched the straps. Ekjinak snatched up a narrow stone and began filing his canines. Itthips hopped about in a cross-legged position, probably to avoid the arrow trees Uhunduni are said to be able to make spring from the ground. Writing this now it sounds cooked for effect. But this (Venice Beach, California) ain't Irian Jaya.

"We wait much longer and that sorcerer's gonna be waving an egret feather over us," said D. B. This was more fun than fact but I got the point and shouldered my pack, listening to the arguing roaring from the elder's hut. Then we slunk into the darkness, at first slowly, till we hit the faint trail at full stride, reversing by daybreak what previously had taken 3 grueling days. And damn near the whole time Justinus was saying, "I think we go now . . . I think we go now," till even he was laughing about it.

They almost certainly let us escape, probably hoped we would so they could be done with the whole problem. Roughing up outsiders usually meant a visit from the military—probably some bored Javanese flunky with a uniform and a rusty .45, who regretted the long hike. I'd bet money that no soldier had ever been there but if we found it, so could they. And who needed that? And in all likelihood, we could have redressed our crimes with some form of payback, the value of which could not possibly have exceeded those things dumped from our packs. At worst we would have had to sacrifice Justinus, which D. B. suggested in jest, though the native didn't laugh, anxious as he was to put further miles behind us.

We joked some more but this was a gut check for two rock climbers clueless about jungle decorum and who'd handsomely bungled a rare encounter with the roots of humanity, with the people we all had been long before Walkmans and Bic lighters. D. B. and I went on to spend memorable days with so-called primitive people, always keeping the fiasco with the Uhundunis in mind. We never managed to keep out of trouble, but the trouble was our own and not caused by accidentally tanking a native's cosmology with a gadget from an incomprehensible future. Of course polluting ancient cultures is a confounding subject, and we fool ourselves by thinking we, as outsiders, can control how it ever plays out. But we'd done nobody proud barging in on the Uhundunis, and we knew it.

We gained the Sungai Pit (Sungai = river) and jogged its banks to its confluence with the great Sungai Baliem, which would lead us back to the government outpost of Tiom, completing this stretch in 3 days, taking in sights and sounds only the Ndanis could supply.

Through open terrain we passed startled natives, saying "Nyak" to the men—lithe, greased, plumed, and empty-handed— and "Laok" to the women, slumped under cords of firewood, lips stained from betel nut, bark thread bag harboring either an infant or dozens of sweet potatoes swinging to and fro, a dire metronome of their tired dance. Gardens extended from river line to lofty ridges miles above, each neatly parceled and slaved over by wizened mothers of six, hunched over, mechanically chopping the cobalt soil with stone trowels. Under vine bridges shiny-skinned youths swam cold swift rapids for sport while lanky bystanders skipped wafer rocks from one bank to the other.

We worked along thin trails carved into 45-degree slopes— up, and down, and up—stopping to munch molten yams and steaming greens, cooling them down with crystal water from thin bamboo tubes offered by pert-breasted, ebony-skinned girls looking so fine in their reed dresses before their years of childbearing and raw labor. Rain came and went with rainbows arching across rumbling skies. Back on Justinus's native turf, a gardener spotted him. A hoot followed, then another, and another, until the whole valley thundered with mirthful yelps, hundreds of voices volleying from the water to gardens in the sky.

The administration at Tiom proved thin—one military man (armed), two policemen (unarmed), and a government official, his wife, and seven kids. We had no permission to visit Tiom, but this requirement was waived for a pack of clove cigarettes. We were led quickly to the home of the Indonesian official (who had never seen an American) and soon we were eating buckets of rice and fanning our mouths from the torrid *sambal* sauce. Two days later a Mission Aviation Fellowship bush plane landed on the grass airstrip. Seventy bucks later we were in Wamena, where we caught the daily flight back to Jayapura and its repugnant brand of "civilization."

It took some local currency and several dollars to get permission to cross the volatile Irian Jaya–Papua New Guinea border, but money always wins in Indonesia, and we soon found ourselves flying for Vanimo and phase two of our expedition.

PART TWO: BIKPELA HOL

Dwight: The thorny business of entering Papua New Guinea (PNG) from Irian Jaya involves leaving a police state, where the colonial administration's main activity is contending with the daring guerrillas of the OFM freedom fighters, and crossing into an independent nation, booming and upbeat. PNG welcomes visitors, has ethnological and topographical diversity surpassing Irian's, and places few, if any, restrictions on those keen to explore the wilds. Many have done just that. The 20th century had crept in nearly everywhere, largely due to aggressive missionary activity, but a few pockets remain so isolated that no outsider has yet climbed up or down into them.

The problem is to find out where these pockets lie.

While kicking around a bottle shop in Goaribari, we befriended a towering Papuan with a boar's tusk through his septum and a steel axe in his belt. Describing himself as an assistant to the sub-assistant district commissioner, he accommodated us with a wide-ranging elucidation of why the Enga Province was the most barbaric, least developed in Papua New Guinea. Following this conversation, we ran out into the street, hopped onto an aging bus and hung on for 2 days, hell-bent for a census post called Birip, in southwest Enga.

We spilled into the little bush village only to learn that the provincial government had been suspended due to its failure to control the constant tribal fighting. A disgusted Tasmanian anthropologist told us there were no "first contacts" left in Enga, everyone there having been chased from a battle scene by the police chopper at least once. True, there was a certain allure to the plan of photographing Enganese against a backdrop of arrow showers, but we hung on to our initial goal of seeking out unexplored areas.

We did take the time to insinuate ourselves into the Official Satellite Record Bureau of the Suspended Provincial Government. Alone in the office, we read through volumes of patrol reports, apprising ourselves of the current situation and devouring the exploits of forgotten explorers. The name T. Sorari came up again and again, this officer chronicling an unforgettable spate of hair-raising escapades. Assigned to routine village tours, Sorari repeatedly contrived farfetched pretenses for heading off his designated patrol routes into what was then (late 1960s) practically impenetrable bush. We daubed our brows, packed our mouths with volcanic white orbs of betel nut, and excitedly agreed that this guy was worth meeting.

Much later we were unpleasantly rousted by one angry Mr. Clementine Warulugabibi, informed by his secretary, Ululiana—whose breasts resembled ripe Wau pumpkins—that "two pela in de" had been rifling government files for more than 3 hours. He ordered us out, stiffly, threatening to "rifle and shoot" us. John suddenly whirled and asked, "But, who is this man, Sorari?"

Twenty Enganese gathered at the shouting of that name.

"Sorari?" said Warulugabibi, amazed, ejecting his quid of betel. "How would two breadloaves like you know about . . . ?" He paused, sternly. "I take it that you have been looking at Sorari's reports. How would you like to sweat it out in the hot-box and eat sago for a month?"

"We ate sago and less for 9 weeks in the Strickland Gorge," said John.

Here was the macho back-and-forth that sustained life in jungle outposts and established just how far, or not, a man might go in these parts. The wacky drama was enhanced by frontier Australian shadings which most native administrators—and Mr. Clementine Warulugabibi was clearly one of them—had picked up at school Down Under.

I had a Biami sago pounder inlaid with fine slivers of human bone which I produced and invited Mr. Warulugabibi to examine, hoping this might win his regard. It did not.

"So you think you're a couple of real bush kanakas, do you?" Mr. Warulugabibi said, flipping the pounder in his hand. All along, the number of steel axes in the immediate vicinity had been swelling.

"Pretty much," said John. "Besides, those bare feet of yours look plenty soft to me. Where you been lately, wantok?"

"No place you'd stay alive very long," Mr. Warulugabibi howled, then suddenly cut himself off, pausing a moment to consider something.

"*Mi no laikim go long calaboose,*" I said to Mr. Warulugabibi, taking advantage of the pause. I'd spent a night in the swamp jail at Daru the previous year, and had no interest in sampling a highland facility.

Mr. Warulugabibi laughed. "A service to Papua New Guinea, yes, yes. I've changed my mind. You'll find Sorari in the Gulf Province, our Siberia. That is where the board that drafted his last reprimand sent him. A patrol post called Kaintiba. Of course, to get in there you may have to face Kukukuku along the way. You'll need more luck than I can wish you, but," he looked up at the blackening sky, "I am not going to wish you any luck!"

The door closed. We knew about the Kukukuku. Once a feared highland tribe, they were still treated cautiously by the government and isolated groups of them were rumored to inhabit nearly inaccessible nether regions of the Gulf Province.

We'd just missed the bush plane that made weekly flights to Kaintiba, so we snagged a ride with a road crew to the malarial coastal village of Moveave, and started marching, swallowing gooey sago and sidestepping *puk-puks* (crocodiles) along the route. We saw no one.

Kaintiba gained, we made for the village men's house, inside which were stacked two dozen cases of South Pacific Lager, the pride and joy of District Commissioner Tsigayaptwektago Sorari.

Initially surprised at our arrival, the 50-year-old commissioner, barely 5 feet tall and reeking of drink, welcomed us emphatically, inviting us in to inspect the hang, and in particular, its trove. The vestibule was guarded by a Sergeant Wanyagildlili, who brandished an M-1 rifle of Second World War vintage. While in no way inclined to refuse the ninth bottle offered him, purchased by us from his stock, the Darwin, Australia–educated Sorari proved himself an astute, witty, and fascinating conversationalist. He sized us up quickly and began talking about various patrols he had made in the surrounding bush. Although cutting a deceptive pose, grinning wildly, bottle in hand, he had noticed the rising enthusiasm in our voices the further out his narratives led us. After several minutes we were grilling the man for a unique destination.

"First of all, boys, no guarantee. You may go a very long way hunting down what may be only rumor. But, I'll tell you, I think there's something to this. For many years, stories have trickled back here about a cave called the Kukuwa Wantaim Kapa Ston, a very gigantic cave; very, very gigantic: truly a *bikpela hol*."

"*Ya-Wa! Nogat! Nogat!*" shouted Sergeant Wanyagildlili. "*Duk-Duk, i stap de. Ern i got wanpela bikpela sinek ern i gat sixpela het, fipela tail, ern i tausen foot long. Nogat! Me no laikim lukirn!*"

Minogat tok! Mi go long haus bilong mi!" With this, he thrust the rifle into Sorari's hands and bailed.

I dropped a kina coin into the skull-bank and withdrew another bottle for our friend as John asked what that was all about. Sorari laughed, pried the cap off with his teeth, handed John the rifle, and took a long pull.

"Well, that's the problem. The local people are afraid of the cave, the *bikpela hol*, and not one of my officers will patrol out to determine whether or not it even exists. Supposedly, it lies 10 days' walking from the nearest habitation, and that place, about 7 days from here, is not a village, only what we call a *liklik plies*, or small place. Most everyone there has died from malaria and sorcery." Sorari shrugged.

"Now, Sergeant Wanyagildlili said there is a ghost in the cave, and a snake. The snake is a thousand feet long, with six heads and five tails. He said he is going home because he and this talk about the cave cannot sleep in the same village. His home is about 12 miles from here. I am a fairly civilized man, but I do not know what to think. I would love to go, but I can't get away. They'd catch me absent, and I'd be sacked. I'm chained to the radio nowadays, relaying messages from outstations to Moresby."

The next morning Sorari drew up papers making us temporary Government Patrol Officers (which he had no authority to do) and provided us with a guide willing to lead us as far as Hapayatamanga, the last Kukukuku village before the liklik plies, but not one barefoot step farther. In Hapayatamanga, we were to seek out Irtsj, who was under government employ and who would lead us on to the liklik plies, Imanakini.

"Irtsj is a sort of a good-for-nothing," said Sorari. "He won't want to lift a finger, and you have my permission to be as firm with him as you feel is necessary."

From Imanakini we would have to rely on an elusive individual called Ofafakoos, who lived with four wives and many children, some of whom, it was said, had recently been killed and eaten alive by unknown tribesmen during a payback raid.

We stomped out of Kaintiba on a muddy track that snaked wildly along the contours of a luxuriant ravine. Soon, we were trudging up and down wearisome inclines choked with skin-slashing vines and seething with primordial leeches. Walking on newly fallen *dipterocarps* trees was fine. Those recently fallen, still hard though shorn of bark, were slick nightmares indeed. Trees long fallen usually looked recently fallen, which meant we had as good a chance of enacting cartoon cartwheels as we had of plunging into rotted pungent trunks to our knees, and mingling with the translucent larvae of rhinoceros beetles, discreetly squirming in the friable wood.

Mazes of steep rivulets ran everywhere, and were soothing to climb or descend in. Moss, orchids, lianas were everywhere, large flying things constantly startled us, and our evasive dives were monitored by intelligent lizards. We slogged up to Hapayatamanga after only 5 days.

The enthusiastic reception the machine-gun-speaking Kukukukus gave us was encouraging. That good-for-nothing Irtsj, a gangly beast with a walking stick on his shoulder, earnestly translated as much talk as we cared to hear, but he flatly refused to march on to Imanakini, a dangerous place, he said, where the people were controlled by vicious bush spirits who made them harm each other.

But, Sorari had sent orders for him to lead us.

"*Samting Nating!*"

But we had hiked 200 hours to get there. He laughed.

We had trade goods with which to pay him.

He said he was sure we would leave Hapayatamanga without them, and laughed again. We didn't, and only after John had threatened his very hide did he agree to roust a couple of bolder village boys to lead us off.

Nippongo and Timbunke, perhaps 15 and 17, had just returned from a 40-day cruise in the Western Province, apparently all the way to the Irian border, and maybe a little farther, since the ragged clothing they returned with bore labels reading "*Dibuat di Jawa*" (made in Java). They did back flips when their fathers cut them loose again so soon. They didn't want money, just buai (betel), tobacco, and any excuse to get right out into the bush again.

These guys were unbelievably industrious. They'd lead, chattering and laughing, boosting exotic fruits and sweet nuts we wouldn't have found if our lives had depended on it. They built rafts in minutes for the gear, then swam the rivers four or five times each. Of course, they'd also have to run half a mile up the bank to ride the river down, and all this only after they'd speared a string of *barramundi* and whipped up an impromptu barbecue. Rice? They'd rip the bark off a certain tree, fold it into a sturdy wooden trough, build a fire, and boil it up. The trough never caught fire.

Their bush craft was ingenious, and we began to see there really wasn't any limit to how resourceful one could be. They were having so much fun maxing themselves they got euphoric. The going was treacherous, no doubt about it, but Nippongo and Timbunke completely transformed our way of looking at the jungle.

During the last 20 minutes before the liklik plies, irregular snaps and rustlings convinced us we were being shadowed by men with stealthy gaits. John was tense. Anyone watching the execution strokes of his bush knife could plainly see it. We paused a moment together and strained our ears. Nothing. John made it clear he had little interest in establishing a listening post, and blasted off anxiety by screaming up the last incline like a cruise missile. I couldn't match the clip, so I brought up the rear wide-eyed, figuring I'd run straight at anyone making a hostile move and nail him.

Then we hit Imanakini—all two huts, four men, thirteen wives, and nineteen kids of it. The people were jittery, freaked by us we thought, but soon realized it was something else when no one had relaxed a bit an hour after our arrival, and every kid old enough to run was kept prowling the perimeter.

Whoever the stalkers were, we never saw them. They might have been a group of raiding Kukukuku spooked off by the odd double-white sight. Fatigue eventually supplanted anxiety, however, and we took turns sacking out beneath a teetering lean-to on a bed of fronds, food for every fly, mosquito, ant mantis, beetle, scorpion, spider, and kissing stabber in the whole territory. One old fellow, betel-eyes out in the Crab Nebula, sat up all night chanting protective spells and exorcising his horrendous hacking cough. Another, his toothless mouth a blood-bin with red betel, was so paralyzed by fear he never suffered himself to move, save for the spasmodic demands of his frame.

The women, meanwhile, did all the work. John and I swapped watches, slapping bugs, eventually giving up, hosting all arthropods, desperate by turns to doze. As the night wore on we convinced each other no one was out there, each of us fully aware that in the Asmat, headhunting raids usually took place right before dawn.

Then we both went to sleep. Worse, however, than falling victim to any skull hunt was putting up with the infuriating gibberish of a cock pecking tediously 6 feet behind our heads. Once home, I would buy a rooster for the sheer pleasure of shooting it.

We slipped out of Imanakini before dawn, following Nippongo along an unobvious brawl of rotting trunks that gave passage through hectares of flora deep enough to swallow a man whole. Eventually we arrived at the bush hut (*haus bilong bus*) of Ofafakoos, the bitter-end of habitation. Queried about Kukukuku raiders, he acknowledged they did sweep through there from time to time, but usually harmed people only when fruit trees they considered their own had pieces missing. Upon being offered one kina per day to lead on to the cave, purportedly 8 days away, Ofafakoos grinned extravagantly, thick lips framing a mighty red orifice and two rows of black teeth. He said betel nut offerings tied to certain trees would assure the Kukukuku of our good intentions. He snatched up his bow, six types of arrows, his bush knife and *bilum* bag of *buai*, chatted with each of his four wives in turn, glanced askance at John's hand ferreting out several stimulant bulbs or buai for the white man's consumption, then took off through the dripping blade-like leaves like a track athlete.

The unrelenting flurry of machete slashes plied against the untracked jungle by this superb bushman filled us both with enthusiasm and distracted us from the starchy, spice-less, boiled gunk of forest tubers we'd gagged down at Imanakini.

Six days followed, during which we traveled in great arcs and weaves, typically climbing gooey walls dripping with flesh-blistering poisons, needle-like vines, and invidious foot-snaring creepers. We'd top out on choked razorbacks, rest the duration of a smoke, then improvise descents down walls where pitching off meant a 100-foot fall. The only white men who had ever been within 50 miles of these locales were the bold Aussie patrollers who'd slogged around from Kerema, Kikorl, and Malalaua during the 1960s.

Ofafakoos would lead a knee- or waist-deep wade for an hour or so, only to step out with spooky acuity and start up another hideous wall. We were truly amazed by his sense of direction. Fathom it? *Nogat!* Wall, ridge, wall, river; over and over and over.

Understandably, we both began to wonder if he did indeed know where we were going, other than into unfrequented reaches, laced with odoriferous bogs and impenetrable clumps of pink lotuses, 14 inches across. Day 6 gave us a view of a forbidding limestone escarpment, a sign that rejoiced us, hinting as it did at cave territory. Next day, after scaling a mud wall on which ice tools and crampons would have been sumptuous aids, I looked at where Ofafakoos had elected to descend. Two 10-foot-high Urama Taboo Goblins, their bamboo, human hair, spider web, rattan, human bone, sennit, hornbill-headed, pig-tusked, red and gray spiral-beaded eyes frankly terrifying, were staked out as an explicit warning not to continue.

"*Dispela olgat det longtim,*" Ofafakoos remarked uneasily, then spun around convulsively at what proved to be only the loud, chugging huff-huff of a hornbill. Apparently, the people who made these effigies were all dead now, having succumbed to the raids of the Kukukuku. We didn't frankly believe a word of this talk about furtive raids and cannibals, though both were occurring in the Balkans as we marched. With an upward flick of his blade, Ofafakoos severed the fibrous weave linking the eerie totems and bolted through.

JOHN: WE hurtled down, legs moving like pistons to avoid cartwheeling toward the glint of water 1,000 feet below. Slipping, bashing, and heel-digging through ripe mulch, we slid the final 100 feet on our backsides, sailed off a mud bank and splashed into the creek. After plodding downstream for an hour, under triple canopy, Ofafakoos zagged left into dense thicket. Twenty paces and we ran into a limestone wall stretching overhead for 500 feet and melding into a tilted mesa carpeted with ferns.

Around us loomed the strangest topography imaginable, as though some giant had grabbed the craggy jungle and twisted it into a green jigsaw. The land flowed in and out of itself with such confusion that getting a bearing was futile since one's other points of reference appeared upside down or backwards. Huge trees grew askance from cliffs and buttresses teetering at impossible angles. Waterfalls looked to fall sideways, creeks ran the wrong way, and grass hung down from the ceilings of mottled grottos. We'd be lucky to cover a mile a day in such terrain, and likely would end up where we started.

Skirting right along the stone wall, we finally gained a clearing and collapsed. Ofafakoos pointed to a tiny black hole. The cave entrance? Hardly the Gothic job we'd expected. More like the entrance to a doghouse. Native eyes peered in for *sineks* (snakes) as we wiggled out from underneath our packs, glad that for a while anyway, the trudging was over.

D. B. dug out some dried swine from his pack as Nippongo, who never tired, laid his bush knife into a 60-foot tree, showering us with wedges of meaty wood. Timber! He ran to the high bough and plucked just the right leaf with which to roll his black tobacco.

"*Nogat*," said Timbunke: too green. Nippongo shrugged and layed into a 100-footer, felling it after a pumping ordeal.

"*Nogat*," said Ofafakoos: too dry. Running sweat, Nippongo smirked, then went for a mammoth hardwood, stopping only when I tossed him a pack of Djarums, ferried with much devotion from the Indonesian pirate port of Ujung Pandang. We all howled. Nippongo bounced a pebble off my head.

After 20 minutes, when our legs stopped cramping and we had some food on board, we couldn't wait any longer. D. B. and Ofafakoos dove into the little cave entrance as Nippongo stared, carping about the 1,000-foot *sinek*.

"*Nogat!*" echoed from the chasm. Let's go.

Nippongo and Timbunke queued up behind me. We wiggled in. The tight entrance immediately gave way to a stupendous tunnel, where many branches shot off into velvet nothingness. Thousands upon thousands of bats were startled into wayward flight. And the huge ochre walls, stripes of red and orange, swirling dikes of Pan-Ethiopian ivory. Down, down we went, through crawlways into vast, dripping arenas where fang-like columns, seemingly half-melted, loomed enormously. The Papuans were forever on guard for the *bikpela sinek* or its traces. Onward, we squirmed past clusters of golden stalagmites, crawled through odorous guano under a 2-foot ceiling, treaded around oceans of vicious quickmud. We long-jumped over clefts, hooking into warehouse-sized antechambers and dead-end vestibules. I paused at a clean pool, pointing wistfully. Confused, Nippongo trained his gaze, just long enough for me to boot him in.

We'd been inside 6 hours, wandered 2, maybe 3 miles. Though the way meandered, sporting many aberrations, all now explored, we invariably returned to the principal shaft tunnel.

The tunnel ahead looked uniform, extending beyond eyeshot, but in 200 feet it started shrinking, the corrugated floor angling down at a 10-degree rake. The bats were gone, likewise the guano, so our little passage was hospital clean. Bubbling pot-holes appeared—little carbonated springs—with the overflow racing down the incline into pitch darkness. Water dripped from the seamless roof. It was probably pouring outside. A squall could trigger an interior flood, but we figured this cave too vast to cause a problem. As Nippongo rolled a smoke, we washed off layers of mud from sweat-soaked bodies. The beastly humidity made our breath thick as cigar smoke.

We'd marked strategic bends with chalk—about forty marks so far—but now everything was too soaked to hold chalk marks so we simply pushed on, and the rays of our flashlights disappeared 50 feet beyond. The shaft angled down sharply, maybe 15 degrees. Worse, the ceiling was now only 8 feet above and the walls barely 10 feet apart. After 100 yards the water ran knee-deep, with wall fissures belching blades of clear juice into our dwindling passage. Suddenly, Nippongo stepped into a pothole and disappeared. Ofa-fakoos shrieked, "*Bikpela sinek em i kai kai* (eat) *liklik Nippongo!*"

Nippongo popped back up, laughed, pointed down the tunnel and said, "*Yumi* go now."

This kid Nippongo—we wanted to slap him silly half the time. But in fact Nippongo was the gamest person I had ever seen and a source of confounding amusement guaranteed to lighten us up when legs grew weary and the leeches too thick to bear. The struggles we had in that cavern might someday fade to black, but never Nippongo.

Nippongo led down the dark corridor. We followed.

The floor of the corridor angled down slightly; the walls were only six feet apart and the ceiling just a few feet over our heads. With every step forward the water level rose till after maybe 100 feet the ceiling curved down to the waterline.

"Fudge," I said. "Dead end."

"Lot of ground we covered, just to bail," D. B. said. "I say we try and swim for it."

"Swim for what?" I asked.

Nippongo and Ofafakoos must have caught the drift because they started spewing incomprehensible *tok ples* (place talk dialect), Afros flush to the ceiling, mouths taking in water. A novel sight, all our bobbing heads, like apples in a barrel.

"I don't know about any swimming," I said. "We got no line and no idea where the thing heads, if it leads anywhere. Plus once you're under, you can't see shit."

"I'll just have a look," said D. B., who drew a deep breath and slipped into the underwater tube.

D. B. re-emerged 5 seconds later, wild-eyed and rambling.

"Man, is that spooky! We'll have to work it out 5 feet at a time. Just draw your hand along the wall so you don't lose direction."

I guess that meant it was my turn. Nippongo shouted that the tube was the gullet of the thousand-foot sinek, then laughed. Glug, glug, and into obsidian. Free-floating in liquid space. When my stomach turned to stone, I reversed.

"I don't know about this one!"

But in half an hour we'd ventured out a dozen times each. The shaft ran straight ahead—simple to reverse so long as we turned around with enough air. But we weren't really getting anywhere. We needed another approach. Yes, forget feeling the wall, I thought. Put in a few big strokes and see where it puts you.

"OK," I said. "I'm going out 10 seconds, taking two big strokes, and coming back."

One stroke out, gliding directionless through this ink, and I freaked, clawed for the wall, then groped back to the fellows.

"That's it. That's my threshold. I think I'm finished here."

Ten minutes later, we'd both gone in twice more, taking three strokes each. Still, we were only staying under about 30 seconds, max. I decided to push it a little more.

"All right. I'm going for four strokes."

I dove back under. Ten seconds, one stroke, two strokes, three, gliding blindly, untethered in space. My arms dovetailed forward and I pulled hard for this last thrust, bringing my arms to my sides, knifing further. Then—*Bonk!* A stalagmite.

My hands wrapped my ringing head, and for several seconds I drifted on the shadow line between consciousness and coma. I grasped for the stalagmite, which was nowhere, then for the wall, which I found. Except I didn't know which way was up, or which way was back. With seconds of air left, I stroked out right. My left hand felt odd, different, and my head raised instinctively into an air pocket, black and soundless. I broke down, gasping, hyper-ventilating, rubbing my dazed head.

Sweet Jesus, I've done it now. I'd known some lonely places in 32 years, but that air pocket—dark as the Devil's heart—made the North Pole feel like Trafalgar Square.

Then a thought. *Find the stalagmite!* That was my best hope, believing as I did that the air pocket was past the stalagmite. Finding it would at least point me in the right direction. A sound plan, but even brief exits from the pocket were terrifying. Again and again I ventured out only to return to the pocket and hyper-ventilate in the darkness till I finally calmed a notch.

Finally I found the stalagmite, 15 feet away. Then back to the pocket. After a minute of big breaths, I glided out, slithered past the stalagmite, hand dragging the wall—but flashed on the fact that I might still be going in the wrong direction and panicked and started stroking for all I was worth. My arms shot out and heaved back, then out again; but with this last pull, I hit some-thing, something moving. It's alive! The *sinek!* Some massive freshwater eel! I reflexively grabbed the snake—which turned out to be D. B.'s leg. I was seconds away from sucking in water when he hauled me to the thick air.

The oxygen and headlamps was heaven attained, but my nerves were shot and not until grappling to a dry porch and gasping for minutes could I start talking. Nippongo thumbed a thin trickle of blood from my forehead, then rolled me a smoke which I zipped in about four draws. D. B. reasoned that since the air pocket was so close to the stalagmite, he'd go have a look. I was too whipped to argue. The few minutes waiting seemed like an hour, and my mind cooked up all kinds of crazy things. Then D. B. burst back, his face awestruck.

"It's there! It's true! No myth!" he shouted.

Ofafakoos's eyes popped, thinking D. B. found the sinek.

"The shaft ends just a few seconds past the air pocket—inside the bikpela hol! There's a river the size of the Mamberambo flowing through the bottom of it. You gotta check it out!"

"Just give me a minute."

I had no idea what I was saying, and wouldn't till I was fixing to swim back into the black tunnel.

Without hesitation, D. B. swam back under. Ofafakoos, Nippongo, and Timbunke set off immediately to find their way out, for the water level was rising by the second. I wasn't entirely sure I'd talked myself into going back under. But now I was alone, which is so spooky in such a place that you're urged to action, however crazy.

Finally, my mind went blank and I dove back into the inky tunnel, too frightened to stop at the pocket, finally popping up with a swift revivifying lunge to the flash of D. B.'s Nikon, feeling like I'd just been born.

"What's with the light?" I asked out loud as we scrambled from the pool. We were clearly inside something very large, yet the cave was full of subdued natural light. A little easy climbing over mossy blocks and we were onto solid ground.

The *Bikpela Hol.* That first open vista defied words. I honestly believed I knew what the Spanish conquistadors must have felt when first gazing into the Grand Canyon, or when ancient Miwok Indians first entered Yosemite Valley and peered up at El Capitan.

It took many looks, this way and that, to fathom the size, later calculated at 11 million cubic feet. We'd been treated to the rarest find—a natural wonder of the first magnitude.

Several years later, once the word got out, a New Zealand team battled to the cave and conducted a proper survey. The following year D. B. and I were credited with "discovering and exploring the world's largest river cave." Nippongo, Ofafakoos, and Timbunke were not mentioned. Not that they would care. For D. B. and me, the real payoff was that first view.

The river, some 150 feet across, entered through a 400-foot arch, flowed through a half mile of open cave, and then exited through a 200-foot arch. Between the giant arches the versicolored ceiling soared to an apex of 800 feet above the water. A 100-foot maw slashed the roof at center-point, rife with flying foxes (Southeast Asian bats) maintaining a clockwise circuit between the dark ends of the massive gash.

The swim had gained us a balcony of sorts, 300 yards long and extending at a gentle angle 100 yards ahead, ending sharply at a suicidal plunge straight into the river, slow and wide, hundreds of feet below. Light flooded through the colossal entrance and exit taking us back to the Stone Age. Never before or since have I felt such awesome natural forces.

At the balcony's far right margin, D. B. discovered a tree-lined tunnel exiting to the original limestone buttress, a quarter mile downhill from our entry point: We could walk in and out of the main chamber easy as climbing a flight of stairs.

"Too bad," I said. "Everyone should have the pleasure of swimming in."

After an hour's gawking (and trundling boulders into the river), we exited into a downpour for the 45-minute trek back to the entrance. After two nervous hours, Nippongo, Timbunke and Ofafakoos emerged, battered, with horror stories of their own.

Constant rain had made for treacherous flooding, and twice they'd nearly been whisked into oblivion by rising currents. By the time they battled back to the light, only Timbunke's headlamp was still working. I quickly dressed wounds more painful than serious, then we charged for a bivouac in the main chamber, vast and dry. En route, we marveled over how the terrain could mask our perception of both the cave and its river.

The river, so distinct a quarter mile upstream, flowed through a twisted maze of upheaved crags and ledges overgrown with trees and shrubs so thick that even the huge cave entrance was noticeable only if you were looking straight at it.

Later, stretched out on pads in the titanic chamber, I told Nippongo if he didn't rustle up some food, he'd soon find himself diving into the river several hundred feet below. He said if I could find so much as a seedpod, he'd give me his widowed sister and her four daughters.

The starved march back to Hapayatamanga thrashed us into hallucinations and slurred speech. The kids could find food anywhere but not in the pounding rain, which never let up from the moment we left the cave. The final hours were hateful uphill battles, our only aid the knowledge that we'd stashed four tins of Torres Strait mackerel in the hut of a Hapayatamanga sorcerer. One tin lay conspicuously open: Nippongo's sister told us that some of the men had been dipping their arrow tips into the uneaten fish. The other three tins went down faster than we could wince.

———————————

THE GULF Province averages 20-plus feet of rain a year, and I swear we got half that in the following days. Bivouacs were sleepless disasters and the food was long gone. When we finally plowed into Kaintiba, we literally dropped, not rising for a day. We later snagged a lift on a Pilatus Porter from a Kiwi mate bound for Lae, a coastal haven, and spent the next 4 days at a ritzy expat yacht club, eating and drinking and drinking and eating.

The Howling

THE PLACE was Pentecost Island, way down in the South Pacific, "where people wear bushes for clothes" (according to an in-flight magazine from Cathay Airlines). The subject was Timu, who had a toothache. And not a dull little pang but a thunderous throbber. Timu had scary red eyes and the frame of a black Achilles, and was a man of influence on Pentecost. But just now his face had swollen shut, his hands shook, and he'd gladly have shot a fellow native, or the nearest white man, to ease the pain. D. B. and I were the only white men.

Pentecost Island, in the Republic of Vanuatu (formerly British New Hebrides), is home of the legendary land divers, who build a bamboo steeple upwards of 100 feet high and dive off the zenith with 90-foot-long liana vines lashed to their ankles. The practice derives from an ancient fertility rite, staged to ensure an abundant sugar beet harvest. *National Geographic* ran a feature article on vine diving some years before, which gave it anthropological cachet.

Once a ritual gets objectified in photographs and descriptions, the conception and the deed often morph into different things. Sure, once upon a time vine diving bespoke a primitive cosmology; but like many rituals in many lands, vine diving also provides local fellows a huge rush and a chance to impress the girls. And it was this dynamic, and never mind the gods, that got their motors running, a simple truth never mentioned in Nat Geo.

But the ritual has its risks. If a vine should snap during a jump, it's a head-plant into the turf. So every inch of surrounding jungle is scavenged for loyal vines, which the tribesmen select judiciously. D. B. and I had joined a dozen or so would-be divers on an overnight vine search when Timu's tooth, troublesome for a week, finally took him down.

We forded a big brown river near the eastern divide and began slogging up the muddy bank when Timu's legs buckled and he dropped to his knees. D. B. and Taru, Timu's eldest son, helped him over to a boulder where he put his hands over his face and rocked back and forth like a lunatic, but didn't say a word. A Pentecost man can betray no pain. That's bad form, a disgrace to himself and his clan. And whoever dreamed up that code never suffered a toothache. Not the kind Timu had.

When Timu's hands came away from his face, his eyes ran like a tidal drift and he mumbled something to Taru in dialect, who translated it into pidgin, but too fast for me to catch. D. B.—who'd been kicking around the South Seas for 2 years now and was fluent in pidgin—looked at me and said, "Timu says the tooth has got to go. Like, now."

"I got that part," I said, "But what about the last bit?"

"He says you're going to pull it."

"Me?!"

D. B. dropped his pack into the mud and said, "I'll get the tools."

"Hold on," I said.

"Well you can't yank the man's tooth out with your bare hands."

"Who said I was yanking anything?"

"Timu said."

D. B. opened his pack and rummaged around.

"What the fuck did his ancestors do when they got a tooth-ache?" I asked.

D. B. kept rummaging and I wondered how come, in all my scattershot reading, I had never come across an antique dental epic? Not a single mention of it. What had Socrates done? And George Washington? I read somewhere that George had wooden teeth, but who had pulled the real ones, and how?

"Pliers," D. B. said. "And we got a pair here somewhere."

He began ferreting through the side flap of his pack for our little tool kit and showing an eagerness I didn't appreciate. Tent poles, the stove, the ten-piece frame packs—they all required occasional tweaking, so we carried a tiny tool kit with a few nuts and bolts and screwdrivers, though I didn't recall any pliers. But there they were, a rusty pair of needle-nosed jobs. D. B. fired up the stove, boiled the pliers in a billy can, and declared the appliance "ready."

I cursed because I felt like it, but from the moment that Chinese junk had dumped us on Pentecost I'd set myself up for this assignment. Over the last few days, hoping to get his endorsement so D. B. and I could take a crack at land-diving, a practice strictly forbidden to outsiders, I'd done everything but kiss Timu's ass. When Timu got a headache, I fed him aspirin; when Timu's back hurt, I cracked it; when Timu's flashlight went dead, I gave him D. B.'s. So when Timu's tooth supernova-ed, the dental chores naturally fell to me. But the story ran deeper than that.

White folks were rarely seen on Pentecost before World War II, and during the war and after, the most jackass thing they ever did was to promote the old Kipling hogwash that it was the "white man's burden" to manage and better the tribesmen. Of course they rarely tried, unless there was money to be made off native backs. Everyone Taru's age already knew the score. But some of the old farts like Timu still held out hope that the Caucasian might save the day. Taru, snickering like a thief, knew damn well I was no more qualified at dentistry than anyone else in our group.

It was a trade-off, really. If I handled the job gracefully they'd surely let D. B. and me take a few dives off the bamboo tower. Not that I, or the president of the United States, could refuse Timu anything. When a Pentecost elder sires thirty kids, owns half a dozen long houses, forty canoes, and three hundred porkers, his wish is your command or you find yourself treading water in the Big Pot. Not literally, of course, but you would never be invited to participate in a sacred ritual, which is the reason we'd come to Pentecost Island in the first place.

That's not quite true. Officially, we were down there to scout vine diving as a possible segment for the joint BBC/ABC show I was helping to cook up, based on the *Guinness Book of World Records*. The vine divers weren't breaking any acknowledged record, but the activity was so visually spectacular and little known that eventually, we just contrived a record and went down to Vanuatu to break it, our cameras running. That was still a year off. This was our first look, in person, and as usual we fell in with the natives straight off, resolved to make a jump or two ourselves, since we were already there. After talking it over with D. B. for a few more minutes, we figured if yanking a native's tooth was the price of admission, it was worth trying.

I moved over to the boulder and peered down Timu's gullet. Sunlight flashed into his mouth and I saw a gaping cavity that went down to his very soul.

"It's badly abscessed," I said to D. B.

"Looks like your work is cut out for you then," he replied.

I wanted to ask what made any of this my work but we'd already been through that. D. B. handed me the pliers. I grabbed the instrument and drew a breath. The natives' chatter suddenly died off. I held up the pliers and it grew as quiet as when a conductor taps the lectern with his wand.

Timu opened wide and I began probing with the pliers. With the first clutch of steel on his abscessed tooth, Timu shot off the boulder like it was the electric chair, dropped to his knees, and rocked back and forth again, both hands pawing his jaw. This went on for several minutes, then Timu gushed out a few sentences to Taru who translated it into pidgin.

Timu didn't trust himself once the procedure got underway, and wanted me to promise that I would finish what I started no matter what he said or what he did in the meantime.

"In other words," D. B. said, "you leave the job half done and we're all dead."

I told Taru he'd better get the boys to hold his father down or we might never resume the job. Whatever transgressions the big man had ever pulled on his fellows, here was the chance for them to get even, and several wore tight little grins as they sat on each limb as Taru locked Timu's head between his knees and pried his mouth open with his hands. I nodded.

"Here goes nothing."

That second grip of steel to Timu's tooth annoyed him every bit as much as the first one, judging by his reaction. To make matters worse, the tooth was of the wisdom variety, set so deep in his jaw that I might as well have been working on that punching bag at the back of his throat. Taru's legs, clamped tight around Timu's head, flexed mightily but the big man's head kept jerking about, leaving me to try to clasp a moving target, the pliers biting variously onto Timu's tongue, his cheek, then finally back onto the tooth. A quick reset and I got decent purchase and starting cranking, gently at first, but the tooth wouldn't budge. More cranking got me nowhere.

"Okay," I said to D. B. "There's no coaxing the bastard out. I've got to try and muscle it, so have the boys bear down."

D. B. said as much in pidgin. The boys got set and I put all my 205 pounds into the work, twisting those pliers with a vengeance, torquing Timu's head side to side. Timu started howling, his legs bicycling in the natives' arms. I tugged and wrenched till the pliers sang. But that tooth still wouldn't budge. I tried again, two-handing the pliers and twisting so hard my hands went numb. Timu thrashed and howled; the natives struggled to hold tight; Jesus wept. And that blasted tooth still wouldn't budge. I withdrew the pliers and stepped back, frustrated and sweating all over.

"Don't let him up," D. B. yelled to the men.

"I don't know if I could get that thing out with a pair of foundry tongs," I said.

"You'll have to stay with it," D. B. gasped, struggling to hold onto Timu's left leg.

"Oh, I'll stay with it," I said angrily. "I'll have that tooth if it's the last thing I ever do!"

"It might be—if you don't get it soon."

Timu's eyes begged for mercy but if I showed him any, I'd quit muscling that molar, and the chief could only howl. So it goes sometimes in the wild places, when empathy is forsaken just to keep it. I hated the job but that tooth had to go, and tender feelings couldn't help. Only the pliers could. I grabbed them.

If suffering is the gateway to wisdom, Timu was a sage, although an angry one. How angry we didn't realize till, just as the business end of the pliers neared his face, he got an arm loose and started groping alongside his waist for his machete. He got it, too, and we all scattered for our lives.

Timu roared and nearly turned himself inside out twirling in ten directions at once, flailing the air with his blade, totally out of his mind. He quickly exhausted himself but kept spinning in place like a buzz saw, murdering the air till his grip tired and the machete whirly-birded over a native's head.

"*Grab 'em bikpella!*" Taru yelled, and we all gang-tackled the big man—who went at about 6 foot, 220—and got him pinned back down on the boulder. Taru locked his legs back around Timu's head as he spat, writhed, and ranted, promising to slaughter his tribesmen to the man unless they let him up. Taru said he'd do worse things if we *did* let him up, so the natives held fast and I again bore in with the pliers.

This time I braced my knee against Timu's chest and started cranking hard enough to twist the top off a fire hydrant. I was really earning my money now, drunk with the dementia of the jungle dentist.

Suddenly, a dull pop. I removed the pliers, and gripped in the end was a gory tooth. Or rather, half of a tooth. It had snapped almost flush with the gums.

"*Caramba*," I grumbled, glancing at the crown of red tooth, then flicking it into the peat. "It's no good. I only got half of it."

Timu was now too far gone to hurt anyone. The boys let him go and he started rocking and sobbing and clawing at his jaw again. So much for the code of honor.

"Liquor," D. B. said, "The man needs strong drink or we'll never get through this."

It's unusual to administer liquor before surgery, but then, I was no surgeon. The natives had a couple bottles of urgent jungle shine, and we'd have to pour it all down Timu's drainpipe if we were to ever carry on. Tara fetched a bottle and gave it to D. B., who put the bottle to Timu's lips where it rattled against his buckteeth. Between pants and whines, perhaps half the bottle went down his throat, while the rest streamed out the sides of his mouth.

Once Timu had slumped down in a daze of shock and drink, the men took his limbs again, Taru pried open his mouth, and I went back at it with fresh resolve. The clamp of steel to his jaw jolted Timu from his stupor and it took all hands to hold him, shrieking and thrashing and sweating rivers.

I worked on that tooth for a full hour before I finally broke its will and it came out. I poured some salt into what remained of the jungle shine and after Timu gargled the concoction the abscess was washed clear and comfort quickly followed, as it always does once a festering wound is relieved. Timu eventually managed a smile. Several of the men had been kicked in the face and Taru's fingers were bitten down to the wood from trying to keep his father's mouth open. We were all glad the business was over.

We arrived back at the village the next day toting several hundred yards of prime liana vines. Timu put our case before the tribal executive board, but fearing our participation might endanger the spud harvest, they denied us permission to vine dive. Two days later we snagged a ride to New Caledonia aboard a Twin Otter owned by a Dutch oil company surveying the island for black gold. All told, it cost ABC about three grand for us to have the pleasure of removing a native's wisdom tooth with pliers. But our contacts were in place and the next year my crew went back with thirty helpers and filmed vine diving for British and American TV. For reasons I can't remember, I didn't go.

Scorched Earth

SINCE LEAVING the swift Bonai River several weeks back, we'd hopscotched from one remote settlement to the next, trusting local native porters to lead the way. But none of the natives had ever crossed the central divide and visited the next village, thought to be Mahak, so we could only press on, adrift in the middle of Indonesian Borneo, hoping the directions given us by a blind, Iban elder were correct.

Then that morning, we'd encountered a band of nomadic Dyaks who said Mahak was straight down the muddy path. Rick was dizzy and hiking slowly, so we told our four teammates to forge on and wait for us in Mahak. Two hours later Rick's symptoms worsened from dizziness and chills to vomiting and delirium.

THE PREVIOUS June we were sitting on the seawall behind Rick Ridgeway's beach house in Ventura, California, sipping beer as we tried to dream up some exotic and historic adventure. A "first." Then Rick remembered a friend who had tried organizing a team to attempt the first coast-to-coast traverse of Kalimantan, or Indonesian Borneo, a trek tried by many teams in a place the world had forgotten. From first mention of "The Great Borneo Traverse," the adventure took hold of us and never let go. As unlikely as it felt to be in Borneo—my first of many affairs with the jungle—it seemed miraculous that we'd raised the money, gathered a six-man team, gotten the permits, and were now 32 days out, about halfway across, we hoped, though back then, before satellite imaging, the government topographic maps showed a huge blank in the jungled interior. Now Rick was shivering and gushing from both ends, and I wondered if we'd need an even bigger miracle to get him back home.

I pulled Rick to his feet and with his arm over my shoulder, we wound down the tangled path. Proboscis monkeys screeched high overhead as orange birds shot through bars of jade light between the banyans. We could hear the monsoon drumming the canopy, woven tight as trellis mesh, high above. By the time it seeped through, the hot rain fell in a misty drape that kept our skin fouled with leaves and clammy peat. Twice we forded steaming tongues of ruddy, shin-deep mud that flowed over the trail.

Rick slumped onto a clump of cane leaves, and I bashed down to a creek to get water, wondering what could have reduced a veteran of K2 (first ascent without bottled oxygen) and Everest so quickly to a shaking, staggering ruin. We continued through the mud, the thorns, the wasps, and the leeches.

Several hours later we broke abruptly into a slash-and-burn clearing hacked from primal rain forest. All flora, including thousands of towering hardwoods, had been felled and torched, the age-old method of creating rice fields. But ironwood burns slowly, so this fallen forest had smoldered in the burn phase for months, never a proper blaze, but never quite out. I had no idea how far the wasteland extended since we could scarcely see 50 feet for the smoke.

I milled around, trying not to think about what happened next, and found a note tacked on a cannonball tree at the edge of the burn zone. The rest of the team, the message ran, had met another band of Punans who assured them they were on the only trail to Mahak. And the trail led straight into the smoke. Good luck.

Rick lay back, glazed eyes rolling and chest heaving. I drank a little water, and gave Rick some, which shot back out of him like Old Faithful. Adventures were unpredictable but in this regard they never were. No matter how thorough our plans, how many vaccinations we got, how cautious we were or how quickly or slowly we traveled, something untoward would happen and somebody would go down hard. Here we were.

Rick was curled up and shuddering. I didn't know if Mahak was 2 or 20 miles away. Should I try to smuggle him through the smoke before he got worse? What if the flames or the heat got him? Maybe I should leave him and run for help. But what would "help" look like crossing an ocean of coals spanned by felled trees where only one person at a time could hope to walk across? Maybe we could walk around but that would take hours we didn't have. The sun hung above the trees like a blood orange. With each moment we waited, black shadows stretched farther through the haze.

Then Rick mumbled about pushing on, reached a hand and I pulled him to his feet. During the past 4 hours he'd managed to stumble only a couple hundred yards before crumpling to the ground. Neither of us knew how far he could go. There was nothing else to do. We headed into the smoke.

The trail was distinct for 100 yards. Then the terrain started rolling and the path disappeared. The only route followed a broken chain of fallen trees spanning a bed of ashy coals. Some trunks were like burning bridges, high in the air, one end resting on a rise or teetering on a stump. My eyes streamed and my nose filled with the copper stench of the hair singeing off my legs. We could not pause for an instant without burning our feet, even through our boots. The temperature soared and the chaotic chain of trunks rose higher above the ground, with several nervous gaps. I wondered what route the others had followed.

Just ahead, a smoldering, 50-foot ramin trunk arched up, across and down over a trench of white-hot coals. We couldn't stop and we couldn't turn back, so I cast off, my eyes riveted on the far end of the narrow bridge, shimmering in the haze. When I was halfway across, the trunk shifted ever so slightly. My hands shot out for balance and sweat hissed on the coals below.

The trunk was easily 2 feet across with an 8-inch sweet spot so there was little chance I'd ever pitch off so long as the trunk stayed put. The fact that it might shift had me breathing in careful, shallow pants, edging forward till just shy of the cantilevered end, where I needlessly lurched forward and sprung onto a hot little knoll.

I shifted foot to foot, listening to Rick's raspy wheezing 50 feet away. It had taken over a month for us to reach this point, but suddenly Borneo and everything in it could go to hell. Rick was already there.

He started across.

He moved like a drunk trying to cross a balance beam. Now over the rise, the trunk started making cracking sounds as Rick's feet skated on the charred trunk. He'd extend his foot like an antenna, rock onto it, wobble, then repeat the move again, sucking each breath. They say if you're walking through hell, keep going, but I could hardly watch Rick try. I looked away many times.

Rick teetered the last few steps and I yelled, "Jump!" But it wasn't in him. He grimaced, groaned, then kicking off the end of the log, he half fell, half hopped toward me. I grabbed his arms and we tumbled back, rolling up with watery blisters on our legs.

Rick draped both arms over my shoulders and I plowed through shallow embers to the edge of the fire, 100 feet beyond. We found a little stream a ways beyond and I toppled in, drinking in gulps. A light rain began to fall and a steamy cloud welled off coals just behind. In good health the crossing would have been far more miserable than hard, but getting Rick across that slash-and-burn area was nothing but lucky.

For the next half-hour we trudged through stalks of sugarcane that hedged the dark trail, lit now by the moon and the swarms of fireflies that follow every rain. We'd been going for 16 hours when we rounded a corner and there it was: a 600-foot-long house with dozens of natives huddled around our team-mates on the veranda. The chief, clad only in a sarong, rolled out a rattan mat and Rick fell onto it. We tried to re-hydrate him, but nothing would stay down. As fluids ebbed out of him, his torso curled into a shriveled fetal knot. He wouldn't last long, but we were rallied to hear that Mahak had a seldom-used grass airstrip and that a missionary pilot from the coast was scheduled to visit the next day. We later learned that the plane, at best, dropped in once a month—a lucky break for Rick, who'd had such bad luck. Now if only he could survive the night.

THE ECHO of an airplane engine volleyed through the haze the next morning. When the craft landed the missionary pilot volunteered to fly Rick to a distant clinic located at an oil field that would, he believed, accept outsiders with dollars. As we watched him take off, none of us believed that Rick, now a shriveled heap, could live out the day.

From Mahak, we thrashed our way to the headwaters of the Kayan River and a straight shot to the coast, still 250 miles away. The Kayan ran smooth for a hundred miles, then narrowed and pitched into unremitting rapids until we had to quit or drown. The portage took 2 days. Twenty-one days after leaving Mahak, our ribs standing out like keys on a xylophone, we inflated the raft, put back in, and floated on.

Tanjun Sellor, the first civilized settlement we'd seen in months, looked like El Dorado but for the sapping heat. Among the natives swarming around the little bamboo dock, there was Rick, withered and sallow, but alive. As our little neoprene raft banged into the pylons, we reached out to make sure he was real.

The next day, we gained the east coast of Kalimantan and dined with the missionaries who had rescued Rick from the jungle in a single engine Cessna—heaven-sent for a man who'd just walked across hell. Then the purgatory of 25 days in a tiny clinic, with hallucinations and toes curling and skin wrinkling into parchment from dehydration during his struggle with typhoid *and* malaria. The vein in the crease of his arm was still black and blue from all the IVs. The missionaries would accept no payment except for the gas they burned in the plane. They never mentioned anything about miracles. They didn't need to. The pilot, who once flew helicopters in Vietnam, served up the food and we ate it.

Adios, Cueva Humboldt

SQUAWKING GUACHARO birds darted round us like swarming locusts, whizzing past our heads and careening off stalactites in a high-vaulted cave corridor large enough to park the Goodyear blimp. We continued ducking, hunched under packs, shuffling down the tourist path we'd picked up after entering the cave through a limestone arch, a mile behind us. Just ahead, the passage pinched down to a keyhole. We shimmied through and into a freezing waist-deep stream that quickly rose to eye level where the ceiling dropped down to a little inverted V-slot known as the "Channel."

Delgado, a local Caripito caver and guide we'd hired to lead us to the climbing, waded into mid-thigh and started gasping as D. B. trained his headlamp down the channel. That was the way, straight down the slot—cramped, but there appeared just enough space to move through without drowning. A quick pant, and in went Delgado, whose teeth started clacking once his chest went underwater. He pushed on, grinding his pate against the top of the slot to keep his nose above water, his limbs churning for minutes. Then, "*Es facil, amigos.*" It was easy.

I drew a breath and waded into my chin. The V-slot looked a mile long and the moment I crammed my head up against the little roof with the waterline right at my nose, I buckled from the bolt-like impulse to turn and clear the hell out. But I could hardly beg off the Channel after conning D. B. to come all the way to Venezuela to go climbing in this very cave.

THE CUEVA Humboldt, known locally as Cueva de Guacharo, is the most celebrated cavern in South America. The name comes from the itinerant German naturalist, Alexander von Humboldt, who first explored the area in 1799. The baron conducted a comprehensive study of the rare Guacharos, as well as some basic ethnology on the local Indians. Two hundred years ago, Humboldt suggested, the horrible warbling of the Guacharos (one who cries and laments) likely discouraged the superstitious Indians from exploring the cave. (D. B. figured it was their dive-bombing, not the birds' sad chorus, that kept the Indians out.)

Considering the remote location, tucked far into Venezuela's jungled interior, it amazed us that a German naturalist had made his way to Caripe in 1799. What kind of man would leave his home two centuries ago and travel thousands of miles on a leaky ship to go caving, study a bird, bone up on the local natives, and become a celebrated naturalist by his own resources? The impersonal, soporific style found in Humboldt's memoirs paints a third-person portrait of a fantastic world, though with the explorer himself, his fears and feelings, longings and dreams, absent from the canvas. There was always a chance that under his cummerbund, Humboldt was someone much like ourselves, rafting though life in the wild places, doing his science. Except me and D. B. were pretty lax on the equations, didn't know ethnology from square dancing and, standing buck naked except for board shorts and approach shoes, probably looked more Indian than Teutonic.

Just outside the cave entrance stood a bigger-than-life statue of the baron, with his noble face, flowing beard, and aquiline nose. The work drew heavily from classic statuary depicting Neptune.

The smart money said it *was* Neptune, a copy of a piece chiseled out in 1744 by German sculptor Johan Christoph Petzold, recently knocked off in plaster by Chinese artisans, with a period appliqué brushed on in Caracas. According to the guy running the little food counter near the cave entrance, the replica was christened and renamed there in Caripe during a historical gala several years before. True or not, the trident was a queer appliance in mountainous jungle. But the baron opened the door.

In the early 1900s, a century after Humboldt's first visit, a second German group survived the first keyhole crawl but held up at a curtain of stalactites. Returning, they punched through with a sledgehammer. The chilling waters rose with each step, and oral tradition says the Germans withdrew, just short of the Channel when, according to explorer Bernhard Graff, their testicles froze "like gemstones of the purest water."

Fifty years later, during a photo-documented exploration led by Remus Octavio Philippi, an Italian team slipped through the Channel to venture another 10 miles, encountering a maze of passages and fabulous chambers. These were all awarded Italian names which were rendered into Spanish in 1964, when a team from *Sociedad Espeleologicolia de Caracas* explored, surveyed, mapped, spray painted, and fumbled their way to cave's end, 15 miles into the mountain.

Aside from the Arctic waters, the Channel, and a few rock steps, it was a safe and sane trek to the Virgin Room, where progress was checked by smooth, featureless limestone, and where a small brass idol of Mary now cradles baby Jesus in a blanket. For each of the four or five (average) annual expeditions, it had become the custom to buff up Jesus's face, giving it a penetrating sheen under a headlamp. Recent parties had produced a cartographic map, which park superintendent Leopoldo de la Rubia had shown me on my first visit.

An ardent caver himself, Leopoldo fetched a stack of maps, then a photo of a gigantic *golina*, a Slavic word for circular valley.

The photo showed a huge uniform crater, ringed by jungle, as though a post-hole plug had been pulled from the escarpment. Leopoldo pushed several maps together on the cement floor, gushing out Spanish while pointing to various contour intervals, erosion features, and alluvial fans on the overlapping charts.

D. B. and I were not master navigators, but we knew our way around topo maps and we couldn't get the numbers to jibe or the features to match up in quite the fashion Leopoldo was insisting. Rather than making things clear, Leopoldo raised his voice, swearing that the golina lay directly above the Italian Room, half a mile short of the cave's end. The Italian Room is a wonder of the world, he said, and is roofed by a great maw, so big that no light can reach the zenith. Nevertheless, he felt that a crafty climbing team might link the cave with the golina—somewhat like scaling the interior of an open hourglass, working through the breech, then popping out into the glorious jungle crater—the kind of thing that cavers and fools dream about. But why would Leopoldo tell as much, unless he too expected to go? He did. But when we returned 9 months later, he was stuck at a symposium in Maturin. There was nothing else for us to do but to follow Delgado through that freezing channel.

IT WAS no great challenge that channel, if you didn't mind raking your head and face across the limestone while fearing the ice water might stop your heart. We stayed where the air was, and it was tight. We made four laps apiece to drag all our gear through, one pack at a time. On the last haul, our 600-foot static line snagged at mid-channel, so we took turns going underwater to feel for the hitch, later to lurch up and bang our heads on the rock. We almost left it.

I finally stopped shivering after stooping and crabbing beneath a low ceiling for most of a mile, just as we gained the first rock step, where a greasy rope hung over a vertical tongue of flowstone. Delgado hand-walked up without a word. D. B. followed, muddy shoes scrabbling under his 60-pound load, variously scattered between soaking ropes, racks of pitons, and two unwieldy packs. I followed, wrestled the 600-foot rope back onto my shoulder. We pressed on into darkness.

Considering the cave's great size and the countless aberrations, the going was pleasantly direct, mostly scrambling, a little groveling over and around hazards, with limited crawling through thick mud, a murderous job with our loads. Colossal chambers bore square, milky boulders and telephone-pole stalagmites. Diaphanous crystals studded the walls, twinkling like rhinestones. Only a troop of spotlights could reveal the cave's secrets. Struggling with loads in 100-percent humidity was a cruel contrast to the glacial waters in the Channel. But what did we really know about caving? We were climbers.

I had puttered around a couple of easy caves in the California Sierra and D. B. and I'd nearly died in a Papuan cavern. Otherwise, we had no caving experience at all, and after about 5 hours of slogging, I started getting spooked. *It's just the velvet darkness and the misery of these loads*, I thought.

When we finally arrived at the Italian Room, 7 hours in, we were mud-covered and bushed. A glance at the labyrinthine ceiling showed us that the climb looked anything but the direct affair that Leopoldo de la Rubia had promised. We'd expected as much, though perhaps not this much, and had brought along a Yosemite-style big wall kit.

"This thing looks pretty grim," D. B. said, peering up into the blackness.

We dumped our loads and started scanning the huge roof with our headlamps. We had a big police-style torch that cast a beam like a tugboat light, but the void seemed to swallow it whole. D. B. said he felt like Tycho Brahe, the ancient astronomer who had worked mostly with the naked eye and who often was entirely wrong. The ceiling was a confusion of twisting tunnels, spiraling arêtes, gaping shafts—like a dome of wormwood—and we didn't have a clue where to start.

"This thing looks totally horrendous," said D. B.

We went with a ramp and gully system that appeared to gain the upper wall most straightforwardly, not that we could tell one way or another. Without a couple 4-K lights filched from a film set, any choice was literally a shot in the dark. As I rooted through the climbing gear, Delgado wished us luck, then left, promising to return in 2 days. Delgado hadn't said ten words the whole day, so we had little idea about his reliability.

"Think we can find our way out of here?" I asked D. B.

"Guess we'll find out," said D. B. We didn't expect to see Delgado again.

D. B. climbed up to what we had hoped was a generous ledge below the first ramp, but it turned out to be a "big-ass sump," the bottom bristling with stalactites. Hand traversing to the ramp would require skirting the sump, and finding some sound protection, in case D. B. ripped off and got shish-kabobbed on the stalagmites. He banged in several poor pitons, clipped the rope through, then shuffled across the ramp on sloping holds, fighting the rope drag. The lead rope, soaked from the channel, easily weighed 40 pounds, and the 600-foot trail rope handled like a ship's cable. We were mud covered, steamed like smudge pots at the first exertion. Things were getting real in a hurry.

"Watch me close!"

D. B. scraped the mud off his shoes and headed up, splaying his legs on the offset walls, blasting in pitons and grunting. After 80 feet, D. B., now just a faint glow, said he needed some "testosterone poisoning" to give him a needed boost. I rooted out an old ZZ Top tape and plugged it into the box. Owing to the cave's fantastic acoustics, my two-bit Indonesian tape deck roared. The rope snaked out smooth and steady till D. B. yelled down that he'd reached an alcove. As I ascended the fixed line, the pitons came out all too easily.

We walked 30 feet from the alcove to where the gully resumed, quickly giving way to a rubbly slot leading to a bulging, geological wonder—huge ivory horns, horizontal purple spears, teetering smoked crystals, and countless stone roots twisting in bizarre, electrified patterns. My pitons sucked, but tying off an organ-pipe crystal offered no help. Too fragile. The holds were crumbly or detached, and when treading them grew too nervy, I burrowed deep into the vertical gully.

Just above, a huge chockstone blocked passage. A mystery held it in place, and a whisper might dislodge it. I hadn't set a decent piton in 100 feet and clawing over that chockstone wasn't an option: too big and too loose. So I started shimmying up behind it, holding my breath. I stretched up for a big hold, then started yanking my hips through the wee space between the chockstone and the main wall when the chockstone suddenly pivoted, then popped, roaring down the gully. D. B. dove for the alcove as the glittering chockstone exploded into fifty ingots.

"Nice shot!" D. B. yelled.

There was a big powder mark close to where he'd been standing.

Six hours and 300 feet later, I tiptoed left to start free climbing up a loose flake. After 20 feet without protection, the wobbles came on and I just managed a piton before my muddy boots blew off the holds and I wrenched down onto the peg. From there I found continuously grim artificial climbing, gingerly clipping my three-step stirrups into a creaking string of pitons. I ran out of gear after 100 feet, whaled in the last pins—which were piss poor—then set up a hanging belay.

D. B. came up, re-racked, and led off. By the sound of the pitons and his constant cursing, the rock quality was not improving. Two hours and three tapes went by, as the *thunk-thunk* of pitiful pitons bandied about the pitch blackness.

"Hey, there's a cave up here!"

"We're in a cave."

"Okay, a hole in the wall, a tunnel, a cleft, whatever. How much rope left?"

"Twenty feet."

"I'll just make it."

I turned the tape deck back up and smiled at the notion of escaping these hanging stances, if only momentarily. After another few songs I got word to ascend the rope nice and easy since the only anchor was "a sling looped around a schist gargoyle."

I tested the rope, and started up. Some of the pitons had already fallen out, and the bulk of the others didn't require a hammer to remove.

We hoped to find the bottom of the golina soon, or some escape. We'd better. My conservative estimate had us about 500 feet off the cave floor. The rock had devolved into flaky trash, and the prospect of more artificial climbing was hateful. Fifty feet shy of the curious anchor, I started yelling for details, got none, and arrived at the subway with D. B. absent.

That bit about a schist gargoyle was a gag; the rope was secured to a spider's web of stout chockstones. I dumped the gear and made my way down the flat subway-sized tunnel, banking that it led to the golina. D. B. appeared just as the subway opened and turned snow white with reflected light. From nervous release, or amazement, we both started laughing. What could ever match this passage, decked in thick, alabaster crystal? For all of creation this little patch of space and rock had been here in dark silence and with a flick of a headlamp a fantastic world was struck to life. What, I wondered, did our gratitude mean to the mineral world? What is beauty—or anything—if it's never perceived?

We crawled, shimmied, and walked another 30 minutes. A porthole-sized slot veered off our ivory shaft, but we kept on, hoping for something direct, and more importantly, one beam of light from overhead that would mark the bottom of the golina. Soon the subway angled down abruptly into what our headlamps claimed was another big chamber. We'd need a rope to descend, which entailed a long round-trip to the gear and back.

When we'd returned to the edge, I peered over the lip of the subway, gazing straight down into the void and the climbing we had done but couldn't see.

Over the last decade we had banged our way up hundreds of rock walls, though never inside a cave. Exciting, for sure, but we were in no hurry to resume that blind, hideous aid climbing. We hustled back to the new chamber, set an anchor and roped down—not into another gorgeous room as we'd hoped, but straight into a small mud pit. The walls were featureless, the air dank and heavy.

Then D. B. spotted a little tunnel at the mud line. Our headlamps revealed that it opened up to a bottomless hole or perhaps another crystalline ballroom—we couldn't tell. I crawled in feet first, boring the chest-tight slot with my feet churning like a backhoe.

Once we could snake in two body lengths, we started talking about a rope; but that rope presently hung over the rappel and wouldn't quite stretch to the crawl. D. B. wallowed back in. A muffled sound, silence, then a distant *splat!* Wild cussing fired from the hole.

I quickly snaked in head first, an inconceivable concept a minute back. The floor had collapsed just short of the new room, plunging D. B. into a quagmire below. Closet sized, the new room led nowhere. D. B. was knee-deep in primordial ooze and didn't look pleased. He raked his hands through the gumbo, vainly searching for his headlamp. He could no more claw out of that mud hole than he could swim through the La Brea tar pits. And I didn't have anything long enough for a hand line.

As a cornered rat circles, my mind raced, unable to grok onto our no-exit jam, the whole thing made worse by D. B.'s flailing down in the sump. There had to be *something* we could do. But I couldn't jump down in there or we both were finished. I couldn't lower down and offer my legs to grab because my gooey stance offered no such purchase and my shoes would still be a dozen feet shy of D. B. I couldn't tie together my pants and shirt and lower those like they do in prison escape films because all I had on were gym shorts. We were, quintessentially, fucked. I blathered out some crap about options, my breath fogging in the humid air, but there was only one thing I could do and we both knew it.

"Go get the fucking rope!" said D. B.

That meant grappling back to our packs, a long ways away, to fetch our remaining free line. We didn't have a second to lose. So I left D. B. in the darkness, knee-deep and sinking in a sewer, 20 feet down a mud closet, a mile into a virgin shaft, 500 feet up a limestone wall, over 10 miles inside a cave, in Caripe, Venezuela, South America.

My headlamp started flickering just past the white room. Considering my breakneck pace, my guess had the gear only 5, maybe 10 minutes away. I started moving as fast as possible, which wasn't fast at all. When my headlamp tapered to a candle, I raged. I'd paid 28 bucks for the special lithium battery in my headlamp (LED headlamps were several years off), said to be good for 24 hours, and now the bastard was failing. I slouched back and checked my watch. Damn, we'd been going strong for almost 30 hours. Then my headlamp died.

A wave of terror snapped me upright. My head banged off the low ceiling. I screamed and sat back down. My cigarette lighter was more psychological relief than anything, since I could only keep it going for 20 seconds before it felt like a meteor in my hand. The journey to the gear, probably 200 feet, took an age of fumbling, bashing, falling, and raging, during which I discovered every ankle-wrenching slot.

When the lighter finally melted I was close to the gear, but took to crawling to avoid a free-fall exit from the subway. At last I stumbled over the packs and played blind man's bluff rooting for the spare lights. Then, with a click—light was reborn. We had four extra headlamps and loads of batteries. I grabbed the essentials plus the spare rope and bolted for D. B., pressing for greater speed, paying the price in contusions.

Once down in the mudroom, I tied the new rope off, clipped on a pair of ascenders, stuck a bight of rope in my teeth and burrowed back into the pit. D. B., sunk to mid-chest, was so unresponsive that minutes passed before he came around, squinting and mumbling. Shortly after I'd left he'd flipped his lid and started churning the mud, clawing for his headlamp and sinking deeper. When he couldn't move at all, and submersion felt imminent, he plunged into a fugue state and started hallucinating. I crawled back into the mudroom. Soon the line came taut and when D. B. re-emerged, wild-eyed and covered with mud, he looked like something from a Japanese horror film.

The hump back to the gear was slow going. When we stumbled into the one and only aberration, the little porthole walkway, I joked that we should immediately explore it. D. B. didn't break stride. Back at the gear we swilled a gallon of water and started rifling for food, but we both slumped back unconscious before the first can got opened.

When we woke up 10 hours later, I was ready to quit the Cueva Humboldt, but after wolfing down most of our food, we psyched for a last jaunt back into the subway to inspect that porthole passage. If our estimates were remotely accurate, we had to be close to the bottom of that golina.

We had three headlamps apiece, plus pockets bulging with batteries. We powered past the white room, gaining the porthole crawl soon enough. I headed in. Once through the stricture, the shaft merged into a massive, multi-layered catacomb of meandering tubes. I quickly retreated for a guideline, and we spent the next hours groveling through the vast arteries, pursuing independent lines. After half an hour of belly crawling, my knees and elbows were raw. I'd kept praying to see that little shaft of light that would indicate the bottom of the golina, but apparently no god was listening. We might spend years groping through, in, up, and around this cave, never finding that damn golina. On the crawl back to the subway, my headlamp flickered, and I cussed. Later my chest got stuck and I nearly wept.

"Let me out of here!"

We lumbered back to the gear, resigned to give the climbing one last shot.

The wall above the subway overhung gently, but a flared crack reluctantly accepted gear. After 40 feet, the crack melted into a rounded groove, with no crack and no chance to place any kind of pro. The rock degenerated into loose mortar, and, as before, it simply flaked away when drilled. Free climbing was out of the question. I swung around, looking for options. Then the top piton popped and I dropped 20 feet.

"That's it," I said. "I'm done with this."

"Let's get the hell out of here," said D. B.

I lowered back into the subway. In 1 minute, we didn't care that we had come all the way to Venezuela and still failed. It was get out or go mad.

The descent was tedious and dangerous and took hours. On the long trudge out of the main chamber, we were amazed to run into Delgado. I'd spent enough time in South America to appreciate that, "Your tire will be repaired in an hour," usually meant they might get around to fixing the thing in a week—if ever. It was unfair to paint Delgado with the same brush, but we had anyway, so his returning like this, as promised, made him a hero in our eyes.

We reached the rock step knowing only 2 miles remained to open air, food, girls, and sandy beaches. Once down into the main shaft, we made good time because Delgado knew all the shortcuts. Then, in the process of dragging our packs through that blasted channel, Delgado went and got his foot stuck. After about 10 minutes of wiggling, yanking, and freezing, we were not only hypothermic, but confused. It didn't seem that Delgado's foot was all that lodged. He could wiggle it around but it still wouldn't come loose.

An absurd idea occurred to me, and finally Delgado admitted as much: he wouldn't pull so hard as to lose his shoe. When D. B. told him he had 30 seconds before we left, his foot slid out of the constriction just like that. But Delgado was heartbroken, so I swam back in, searching for his goddamn shoe. After another 15 minutes, D. B. said he would buy him 10 new shoes. No good. I finally found it floating just past the channel.

We all were shivering convulsively by the time we made the tourist path, breaking into a jog and ducking the whizzing birds, hoping to warm up and possibly exit before dark. Soon the cave's ragged lip arched in faint relief against the darkening sky. Thousands upon thousands of Guacharos swarmed into the twilight, where clouds and stars and moon and all kinds of open space kept my feet shuffling until I nearly tackled Humboldt's statue. For no reason whatsoever, I surveyed the baron's face, actually touching his hair and beard and clutching his trident. Then we went over to a little trailer that sold empanadas, coffee, and candy to tourists, all gone at this late hour. The trailer was shuttered and chained shut but there was a hose beside it with some water pressure so we stripped down and washed off the mud and grime and fatigue. It felt like we'd narrowly escaped doom, yet standing there wringing wet, neither D. B. or I had a scratch. Not a mark. None of our fears came true. Nothing lasting had happened but the passing of time. We had been inside for about 65 hours, had slept 10. I dropped to my knees and kissed the ground: Adios, Cueva Humboldt.

My Friend Phil

MRS. DAVENPORT screamed bloody murder. Phil and I were in the next room, swinging face down in hammocks and trying to spit through rifts in the floor, when the fiddler crab scampered across Mrs. Davenport's bedspread. I'd been counting the hours for what felt like a year to blow town and spend Easter vacation in Baja, California, with the Davenports: my best friend, Phil, his folks, Harold "Pops" Davenport, and his wife, Katherine Putnam Davenport, a Jane Eyre on triple sec and valium. We'd only arrived in Mexico that afternoon, but Mrs. Davenport couldn't stay in the *casita* another second.

Pops loaded Mrs. Davenport's three Rimowa suitcases into the rental Jeep for their evacuation to the Hotel Rosario La Paz, a few miles away. We could come if we wanted to. We didn't. Pop would swing by in the morning to take us out for breakfast. The Jeep wheeled off, and Phil and I were alone. We were both 16 years old.

The Davenport casita lay just off a dirt road, in a copse of bamboo, set up on oak pylons and cantilevered over gulf waters famous for sport fishing. The front of the house had a plain wooden door, whitewashed plaster walls and no windows, probably to limit break-ins. Pop had spent a bundle trimming out the inside, with portraits of Aztec noblemen and a few San Sebastian bullfighters on the reed walls, combed steer hides on the wooden floor, and a collection of faux Olmec artifacts staged in cabinets against the den walls. But this was Baja, so the electricity was off and on, mostly off, the humidity was terminal, and the flooring in the bedrooms was so warped you could see the anxious ocean through the gaps. A chrome-plated horseshoe hung over the kitchen door for *suerte*, or luck. And now we had the run of the place.

Phil rifled the liquor cabinet and came away with a black earthenware jug, sealed with a waxed cork. "The real *mierda*," said Phil.

He drew out the cork with his teeth and drained off an inch of tequila. He shuddered, trying not to, and handed me the bottle. We'd watched *Fistful of Dollars* and *The Good, The Bad and the Ugly* ten times each, and studied how Clint Eastwood tossed off 100-proof hooch like it was branch water, so we had to drink our liquor with impunity. We moved to the back of the house where a plank staircase descended between two rotting pylons, from the den straight into the sea.

At the bottom step, tied off a pylon, bobbed a frail-looking dinghy. We sat on the last step with our legs in saltwater and gazed out over the moon-rinsed gulf, talking about climbing up at Tahquitz, and maybe doing some bullfighting here in La Paz, if they'd let us. The tequila burned all the way down to our toes.

Then we spotted the giant cutlass carving through the water, flashing like mother-of-pearl as it swiveled into a shaft of moonlight.

"Shark," Phil whispered.

I moved up a couple of stairs as Phil jumped into the dinghy, snatched an oar, and started bashing the water.

"Frenzied movements attract them," said Phil. "I read so in *Argosy*."

"Man, that fin's big as a surfboard," I said, clinging to a pylon. "Sure you wannabe fuckin' with it?"

Phil thrashed the water harder still. I moved to the top step as the fin swept close by the dinghy, circled under the house and plowed back into the deep. Phil jumped from the dinghy, splashed up the stairs and into the house, returning with the remains of our chicken dinner, chumming the water with bones and gizzards. Several times the gleaming fin cruised past but never as close as the first time.

"Blood," Phil said. "We need blood." And he hurled the jug into the sea. It was nearly dawn before I drifted off in my hammock, picturing that great fin circling under the bedroom floor.

WHEN I woke the next morning, Phil was in the kitchen, studying the chrome horseshoe hanging above the door. Pop Davenport had already come and gone, and Phil showed me a wad of pesos to prove it. His mom had a fever and Pops couldn't leave her alone in the hotel. We'd have to fetch our own breakfast.

Phil reached up above the doorjamb and yanked the horseshoe off the wall, his eyes burning.

"We're going fishing, amigo."

We jogged up to the paved road, swung up onto an *autobus* and were soon scudding around central La Paz, grabbing a shrimp cocktail in one stall, ogling the *senoritas* in others. We found an old man, hunched over a foot-powered grinder, and he milled one end of the silver horseshoe into a pick. I watched the fury of peso notes changing hands, Phil rattling off *Español* like a local. He'd mostly grown up with Pop, a kook gentleman anthropologist who had fooled away nearly 30 years annoying natives and "studying" antique cultures deep in the Peruvian rain forest. So Phil could speak Spanish like Zorro.

We hustled on through the fish market, ankle deep in mullet offal. At another stall a fleshy woman, her cavernous cleavage dusted with talc, cut 10 feet of chain off a gigantic, rusty spool.

"For leader," said Phil, grabbing my arm and racing off.

Phil bought 200 meters of stout polypropylene rope from another lady in a booth hung with crocheted murals of *Jesu Cristo*. Meanwhile, her husband welded the chain leader onto the sharpened horseshoe, sparks from the acetylene torch raining over Jesus like shooting stars.

"Now for the bait."

We took a cab to the slaughterhouse on the edge of town. Outside the reeking, sheet-metal structure, Phil waved through a curtain of flies and stopped an Indian girl, around our age. Her hair was pulled back in thick black braids and her oval face was a picture. She was selling fried pork rinds and sweetbread, and when Phil asked her a probing question, she killed him with her eyes. Phil kept talking in dulcet Spanish and the girl started to snigger. When Phil's hand went out with a 10-peso note, she glanced around at empty streets, then hiked up her white muslin blouse and for about one thousandth of a second my eyes feasted on her perfect brown globes crowned with two perky, pinto-bean-like nipples. Then her shirt was back down and the bill was gone from Phil's hand and all we saw were two golden heels hot-footing to some shady nook to admire the gringo boy's money.

"I'd marry her in a second," Phil said, "if I was old enough."

An autobus took us back to the casita, me laden with a giant bull's heart wrapped in brown paper and a plastic bucket of bloody slop so heavy it put my hand to sleep. On the stairs behind the house Phil baited the sharpened horseshoe with the ruby bull's heart, duct taped a soccer ball to the chain leader just below where he'd tied on the polypropylene rope, then coiled the rope on the stairs and lashed the free end round one of the creaky pylons. Then he hefted the bucket of entrails into the dinghy.

"You either watch the line here in the bow, or row. Your choice."

"I thought we were going to just chuck the thing in from here."

"Shark won't go for it. You saw how he shied away last night. And anyway, I bought all this rope."

Two hundred meters of nylon rope seemed a poor reason to row into shark-infested waters in a leaky dinghy full of blood and guts, but Phil was already in the boat, yelling, "Come on, John. It's a 2-minute job."

I took the oars and rowed straight out into the gulf, my limbs trembling so hard I could barely pull. The dinghy was overloaded and tippy and little geysers spewed up through gaps in the hull. I watched the house slowly recede, the line slithering out from its coil. The water rose to ankle level around my sneakers.

Fifty yards out, Phil tossed the bucket of gore overboard and a red ring bled out around us.

"That sucker's any closer than Acapulco, he'll smell this," said, Phil. "Believe it."

"I do."

Phil hurled the big heart overboard with a plunk, the weight yanking out the chain leader, which chattered over the low gunwale of the dinghy. The soccer ball shot out and sank. Phil panned the ocean for a moment. Then the ball popped up near us, the waters churned, and he screamed, "Pull, man, pull!"

I heaved at the oars, my heart thundering in my ears, the dinghy fairly hydroplaning, Phil bailing with the bucket and screaming, "Put your back into it or we're goners!"

I pulled harder and faster, trying to retrace the line floating on the water, marking the way back home. The flimsy oars nearly bent in half as Phil screamed to go faster and faster till my oars were driving like bee's wings. Twenty yards from the house we were both screaming, breathless, and terrified, the dinghy shin deep and sinking by the second. A final heave and I powered right into the stairs and we stampeded over each other and through the house and out the front door, finally collapsing in front of a man selling shaved ice from a pushcart.

Phil lay in the dirt, sucking down breaths.

"Not that we're afraid to die or anything," Phil laughed.

The man with the pushcart couldn't have looked more surprised had a burro pranced by on its hind legs.

After a few minutes we stole back into the house, tiptoeing through the hall, through the narrow den, past the wall of glassware and artifacts, pausing at the open door and the stairs below and staring out over the gulf at the line sleeping on the surface and the soccer ball bobbing peacefully fifty yards away. There wasn't so much as a mackerel on the line. Never had been.

"Chickenshit shark," Phil mumbled.

For several hours we sat hip to hip on the stairs, talking about the Indian girl as we stared out at the bobbing ball so hard that the flat horizon and the heat of high noon put us in a trance. Then everything went quiet.

"Wonder where the gulls went?" I asked.

The rope suddenly jumped out of the water, the staircase groaned, and splinters flew off the pylon as the line lashed itself taut as a bow string.

"He's hooked!" cried Phil.

We leaped up and grabbed the rope as the pylon bowed against the stairs. Rusty nails sprang up from fractured planks and sand crabs scurried from dark places. Far out on the water we saw an invincible fin, a roil of water, and a jagged snap. A scythe-shaped tail curled on itself and the rope went slack against the pylon. A gathering surge was tearing straight toward us, looking like a submarine surfacing as the line doubled back on itself. Then the fin swerved maybe 10 yards off and headed out to open sea fast as a cigarette boat.

"Grab the rope, or the house is going with him," Phil yelled, lunging for the line.

There was no checking that monster, but I grabbed the rope anyhow and when the shark hit the slack line it wrenched me off the stairs and straight into carnivorous waters. I crabbed from the water and up the stairs and didn't stop running till the den, where I stood, shitless, my trunks draining onto the rug. I was nearly dry before I crept back out to the stairs.

The line went slack, then taut. Then slack again. We pulled like mad. "*Eres tan ugly que hiciste llorar a una onion you pinche cocksucker!*" Phil yelled.

The rope smoked through my hands. We pulled some more and Phil kept swearing, calling up the remotest, most colossal vulgarities, so piquant with the odd Spanish word tossed in that I could only pull in awe. It was genius.

After an hour we'd gained a little. With the rope doubled round a pylon, we had just enough purchase to lock the beast off, even gain some little rope when the tension eased for a second. After 2 hours we'd reeled the creature a quarter of the way in. Several times it broke the surface, obsidian eyes glinting in the sun. The monster would relax for a moment and we'd win a yard, then the line would twang tight, the pylon would creak and the stairs would twist and shudder under our feet. The line dripped red below my hands and the saltwater stung like hell.

"Pops got this place from Old Man Daley," said Phil, when the line went lax for a minute. "Or from the widow Daley," he added, spitting into his palms and rubbing his hands together, saying that Old Man Daley—whoever he was—used to come down there on weekends from San Diego and drink some and fish for tiger sharks. Then one Sunday he didn't return home so a brother or cousin came down looking. "'Cept all he found, washed up under the house, was part of a leg and a *huarache*."

Phil was hopping up the story because he couldn't stand it when things simmered down, even for a minute.

"This ain't working," said Phil, staring out to sea. "Just lock that *chingadera* off for a sec." He stomped up the stairs and was gone.

I braced against the pylon and held fast as the house behind me filled with whoever Phil could snag off the dirt road—dark-haired boys, street urchins, even the man with the pushcart. Phil returned to the steps and when the line went momentarily slack, Phil unwound it from the pylon, ran the rope in a straight line from the water up the stairs and through the den, down the hall, and right out the front door.

The brown crowd turned its back on the casita, each man and boy clasping the rope over the shoulder, Phil yelling, "*Hale, hale, caballeros!*" And the tug-of-war was on, "*Tiburon! Pinche tiburon!*" yelled over and over like a chant at a soccer match.

Phil joined me once more on the crumbling stairs, hauling hand over hand. Out in the gulf, a huge swell spooled toward us as the shark, big as a four-man bobsled, b-lined for the casita.

"Let off," I yelled, releasing the rope and backpedaling away, "Tell them to let the fuck off."

But it was no good. The gathering crowd was well past the front door, 30 feet churning the dust. Phil and I jumped to a pylon when, with one titanic lurch, they hauled the opalescent monster to light. It flopped lengthwise onto the buckling stairs, the silver horseshoe hooked deep through its saw-toothed lower jaw, the line taut as a guy wire.

The beast lurched a yard straight up the stairs and was yanked right past us. Its bear-trap maw snapped and a sandpaper flank rasped the skin off my arm as he jackknifed over the stairs through the open back door and into the den where, with a snap of its jaws, it clipped the legs off the rosewood table.

"Let off, for Christ's sake," I screamed from the stairs, "Let it go!"

But every able man along the dirt road had latched onto that rope, and every last one was hauling for pride and country. And half a ton of shark wasn't going easy.

A smashing tail, and the cabinet was gone, the Olmec artifacts so many shards, the Spanish glassware, sand. Colossal teeth shredded filigreed wood, ripped the hides off wicker chairs. A flip and a twirl and he unraveled the Malagan rug.

The heaving crowd dragged the monster farther through the narrow den. Purple blood splattered white partitions. A deep-water kip, an airborne nose butt, and a wall caved in. Salt-rotted wood fractured and floor slats snapped to attention as the ceiling dropped a yard and parted to show a splintered smile of Mexican sky.

"Jesus almighty!" Phil screamed. "*HALLLLLLLLLLLLLLLE!*"

And the brown mob pulled. The great monster died ten times, then erupted back to life, knocking plaster off the hallway walls, murdering grandfather clock, blasting the front door off its hinges.

At last the noble creature lay outside, its hornblende eyes locked on infinity, its jagged mouth open. A tough with a ball cap probed the cavity with a tree branch, and in a final show of sea force, the huge mouth snapped shut. The tough jumped back with a wooden stub in his hands, yelling, "*Que barrrrrrbaro!*"

WE ALL stood in a daze, staring at the great monster as kids prodded it with branches. Word of the conquest spread down the dirt road. Several *Federales*, who gathered with the crowd, posed for pictures taken with an old Kodak Brownie Phil swore had no film in it. Then a flatbed truck from the fish market sputtered up and it took ten of us to logroll the creature onto the lift and then into the bed of the truck. In 5 more minutes the shark was a memory. The crowd wandered off, thumping each other's backs, and once again Phil and I were alone.

I was grated raw, rope-burned, sunburned, splintered, and bloodied, my trunks and shirt in tatters, one sneaker gone, my hands two oozing, pulpy knobs. Phil was hardly marked, but the casita was trashed.

We tried a dozen different lies on each other but couldn't build an excuse as big as that shark or the wreckage it caused. Finally, Phil went to the Hotel Hidalgo to try to explain, and in an example of his transcendental luck, he found his parents packing to leave on the next plane for the States. His mother thought another night in Mexico might kill her. Without reservations, they were able to secure only two seats on the afternoon Air Mexicana flight to Los Angeles. But Pop had booked us on a later flight that same night. The Davenports would wait for us at the airport in L.A., and the next day we'd all go to Disneyland.

We raced back to the casita and, after wandering through the ruin for several minutes, Phil said, "Shark left us no choice here but to torch it."

"Torch it?"

"Yeah, burn the place down."

I pictured myself in a Mexican jail. Forever.

"You want to try and explain this?" Phil laughed, glancing at the ocean through a 10-foot hole in the floor, then up through the rent in the roof.

"This joint's dusted. *Acabó*."

"How do we explain the fire?" I asked.

"We don't," Phil smiled. "That's the beauty of it. It burns down after we're gone. And it will."

Phil shagged into town and returned with a cab, a gallon of kerosene, and two candles. We threw our suitcases into the cab waiting on the dirt road, then Phil soaked what was left of the den with kerosene, planted two candles in the middle of the buckled floor, lit them, walked out the open door and into the cab.

As we ground up off the tarmac we spotted a plume of smoke out east, rising off the fringe of the ocean. Phil leaned back in his seat and said, "Wonder how big that sucker was?"

When Pops returned to Mexico he found two shrimp boats tied up to the blackened pylons where his casita once stood. Nobody knew how the fire had started, or even when. Years later, shortly after his twenty-fourth birthday, Phil and his two kayaking partners paddled into an unexplored river in Sumatra and were never seen again. Like the shark, like the casita, like an Easter in Mexico, Phil burned and raved "till there came the Destroyer of all delights and the Sunderer of all societies, the Depopulator of palaces and Garnerer for graves. . . ."

Rats

WHEN MY friend Dean Potter crashed in his wing suit, we knew he was gone forever but nobody knew where to. We'd all danced close enough with death to feel it wrapping round us like an iron blanket, but no one ever learned a thing about Dean, or what loomed on the Other Side. What we did learn in the dance were things about being alive we couldn't have imagined through playing it safe.

For our informal group of "Stonemasters," the deepest cut came early, in the 70s when we were teenagers battling up our first Yosemite big walls. Our heroes and occasional enemies were a cult of rogues who landed in the Valley just after the pioneering climbers of the 1950s and 60s, guys who refined the art of going huge. We called them wall rats, or simply rats. Their promise land was terra incognito, and man alive, did they find it.

THE GENERIC term "big wall" indicates any sweep of rock so sheer and so tall it takes days, sometimes weeks to climb. Many big walls lack sufficient holds for free climbing, a catch-all term for hauling yourself up under your own power, using the rope and attendant gear much as a trapeze artist uses a net—as a backup, to check a fall should feet or hands fail.

A dated illustration of a big wall climber is found in old B movies—and sometimes now in redneck beer ads—where the burly mountaineer, like a gnat on the side of a high rise, slowly and precariously hammers up the overhanging rock, stepping from one creaky piton to the next. He looks roughly the same as the bold *grimpeurs* who first bashed their way up the great limestone and granite cliffs in the Italian Dolomites and French Alps, circa 1900.

The mechanics have evolved in a hundred years, but I wonder if the few climbers who make a trade of scaling big walls aren't as wild and lonesome as their soul mates who climbed a century before them, when boots were hobnailers and pitons soft iron, and when hemp ropes sometimes snapped during falls.

The most accessible and most popular, and arguably the finest big walls are in Yosemite Valley. Since the late 1950s, climbers have come from many lands to scale Half Dome, the Leaning Tower, Washington Column, Mount Watkins, and especially El Capitan, the crown jewel of world rock climbing, rising 3,000 feet directly off the scree, a marvel to look at and a miracle to climb.

Several miles from El Cap is a tract of dirt, piñon, and scattered boulders known as Camp 4, a rude and dusty ghetto with a history like Dodge City without the gunplay. Most Yosemite climbers stay there. A mile across the valley is a huge rock spire called Sentinel. John Salathé and Alan Steck, over 5 blazing summer days in 1950, established the first valley big wall on Sentinel's sweeping north face, ever lording over Camp 4 like a 1,600-foot-high talisman to the unknown.

I lived in Camp 4 for eight summers, and though I climbed dozens of walls during that time, I was never a true wall rat. I'd knock off two, perhaps three walls a year. A wall rat might do ten. And not just the trade routes, where the going is straightforward and a fit free climber can really make time. Rather shit-your-pants horror shows, where the cracks are like breaks in an old mirror, where nearly every piton hangs three-quarters of the way out of its slot, where there are no cracks at all and you must hook dimples and scallops and into incipient seams smash malleable copper swages solid as farts in a dust storm. And all on terra incognito, terrain they were meeting for the very first time, "on sight." They'd start at the bottom and in one continuous push, battle their way to the top, encountering cracks, flakes, chimneys and faces much as a jazz musician encounters a solo in the middle of a song, embracing the brand new on the fly and ad libbing as they went, bringing to the encounter their own basic stuff in a voyage where both the immediate terrain and the outcome were unknown and success was never assured. A rational person would never have gone up there or hung so much as their hat on such bogus hardware. A wall rat nearly lived in the unknown, hanging his life on sketchy tackle, over and over again.

I lacked the poise and doggedness to do anything but dabble with these big-time "nail ups." On hazardous leads I'd feel the worm turning as I mounted higher on increasingly fickle gear. Scary, yes, but usually doable, absorbed as I was in the function. Belaying, however—tending the leader's rope, stranded in slings for hours at a go—drove me mad. The intensity of the belay is made so by the long silences. Once the leader is 75 feet out you have to scream to hear each other.

Intensely alone, you have little to do but fantasize about the rock shearing away and the leader plunging down and the whole goddamn sky falling on you, lashed to a stake and powerless to do anything but die, horribly, a hundred times an hour. A couple days marooned at the anchor and I had summit fever, the hysterical desire to get off the climb, and that's just when a wall rat would hit their stride.

Wall climbing peaked during the mid-1970s, then enjoyed a resurgence in the 90s, as speed climbing caught fire, finally settling into a small but avid sub-genre when climbing went mainstream around 2000. The new breed is better funded and better equipped, are better people and far better climbers. But few of this group would identify as wall rats, who are to modern climbers what Ben Hur is to racing.

Early on, Camp 4 was divided between wall rats and free climbers. We free climbers outnumbered the rats twenty to one, proof, they reckoned, that they were the genuine article. Their craft was too chancy and required too much suffering to draw many numbers. Exposed as they were to sun and wind and long nights dangling in hammocks (and later, aluminum and nylon Portaledges) lashed high above the rest of us, they nonetheless lived in a sheltered world.

Their crusade, if you could call it one, had slowly turned in on itself since Salathé and Steck first climbed Sentinel decades before. In the ensuing years the rats had become increasingly detached and self-contained, finding security and even safety of a kind in the yawning void that the rest of us passed through just as fast as we possibly could. They considered us free climbers athletic enough, but lacking the essential steel to manage days, sometimes weeks, stapled to a big cliff. They loved to prove this point and were always goading us to take our lives seriously and join them on some sinister wall.

Many of us were wall climbers, on a limited scale, granted, but rarely did a season pass when a partner in the Yosemite hardcore didn't slug up a couple of walls. So the rats' needling—which for me started the second I showed up in late May and continued till the moment I left in August—had a grating, cumulative effect because it wasn't true. If I said as much, the rats would pipe up.

"Fact is, Long, you're light," some rat would inform me.

"He's sort of perdy, though."

"But he's light."

"Fuck all you rats."

Then they made it personal, with more jeering and laughing till their voices lowered and they'd start waxing rich about some giant new climb up some giant wall that I knew damn well would require great suffering and labor and terror—for me anyway. Then they'd haze me a little more, hoping to stir the embers. No matter how badly my fingers were slashed or my elbows throbbed from too much free climbing, I could almost always brush them off. But if I was reckless enough to let my pride get caught up in the business, if I felt I was losing too much face to guys I'd essentially grown up with, I'd call their bluff (in fact, they'd called mine), and I'd find myself bashing up a wall with a couple of rats.

Like the time I got recruited for a 2,000-foot-high wall in the Sequoia wilderness, just south of Yosemite. "Gonna be some free climbing up there and we could use you," said Gordy B., a Canadian wall climber and El Capitan champion thirty times over. "But there's a bit of a hike to get there," added Walter, Gordy's longtime partner, also Canadian.

The bit of a hike was 17 cruel miles humping monster loads for a projected 5-day climb. Except at the end of the long march, most of our food got looted by brown bears at our camp in Bear Paw Meadow. The Canucks ruled out a 34-mile round-trip slog to resupply, so we headed up the wall with only Mars bars and a packet of Matador beef jerky so tough "you need teeth in your anus just to pass it," said Gordy, chewing his brains out during our first bivouac.

From the camp the wall was all steeples and towers and glorious minarets, classic as a scaled-up Chartres. Up close it was a regular sand castle. Crumbly rock drove us down after our 3rd day. Fifteen rappels and 18 miles later, slumped against a tree not far from the trailhead, Walter shouldered the pig (haul bag) for the last time, staggered down the home stretch and said, "I'm so hungry I could eat the hind legs off the Lamb of God." He would have, too. And that goes for every rat in the business.

Many rats were extravagant characters I liken to the wandering prospectors of the Old West, private and standoffish. They cared little for glory, nothing at all for fame. Having their exploits publicized or praised was a slur because no rat worth a damn cared about your opinion. However much they liked the hazards, toils, and silences on the high crag, their climbing went beyond liking in almost all directions.

What made them rats was who they became when they ventured out of this world and into the unknown. Several were rich, rebelling against comfortable limits; but most were poor. They all seemed to do just a little better on the walls than on the ground. Most rats had their share of things going wrong, and they all seemed to come from the flat. So they'd jump onto a wall and for a week or 10 days get free of the ground, and the ground of them. Eventually, the walls became their chosen refuge from a world that confused or annoyed them.

A few rats were not so conflicted. They loved the ground, but the high crag even more. Zorba the Greek danced to forget the pain. Yet when he was happy, he danced just the same. I think if Greece had a high crag, Zorba would have been a wall rat.

Necessity determined that they'd haul the duct-taped water bottles, the nylon hammocks and Portaledges, the rain-flies spangled with patches, the Ensolite pads and sleeping bags with names sewn into them (rarely their own). They also hauled boxes of Moon Pies they'd filched from the Lodge store, and they hauled cans of peaches in heavy syrup, greasy foot-long salamis and summer sausages, Pop-Tarts, smoked oysters, Red Vines, Dinty Moore Beef Stew, Cracker Jacks, and Life Savers to slake the "Kalahari Throat." And sodas that would explode when opened but cut through the gum that accumulated in your mouth after a day's climbing and so were treasured like pearls. But it was the other things they hauled that said who they were.

Ron B. was an extraterrestrial buff, and he hauled pseudo-scientific texts about flying saucers and alien sex. He'd also haul a pair of "4-D" glasses, ludicrous red plastic jobs he had paid serious money for that any sane man could have bought at a joke store for a buck. Through these glasses he could "see" the gaseous trails of Venusian ships.

Greg V. and Jean-Paul D. were two of the best rats in the business. One time (along with three cases of Olde English 800) they hauled a bag of golf balls they'd pilfered from a driving range in Palm Springs and teed up on El Cap Tower, a flat, spacious ledge about 1,000 feet up the cliff. Along with 200 golf balls, they'd brought a driver and a thatch of Astroturf, and they spent a June afternoon banging great drives into the ocean of trees below. Several hikers were nearly struck on the trail snaking toward El Cap. The rangers were alerted and fanned out on horseback, looking for a sniper.

Before he died soloing in the Wind Rivers, Joe P. hauled a hibachi up Half Dome and up Mount Watkins, too. Russ W. hauled a small acetylene torch so he could barbecue ballpark franks. Along with half gallons of Diet Coke, Charles C. hauled a burlap bag full of bottle caps, and would flick them off the wall every night, hoping to hear a sound. Once, when the bag went empty, he grew so bored and restless that he led the last 600 feet of an extremely difficult new climb in half a day.

Jeff W. hauled a brass crucifix and a wallet photo of the Virgin, a fake Spanish doubloon, a slingshot and fifty marbles—curious offerings to the unknown. Bernie R. soloed the Leaning Tower and Half Dome wearing a yarmulke—partly from authentic devotion, partly because he was "so bald you could see his thoughts."

Tom hauled a harmonica, a kazoo, and a 10-pound ghetto blaster on which he'd play "Lara's Theme" from *Doctor Zhivago* till we were ready to murder him—and we would have if he hadn't gone 6'3", 225 pounds.

They traded off hauling the bags, sharing the weight of strange lives, dragging up the wall what others did not want, including each other. They hauled the clouds and rain and the sun pounding on their heads. They hauled a lifelong sense of homelessness and squatter's rights to terra incognito. They hauled thirst that would have killed a camel.

Until an avalanche swept him off Broad Peak, Dan R. hauled a medical degree up El Capitan (and a new route on Nanga Parbat). Others hauled scabies and the drip, smashed fingers and swollen feet, cracked ribs and broken hearts, and so much malt liquor (the go-to brew was King Cobra, which "bites hard and tastes like ass") they often needed a separate haul bag. One rat hauled leukemia up El Capitan not once, but three times. They scattered his ashes over Matterhorn Peak from a Stearman biplane.

They hauled the very mountain, shards of it flaking off under 10,000 hammer blows and sticking to their faces and necks and hands, stinging their eyes, blinding them to everything below. They hauled the pull of the earth and they hauled the earth itself because they could never leave it completely behind.

They hauled the stress of men engaged in dangerous work and they made jokes about it. They hauled their honor with them, for they were its only custodians. Some hauled loneliness so deep and so treasured they would share it with no one—like "Private Dave" from Montana, 30-something and heroically laconic, who always climbed his walls solo, which is twice as dangerous, three times the work, and a hundred times more frightening. (If any man should feel like the last soul on earth, he's the one hanging alone on a Portaledge, half a mile up a big wall, on a night dark as a river bottom.)

After a long climb, Dave would join in at every campfire, laugh and carouse with climbers he'd known for 10 years. Then, slowly, we'd see less and less of him, until finally he'd start laying out gear on a tarp and borrowing water bottles. And where was Dave going? "Back to the high lonesome," he'd say, grim as Atlas, "Where there ain't no people at all—yet." "Private Dave" preferred his own company, and up on the high lonesome, he and the work understood each other perfectly.

The sun and moon would come and go but time for a rat was a watch with no hands. They climbed a foot a minute, working toward the clouds, always hammering, beyond willpower and resolve because it was all instinct, an emptying of thought. They had no commission and no guarantees, no boss and no pay. They took insane risks. In the rat's theology, to travel hopefully was better than to arrive. The summit meant nothing, the unknown, everything. It was the blank page on which they wrote their story as they went and however they wanted, though always in bold script.

The new and unexpected first drew the rats onto the high crag, and after a decade, when many rats had climbed upwards of fifty walls apiece, no face or tower or flying buttress held the same secrets as before, when the rock stretched beyond them like unexplored ocean. Their quest stalled out once the untrodden became the beaten path. Some ventured off to the big mountains, searching for the brand new in Peru and Tibet and India and Pakistan, and many were lost. Over time, the others ran out of Frisbees and golf balls, tired of Cracker Jacks and *Doctor Zhivago*, could no longer see anything through their red plastic glasses, could no longer haul a world of their own making. By twos and threes, the rats left Yosemite and the walls were nearly silent.

THE RATS played a radically different game than the modern free climber, with their hired porters, fixed ropes, camera crews, drones and support personnel, including personal "belay slaves" and poop tube gophers.

Because the old ground-up ethic was impractical for such difficult and athletic terrain, the modern big wall free climber often started from the top and rappelled sometimes thousands of feet into position, vetting the unknown and rehearsing the moves till every sequence was memorized and every hold chalked. And when a team started up a wall—a valid "send" (free ascent) must be accomplished bottom to top in one continuous effort or "push"—none hauled Mars bars and packets of Matador beef jerky, golf balls and drivers, or books about alien sex. Rather vegan cheese and canned frappuccinos, solar-powered laptops to post real-time updates on social media, and countless other marvels of technology. And while everything changes, the modern crusher was focused, remarkably skilled, and just as exuberant and driven as any rat who ever lived. The results were landmark achievements in the history of adventure sports.

The essence of the wall rat is why the crusher came to be. Nevertheless the sea change brought about by the free climbing renaissance left little room and less need in the valley for the mavericks who once found solace and purpose in terra incognito. And so the stoic, confidential world of the wall rats, who hauled life and death in the same bag, slowly faded in time, like the slipstreams of Venusian ships.

But not completely . . .

Over the span of several decades, right up to Kevin Jorgeson and Tommy Caldwell's 19-day epic first free ascent of the Dawn Wall on El Capitan—the "hardest big wall free climb in the world"—climbers got better, and the hardest long free routes, over time, became common targets for leading men *and* women. With the experience accrued from years of practice and "sends" of the mega free climbs, what once required top-down strategies and massive rehearsals were now being done, in exceptional cases, in the old ground-up style, where the team tackled the route "on-sight," encountering the unknown with their own basic stuff much as the Rats did back in the day, but this time using hands and feet instead of hammer and steel. In the ways that mattered, some modern free climbers were approaching the big stones just like Steck and Salathé had when they first trekked up to Sentinel in 1950, and climbed the first big wall in America. The game was coming full circle.

ADVENTURE, LIKE the literature that lasts, is not, finally, its medium nor its style; rather something before, behind, above, and beyond all words and all movements. The rats, in name and deed, could not outlive their own time. What could was the precious cargo they always hauled: the magic of terra incognito, and what a person becomes when it's the air you breathe and the ground you cover, a sparkle silently passed on, generation to generation, from one bag to the next, that leads every traveler not up, but into the valleys of the soul.

The Bird's Boys

I FIRST WENT to Yosemite Valley as a wannabe rock star when I was 17 years old, and continued to spend every summer there until I was 25. Like most climbers, I stayed in Camp 4 (now on the National Register of Historic Places), which back then was girded on the east end by the Camp 4 parking lot, an oily acre crammed with the proudest medley of rust buckets imaginable, including an ancient British step van that must have been parked on the street during the blitzkrieg; a dented, salt-pocked Cadillac, now a convertible thanks to a cutting torch; and a red VW van, broadsided, t-boned, rear-ended, and rolled, not a window in it, vise grips where the steering wheel should have been. Few of these ran without priming and a push start. There wasn't a treaded tire in the whole lot, and a live battery got passed back and forth like a gold brick. The license plates were from Canada, Washington, California, Colorado—most of these junkers having been babied down the road with little chance of ever reaching the valley, and no chance of ever leaving it.

Beyond the parking lot lay dozens of colorful tents pitched in a swath of wooded shade. In the summertime, between two cinderblock bathrooms at both ends of camp, many of the world's foremost rock climbers called this place home. Other legitimate campgrounds, full of scrubbed tourists, RVs, and screaming brats, featured kiosks full of rangers, who were full of silly rules; but during the first few summers I spent in Camp 4, I rarely saw a ranger. The park service had essentially roped the place off, much as Hawaii, through the cruel years of leprosy, had quarantined the island of Moloka'i. With no rangers and no regulations, and in the almost complete absence of women to sow shame and keep discipline, the place was basically an international ghetto.

Jim Bridwell—"The Bird" as we later styled him—was de facto lord of Camp 4 and everyone in it. He had a vulpine smile, a gymnast's frame, and big plans. And he always needed partners. That left him to pull a couple of us up to his level, no easy trick, since Jim Bridwell was probably the finest all-around rock climber on the planet.

He'd snag the most promising kids in camp, climb them till they couldn't climb anymore, tie them back in and climb them some more. He never eased us into anything, and never worried about teaching us more than we could learn. In this manner he shifted the sands of daydreams until he produced the solid stuff— the finest climbers and the greatest ascents of the era.

Within a week after I'd first stumbled into Camp 4 (school was now out across the country), every campsite was packed. Of the hundreds of climbers, about six or seven others, of roughly my age and ability, had gone through a trial by fire with The Bird, and we naturally fell in together. We were all the Bird's Boys.

For that first month, most of us slept on the ground. The Bird, however, had a tent, a massive green-canvas affair. When the Bird was handling some personal business inside, he'd pin a cardboard sign on the zippered door: *Keep Out*. This went for fellow climbers, park rangers, the president of the United States, and Jehovah. By morning, the sign usually was gone, and in the faint musk of patchouli oil and K-Mart Chianti, a little group of us would hunker down inside and discuss various climbs, getting The Bird's feedback on routes germane to our curriculum. We covered other topics besides climbing, though The Bird did much of the talking because he was just enough older than we that he seemed to know everything.

Much has been written about the climbs of that era, and the Bird has been lionized for his pioneering ascents up the steep granite faces—exciting stories, but mostly standard hero fare. But "standard" did not apply to the other things about life as one of The Bird's Boys.

LOVE

Our typical lodging was a four-man expedition tent, often on loan or bought secondhand from another climber who had either borrowed it himself or gotten it as a perk from some expedition. No one I knew had actually gone to a retail store and bought one, though Dale stole his, and said so. Even 30 years ago, high-tech tents cost hundreds of dollars—which none of us had—and you absolutely needed one to safeguard your few possessions against varmints, bears, and thunderstorms. Understand that in the daffy parlance of adventure sports, "four-man" refers to an area sufficient for four beanpoles to sleep on their sides, with not space enough between them to drive a knifeblade. So, in truth a four-man tent was just big enough for one climber to have a private space all his own.

We didn't much care what we slept on so far as padding went, but if we had any hopes of luring a girl into the tent we had to have a mattress. These were acquired from girls who worked as maids in the park hotels, lodges, and tent cabins. Since we could rarely nick the precious mattresses outright, we normally had to barter for them. Such transactions took many and curious forms.

Since it was summertime, the Valley was always full of girls, and we always were looking to get laid. What's more, robust sex, and plenty of it, was an indispensable part of our training routine, according to The Bird. The perilous climbs required a Zen-like acuity impossible to achieve when freighted with "urgent fluids."

I never got clear on The Bird's hypothesis, but apparently the terrestrial body could grow dense, and the astral body (so key for legendary leads) distracted, by a surfeit of fluids. In any case, the fluids had to go. But the Yosemite climber worked the field at a disadvantage—barely two nickels to rub together, ragged, torn and aggressive, eating the holes out of doughnuts and trying to woo Helen of Troy. That we might end up with someone a little less than a lady who launched ships was okay.

Many climbers tricked out their tents in the hopes of creating a tender atmosphere. Some had "stereo" sound systems, consisting of several transistor radios tuned to the same station and situated here and there. Others had pictures of sunsets and rainbows taped and even stapled to the nylon walls. Still others hung bead curtains and small mirrors, burned incense, or had fancy bedding (Buddy W. fleeced the purple satin sheets from a whorehouse in Blue Diamond, Nevada—swank merchandise save for the stains). Of course the crux was always getting the girl in the tent in the first place, and some would-be darlings found the décor so ludicrous that the amour stalled out at the rain fly. But kids manage to strike up the band no matter the circumstances, so occasionally we got lucky, and even learned a few things.

I must have been a sophomore or junior in college and had always swallowed life whole, wolfing it down unconsciously, tasting little. My relations with girls were Neanderthal—either wham-bam, or erotic wrestling matches lasting so long the poor, beleaguered *wahine* begged for mercy, and got none. Then one night at the tent cabins over in Curry Village, in the middle of passing the gravy, and for reasons I couldn't imagine, I simply stopped and pushed away to the edge of the bed. Something felt all wrong, but I didn't know what so I looked dumbly at my then-girlfriend, Roxanne—21, tanned, fit, spectacularly naked, perfect in the lamplight. And it occurred to me that I'd hit the lotto—that no man rich or poor could expect much more from life, so I said so.

"What a line," said Roxy, and I asked, "To get what?"

I already had the girl. And what might *better* even look like, if it wasn't Roxanne all over again, tomorrow night?

"Or now," she said.

For a long time we just lay there. I'd always met girls with a terminal libido. Could there be more to it? Either way, just then I had nothing—no clothes, even. And yet everything. Later I would appreciate that these are the moments that make a life.

VITTLES

The business of eating was paramount. The Bird's Boys were all starving all the time. Food was fuel, and we burned immense amounts of it, judging all meals by quantity, not quality. Ninety percent of our money went to food, the rest for weed and beer. Every campsite had a thrashed old picnic table usually shared by six climbers. Every table bore a smattering of pots and pans, black as stovepipes, and an old Coleman stove that broke down so often and so entirely that every Camp 4 climber knew them as well as his very pud. There were some women, of course, and they were equally knowledgeable.

All meals were one-course affairs. The standard entree was a sort of goulash, consisting of rice and spuds as the principal ingredients, enriched with whatever else we had to chuck into the mix—canned vegetables, tuna, acorns, even pie filling—anything to sweeten the pot. The trick was to keep the stove going and to keep stirring the bubbling gunk so that it didn't burn. Once the fare was judged done, we all tore into it and kept eating till ready to explode. Then we'd rest for a bit, maybe walk a few laps around camp, hitting any peace pipe offered, and then eat some more. And we could always eat more. Or almost always.

A favorite stunt was to frequent barbecues and picnics put on by various religious groups that swarmed into the park for week-end retreats. These were strictly private gatherings, though strangers were sometimes tolerated so long as the spirit of the thing was close to their hearts (if you could suffer through a sermon and the singing of hymns and so forth). Kind of like the Salvation Army.

Acting pious and playing along was our ticket to the chow. So we'd all turn out in our finest gym trunks and T-shirts, smiling alongside the righteous, the whole while licking our chops and growing increasingly restless till we could finally break for the grub like wolves. These celebrations were usually large, and our numbers were comparatively so small that we could eat like we'd just come back from Annapurna and no one ever cared. Till they did.

I have no idea how The Bird learned of these affairs, but he did, and so frequently that the late, great Alan Bard claimed a tourist couldn't so much as roast a few marshmallows without The Bird catching wind of it. He usually tried to keep our numbers down to three or four of our little band, but one time the word had gotten out, and about twenty of Camp 4's hungriest showed up for a stiff affair put on by the Four Square Pentecostal Church out of Modesto, California. We were as out of place as arrowheads on the moon, and everyone knew it.

The pastor, a nail-thin southern windbag, sailed extravagantly about the Good Book. When he started in with the flood and the Tower of Babel, we were right there with him, following his traveling hands and the rampage of his fractured drawl. Drifting to Leviticus now, and the law of holiness, I noticed an uneasiness moving through our group. We traversed the plains of Moab, then on to Babylon and Nebuchadnezzar, and the boys were starting to fidget. He touched on the Eight Visions, and Daniel in the Lion's pit, and we wanted to chuck that preacher in there with him, heckled as we were by the smell of those ribs and the fact that he was catching a second wind. Solomon spent 20 years building the House of the Lord and, around half past eight, when we finally rose for a closing prayer, that hayseed seemed to take 40 years closing things out till he finally said, "Ah-Men."

Straight away the climbers stampeded over the congregation and entire tabletops of burgers and fried chicken vanished in seconds. It was like something out of a Fellini film. Guys plunged bare hands straight into great vats of beans and potato salad, shoveling huge and sloppy loads into their mouths. Punch was swilled directly from the jugs, faces were stuck right into layer cakes and pies, and all this before the proper crowd had eaten so much as a carrot stick.

I don't remember what set the thing off, only that one of us crashed the line for the tenth time, reaching for a last drumstick of something, and a deacon angrily grabbed his arm. Words were exchanged; there was some pushing and, as the shocking news spread that the food was all gone, we scattered into the surrounding forest. I had so many franks and ribs and rhubarb pies on board I could barely walk. I caught up with The Bird (an avid reader of both the *Holy Bible* and the *Book of Urantia*) in the darkness of the forest, and we both leaned against a tree and glanced back.

The dust had cleared and the big pastor was up on a picnic table, sweat pouring off his bald pate like the rivers of Damascus. He glared down at the great mountain of rinds and corncobs strewn about him. Then looking at the starving faithful he threw up his hands and cried that the famine was sore in the land—or something like that.

"Stolen waters are sweet," said The Bird, quoting Proverbs.

TREASURE

Climbing consumed most of our daylight hours, and we were generally so exhausted afterwards that our downtime, and the things we filled it with, were seldom remarkable. Until "The Wreck." Twenty years later a fantastically embroidered version of the event provided the basis for Sylvester Stallone's hit movie, *Cliffhanger*. A recent book and dozens of articles about the wreck tell different stories, but the backstory seems clear.

One morning in the dead of winter, two young waiters at the Ahwahnee Hotel (the fanciest lodging in the Valley) set out on

snowshoes for an over-nighter in the Yosemite backcountry, dropping LSD for good measure. Six miles out they found an airplane
wing and a debris trail. Later, once the acid wore off, they alerted
the rangers of a probable plane wreck. Inside of 24 hours, agents
from the National Transportation Safety Board, the Federal Aviation Administration, the DEA, and Customs, had all assembled
in the valley.

Customs sent a Vietnam-era Huey from San Diego to shuttle
the Feds to the crash site, at Lower Merced Lake, 16 miles away
from Valley central, in the rugged and frozen backcountry. Over
the following several days they hauled out over 2,000 pounds of
Mexican red-hair weed. Then logistics and an approaching storm
shut down the operation. The pilot and co-pilot were left behind,
entombed in the frozen cockpit.

Given the waist-deep snow and 16-mile trudge from the Valley floor, the park superintendent chose to wait till winter thawed
before conducting a recovery operation, expensive even in perfect
conditions. So the case was put on ice (in fact the winter of 1976-
77 was one of the driest on record).

ONE OF the dead pilots left behind in the downed plane was
former Army copter pilot Jon Glisky. Glisky's attorney, Jeffrey
Steinborn, was alerted that his client was dead. In fact Steinborn
hated the drug-runner's guts, but still had a shine for Glisky's
wife, who he'd romanced back in college. The widow was given
no information about her dead husband except that his plane
crashed somewhere in the valley. As a favor to his old flame,
Steinborn drove a rental car to Yosemite and spooked around,
eavesdropping on DEA agents still lingering in the Yosemite
Bar, and was able to get the lowdown on the dead pilots and
the salvage operation just abandoned. It's doubtful Steinborn
knew that the night before the crash, at a dirt airstrip in Baja,
California, Glisky had loaded 6,000 pounds of dope onto his

twin-engine Howard 5000. But Steinborn probably figured as much, and he did know that the fuselage was still up at the lake, under the ice, as well as Glisky's and the co-pilot's bodies, along with whatever weed the feds had not recovered.

"On his last night in Yosemite," wrote Greg Nichols in *Men's Journal*, "Steinborn noticed a fire burning in a campground nearby. He lit up some Thai stick and sauntered toward the trees. He found about a dozen young climbers around a fire, so he passed his joint and told them a fantastic story about an airplane full of dope."

"I knew Jon Glisky and Jeff Nelson (co-pilot) were dead," said Steinborn. "I just had this romantic notion that someone should smoke that beautiful weed those guys were bringing back from Mexico."

Of course The Bird got word in nothing flat. Following a confab at The Bird's circus tent, freezing their asses off in blue jeans and tennis shoes, Woody, "Buzz," and "Skillet" trekked up to Lower Merced Lake to find the Howard 500's fuselage augured into the frozen surface. When Skillet reached down into a slushy hole (carved by federal chainsaws) and heaved out what looked like a hay bale, the small talk stopped. They hauled the stuff outside into the moonlight, studied it under their headlamps, sniffed it, ate it, smoked it, and were still disbelieving. But it was true: the submerged fuselage was bursting with 5-kilo bales of red-haired Mexican weed.

The storm never came, rather a heat wave. And since the rangers never stationed a sentry to stand guard, the feds were none the wiser that climbers were looting the Howard 500. The trio made four trips in as many days and each time they hauled out a bale, another one would bob to the surface. Since there was obviously enough for every rascal in Camp 4 to get quickly and shockingly rich, all of The Bird's Boys and all their friends were recruited. (If nothing else, Woody needed a few dozen strong backs to hump his plunder out.) In a matter of hours there was a virtual mule train of climbers making withering loops to and from the lake.

Woody had his load out the first day; then it was each for his own (though most climbers worked in teams of two and three). Some returned with upwards of 150-pound loads, a burden that fetched roughly $50,000 on the open market. "Hiking for dollars" they called it, and in a week's time more than a million dollars' worth of booty had been hauled to light.

The plane had broken up, and after the initial site finally went dry it was discovered that dozens of additional bales were lodged under the ice, some distance from the wreck. The Feds had used chainsaws to extract the obvious bales, but quickly abandoned the effort as the blades got dull and the storm hove to. But "Pepe" got the picture and returned with four Husquvarna chain saws he borrowed from woodcutters down in El Portal. For several days Pepe and his crew skipped around the rink, boring the ice with the buzzing saw. If a blizzard of green stuff shot from the chain, they knew where to dig. By the time the lode was played out, Lower Merced Lake looked like it'd hosted an ice fishing convention.

What followed the strike was a living example of fools and their money. My friend "Horace" was one of the first ones on site after Woody's initial sortie. He probed the wreck for one minute, found a wallet containing nearly $10,000, turned around and walked—and kept walking, right out of the park. Forty-five days later he staggered back into The Bird's tent with a full beard, a shiner, and two bucks in his pocket. "Gene" found a little black book with Italian names scribbled throughout. He burned it on the spot. On the last day, "Steve" returned from Fresno with a diving mask, flippers, and a wet suit. After warming up by a roaring fire for 20 minutes, he lashed a rope round his waist and dove through a hole and into the bowels of the fuselage. Good thing for the rope because after 10 seconds in the ice water his limbs went dead; but when they hauled him out he had a death grip on an attaché case full of greenbacks.

The fuel cells burst on impact and some of the weed was drenched in aviation fuel. If you couldn't smell it, you'd find out the moment you would stoke a pipeful, when a flame like a blowtorch would leap off the hooch. The Bird (who throughout acted as a sort of ombudsman, shipping manager, and logistics director) said not to worry, that the tainted goods could be peddled off at top dollar. In fact, they were, and that's when things got crazy.

"Homer" left for Berkeley in a wheezing DeSoto crammed to the shattered windows with soggy hemp. Ten days later he tooled back into the Valley driving a candy-apple red convertible Lincoln Continental with fleecy dice hanging from the rearview mirror. "Butch" rolled in on a chopped Harley. "Hank" showed back up in a buckskin suit with a Scandinavian bombshell who spoke almost no English and wore almost no clothes. He spent $800 in the bar the first night—even bought the rangers a beer.

Climbers who a few weeks before hadn't had two dimes to rub together streamed back into the Valley and were spending cash with all the nonchalance of a Saudi prince. Goodbye peanut butter and jelly. It was steak dinners forever and cognacs all around.

When the rangers put the pieces together, most of The Bird's Boys cleared out to avoid the grill. The months that followed are best illustrated by a "climbing" trip undertaken by "Buzz" and five others. They took a charter to New York and the Concorde to London en route to Chamonix. They had plans: the North Face of Les Droites, the Walker Spur on the Grandes Jorasses, to name a few. Later, they'd swing by the Eiger. They got hung up at a whorehouse in Bordeaux, however. A few days stretched into 2 weeks. They were still there after a month. In fact, they never made it to the Alps at all. The next spring, the six returned to the Valley, flat broke and about 20 pounds overweight.

So It Goes

I saw Buzz (now a land developer) last year and asked him if he regretted not having banked a buck or two of his plunder instead of pissing it away in a French bordello.

"Not a chance," he said without hesitation. "That's the kind of shit that happens once if it happens at all. You can always make money."

Much has changed with the original group, which numbers attorneys, dentists, Oscar winners, carpenters, producers, photographers, and felons amongst their ranks. But one and all, we'll always be The Bird's Boys.

The Only Blasphemy

A T SPEEDS beyond 80 miles an hour the California cops jail you, so I keep it down in the 70s. Tobin used to drive 100, till his Datsun exploded in flames on the freeway out by Running Springs. Tobin was a supreme artist, alive in a way the rest of us were not. But time was a cannibal for Tobin, who lived and climbed like he had days or perhaps only minutes before life ate him alive. It came as no surprise when he perished attempting to solo the north face of Mount Alberta in winter.

I charge on toward Joshua Tree National Monument, where 2 weeks before, another friend had "decked" while soloing. I inspected the base of the route, wincing at the grisly bloodstains, the tufts of matted hair. Soloing is unforgiving, but OK, I think. You just have to be realistic, and can never stove to peer pressure or pride. Soul climbing, and all that jazz. At 79 miles an hour, Joshua Tree comes quickly, but the stark night drags.

The morning sun peers over the flat horizon, gilding rocks shining on the desert carpet. The biggest stones are 150 feet high. Right after breakfast I run into John Bachar, widely considered the world's foremost free climber. For several years he's traveled widely in his red VW van, chasing the sun and the hardest routes on the planet.

Most all climbs are easy for Bachar. He has to make his own difficulties, and usually does so by ditching the rope. He dominates the cliff with his grace and confidence, never gets rattled, never thrashes, and you know that if he ever gets killed climbing, it will be a gross transgression of all taste and you'll curse God for the rest of your life—on aesthetic, not moral grounds. Bachar has been out at Joshua Tree for several months now and his soloing feats astonish everyone.

It is wintertime, when college checks my climbing to week-ends, so my motivation is there but my fitness is not. Right off Bachar suggests a "Half Dome day." Yosemite's Half Dome is 2,000 feet high, call it twenty rope lengths. So we'll have to climb twenty pitches, or twenty climbs, to log our Half Dome day.

Bachar laces up his boots and cinches the sling on his chalk bag. "Ready?"

Only then do I realize he means to climb all 2,000 feet solo, without a rope. To save face, I agree, thinking: Well, if he suggests something too crazy, I'll just draw the line. I was the first to start soloing out at Josh anyway.

We cast off up vertical rock, twisting feet and jamming hands into bulging cracks; smearing the toes of our skin-tight boots onto tiny bumps and wrinkles; muscling over roofs on bulbous holds; palming off rough rock and marveling at it all. A curious little voice occasionally asks how good a flexing, quarter-inch hold can be. If you're solid, you set curled fingers or pointed toes on that quarter-incher and push or pull perfunctorily. And I'm solid.

After 3 hours we've disposed of a dozen pitches and feel invincible. We up the ante to stiff 5.10, the threshold of expert terrain. We slow, but by early afternoon, we've climbed twenty pitches: the Half Dome day is history. As a finale, Bachar suggests we solo a 5.11—an exacting drill even for Bachar. I was already hosed from racing up twenty different climbs in a few hours, having cruised the last half dozen on rhythm and momentum. Regardless, I follow Bachar over to Intersection Rock, the com-munal hang for local climbers and the site for Bachar's final solo.

Bachar wastes no words and no time. Scores of milling climbers freeze when he starts up, climbing with flawless precision, plugging his fingers into shallow pockets in the 105-degree wall, one move flowing into the next much as pieces of a puzzle match-fit together. I scrutinize his moves, making mental notes on the intricate sequence. After 30 feet he pauses, directly beneath the crux bulge. Splaying his left foot onto a slanting edge, he pinches a tiny flute and pulls through to a giant bucket hold. Then he hikes the last 100 feet of vertical rock like it's a staircase. A few seconds later he peers over the lip and flashes that sly, candid snicker, awaiting my reply.

I am booted up and covered in chalk, facing a notorious climb, which just now is rarely done, even with a rope. Fifty hungry eyes give me the once over, as if to say, "Well?" That little voice says, "No problem," and I believe it. I draw several deep breaths. I don't consider the consequences, only the moves. I start up.

A body-length of easy stuff, then those pockets, which I finger adroitly before pulling with maximum might. This first bit passes quickly. Everything is clicking, severe but steady, and I glide into bone-crushing altitude before I can reckon. Then, as I splay my foot out onto the slanting edge, the chilling realization comes that, in my haste, I've bungled the sequence. My hands are crossed up and too low on that tiny flute that I'm pinching with waning power.

My foot starts vibrating and I'm instantly desperate, wondering if and when my body will freeze and plummet. I can't possibly downclimb a single move. My only escape is straight up. I glance down beneath my legs and my gut churns at the thought of a free-fall onto the boulders, of climbers later cringing at the red stains and tufts of hair. They look up and say, "Yeah, he popped from way up there."

That little voice is bellowing, "Do something! Fast!"

My breathing is frenzied while my arms, gassed from the previous 2,000 feet of climbing, feel like concrete. Pinching that little flute, I suck my feet up so as to extend my arm and jam my hand into the bottoming crack above. But I'm set up too low on that flute and the only part of the crack I can reach is too shallow, accepts but a third of my hand. I'm stuck, terrified, my whole life focused down to a single move.

Shamefully, I understand the only blasphemy—to willfully jeopardize my own life, which I have done, and it sickens me.

Then everything slows, as though preservation instincts have kicked my mind into hyper gear. In a heartbeat I've realized my desire to live, not die. But my regrets cannot alter my situation: arms shot, legs wobbling, head on fire. Then fear burns itself up, leaving me hollow and mortified. To concede, to quit, would be easy. The little voice calmly says: "At least go out trying." I hear that, and punch my hand deeper into the bottoming crack.

If only I can execute this one unlikely move, I'll get an incut jug and can rest on it, jungle gym style, before the final push to the top. I'm afraid to eyeball my crimped hand, scarcely jammed in the bottoming crack. It must hold my 205 pounds, on an overhanging wall, with scant footholds, and this seems ludicrous, impossible. My body has jittered here for close to a minute. Forever.

My jammed hand says, "No way!" but that little voice says, "Might as well try it."

I pull up slowly—my left foot still pasted to that sloping edge—and that big bucket hold is right there. I almost have it. I do. Simultaneously my right hand rips from the crack and my weight shock-loads onto my enfeebled left arm. Adrenaline powers me atop the "Thank God" bucket where I try to suck my chest to the wall and get my weight over my feet. But it's too steep to cop a meaningful rest so I push on, shaking horribly, dancing black dots flecking my vision, glad only that the terrain, though vertical, is casual compared to below. Still, it takes an age to claw up the last 100 feet and onto the summit.

"Looked a little shaky," laughs Bachar, flashing that wry, candid snicker.

That night I drove into town and got a bottle. The next day, while Bachar went for an El Cap day (3,000 feet, solo, of course), I wandered through dark rock corridors, scouting for turtles, making garlands from wildflowers, staring up at the titanic sky— doing all those things a person does on borrowed time.

POSTSCRIPT: ON July 5, 2009, John Bachar died while free soloing on the Dike Wall near his home in Mammoth Lakes, California. He was 52 years old, an iconic rock climber and a legend in the world of adventure sports.

Thirty-one years ago I wrote this essay, stating that if John ever got killed climbing I would curse God for the rest of my life—on aesthetic, not moral grounds. Now, I'm not so sure I want to curse God, or anyone, for the rest of my life, though I'm saddened to have to live it knowing John Bachar is not out there somewhere, tangling with Old Man Gravity. But maybe he still is. He's just higher than I can see from here.

The Green Arch

EVERY SATURDAY morning about a dozen of us would jump into a medley of the finest junkers $200 could buy and blast for the alpine hamlet of Idyllwild, California, home of Tahquitz Rock. The last 26 miles follows a twisting road, steep in spots. More than one exhausted Volkswagen bus or wheezing old Rambler got pushed a little too hard, blew up and was abandoned, the plates stripped off and the driver, laden with rope and pack, thumbing on toward Mecca. We had to get to the Coffee Cup by eight o'clock, when our little group would meet, discuss an itinerary, bolt down some food and stampede for the crags. The air was charged because we were on a roll, our faith and gusto growing with each new climb we bagged. We were loudmouthed 17-year-old punks, and proud of it.

Tahquitz was one of America's celebrated climbing spots, with a pageant of pivotal ascents reaching back to when technical climbing first came to the States. Many legends had learned the ropes there. Our informal band of "Stonemasters" barged onto the scene just as the previous generation of local hardcores were getting broad-sided by kids and house payments. The old guard cared little for us. We were all young, vain and broke, and had grappled up many of their tougher climbs with nothing but gumption and fire. When word got out that we were taking a bead on the hallowed *Valhalla*—a route often tried, but as yet unrepeated—the duffers showed their teeth. When, after another month, we all had climbed *Valhalla*, some of us several times, the duffers were stunned and saw themselves elbowed out of the opera house by kids who could merely scream. And none could scream louder than Tobin Sorenson, the most conspicuous madman ever to lace up *varappes*.

Climbing had never seen the likes of Tobin, and probably never will again. He was a latecomer to the Stonemasters, the last ingredient in a boiling pot. He had the body of a welterweight, a mop of sandy brown hair and the faraway gaze of the born maniac. Yet he lived with all the innocence of a child. He would never cuss or show the slightest hostility, and around girls he was so shy he'd flush and stammer. But out on the sharp end of the rope he was Igor unchained.

Over the previous summer he'd logged a string of spectacular falls that should have ended his career, and his life, ten times over. Yet he shook each fall off and clawed straight back onto the route for another go, and usually succeeded. He became a world-class climber very quickly because anyone that well formed and motivated gains the top in no time—if he doesn't kill himself first. Yet when we started bagging new climbs and first free ascents, Tobin continued to defy the gods with his electrifying whippers. The exploits of his short life deserve a book. Two books.

One Saturday morning, five or six of us hunkered down in the Coffee Cup, a little greasy spoon in the middle of Idyllwild. Tahquitz was our oyster. We'd pried it open with a piton and for months had gorged at will; but the fare was running thin. Since we had ticked off one after another of the remaining new routes, our options had dwindled to only the most grim and improbable.

Ricky Accomazzo had recently scoped out the *Green Arch*, an elegant arc on Tahquitz's southern shoulder. When Ricky mentioned that this classic aid climb might go free, Tobin looked like the Hound of the Baskervilles had just heard the word "bone," and we nearly had to lash him to the booth so we could finish our oatmeal.

Four of us hiked up to the base of the rock: my hometown partners, Richard Harrison and Ricky Accomazzo, along with Tobin, and myself. Since the ~~Green Arch~~ was ~~Ricky's idea, he got~~ the first go at it. Tobin balked, but Ricky started up anyhow. After 50 feet of face work on tiny scallops and rugosities, he gained the arch, which soared above for another 80 feet before curving right and melding into a field of knobs and pockets. If we could only get to those knobs, the remaining 300 feet would go easily and the *Green Arch* would fall.

But the crack in the back of the arch was too thin to accept even fingertips, and both sides of the corner were blank and marble-smooth. Yet by pasting half his ass on one side of the puny corner, and splaying his feet out on the opposite side, Ricky stuck to the rock—barely—with both his ass and his boots steadily oozing off. It was exhausting just staying put, and moving up was accomplished in a precarious sequence of quarter-inch moves. Amazingly, Ricky jackknifed about halfway up the arch before his calves pumped out. He lowered off a knifeblade and I took a shot.

After half an hour of the hardest climbing I'd ever done—we were wearing the old high-top, red PAs (rock shoes designed by French climber Pierre Allain), which had the friction coefficient of a shovel—I reached a rest hold just below the point where the arch swept out right and dissolved into that field of knobs. Twenty feet to paydirt. But those 20 feet looked desperate. There were some big sucker holds just above the arch, but those ran out after about 25 feet and would leave a climber in no-man's-land, with nowhere to go, no chance to climb back right onto the route, no chance to get any protection, and no chance to retreat. We'd have to stick to the arch.

Finally, I underclung about 10 feet out the arch, whacked in a suspect piton, clipped the rope in—and fell off. I lowered to the ground, slumped back, and didn't get up for 10 minutes. I had weeping strawberries on both butt cheeks, and my ankles were tweaked from splaying them out on the far wall.

Tobin—who'd suffered through the previous hour circling and doing jumping jacks—tied into the lead rope and stormed up the corner, battled up to the rest hold, drew a few quick breaths, and underclung out to that creaky, buckled, driven-straight-up-into-an-expanding-flake piton. Had he traversed right from there, the now-standard free route, he would have gained tall cotton. Instead he just gunned it straight up for glory, cranking himself over the arch and heaving up the line of big sucker holds.

"No!" I screamed up. "Those holds don't go anywhere!"

But it was too late.

Understand that Tobin was a born-again Christian who studied God with all his might, who worked the soup kitchens down in Skid Row, San Pedro, and later smuggled Bibles into Bulgaria, risking 25 years on a Balkan rock pile, and none of this tempered the fact that he was perfectly mad. Out on the sharp end he not only ignored all consequences, he seemed to loathe them, pulling foolish, incomprehensible pranks to mock the fear and peril. (The following year, out at Joshua Tree, Tobin followed a difficult, overhanging crack with a rope noosed around his neck.)

Most catastrophic of all was his habit of simply charging at climbs pell-mell. On straightforward routes, no one was better. But when patience and cunning were required, few were worse. Climbing, as it were, with blinders on, Tobin would sometimes claw his way into the most heinous jams. When he'd dead-end, with nowhere to go and looking at a Homeric peeler, the full impact of his folly would hit him like a wrecking ball. He would panic, wail, weep openly, and do perfectly jackass things. And sure enough, about 25 feet above the arch those sucker holds ran out, and Tobin had nowhere to go.

To appreciate Tobin's quandary, understand that he was 25 feet above the last piton, which meant he was looking at a 50-foot fall, since a leader falls twice as far as he is above the last piece of protection. The belayer, tending the other end of the rope, can rarely reel in much rope during a fall because it happens so quickly. Basically, he can only secure the rope—lock it off. But the gravest news was that I knew the piton I'd bashed under the roof could never hold a 50-foot whipper.

On gigantic falls, the top piece often rips out, but the fall is broken sufficiently for a lower nut or piton to stop you. Maybe. In Tobin's case, the next lower piece was some dozen feet below the top one, at the rest hold; so in fact, Tobin was looking at close to an 80-footer—plus a few yards more with rope stretch.

Now as Tobin wobbled far overhead, who should lumber up to our little group but his very father, a Lutheran minister—a sober, retiring, imperturbable gentleman who hacked and huffed from his long march up to the cliff. After hearing so much about climbing from Tobin, he'd finally come to see his son in action. It was like a page from a B-movie script: us cringing and digging in, waiting for the bomb to drop; the good pastor, wheezing through his moustache, sweat-soaked and confused, squinting up at the fruit of his loins; and Tobin, knees knocking, screaming like a woman in labor and looking to plunge off at any second.

There is always something you can do, even in the worst situation, if only you keep your nerve. But Tobin was gone, so mastered by terror that he seemed willing to die to be done with it. He glanced down. His face was a study. Suddenly he screamed, "Watch me! I'm gonna jump."

We didn't immediately understand what he meant.

"Jump off?" Richard yelled up.

"Yes!" Tobin wailed.

"NO!" we all screamed in unison.

"You can do it, son!" the pastor put in.

Pop was just trying to put a good face on it, God bless him, but his was the worst possible advice because there was no way Tobin could do it. Or anybody could do it. There were no holds. But inspired by his father's urging, Tobin reached out for those knobs so far to his right, now lunging, now pawing the air as the falling man grabs for a cobweb.

And then he was off.

The top piton shot out and Tobin shot off into the grandest fall I've ever seen a climber take and walk away from, ragdolling down the wall with dull thuds. But the lower piton held, and he finally jolted onto the rope. For a moment he simply hung there, upside down and moaning. Then Ricky lowered him off and he lay motionless on the ground and nobody moved or said a word. You could have heard a pine needle hit the deck. Tobin was peppered with abrasions and had a lump the size of a turnip over one eye. He lay dead still for a moment longer, then wobbled to his feet and shuddered.

"I'll get it next time," he grumbled.

"There ain't gonna be no next time," said Richard.

"Give the boy a chance," the pastor said, thumping Tobin on the back.

When a father can watch his son pitch 80 feet down a vertical cliff and straightaway argue that we were shortchanging the boy by not letting him climb back up and have a second chance at an even longer whistler, we knew the man was cut from the same crazy cloth as Tobin, and that there was no reasoning with him. But the fall had sucked the air out of the whole adventure, and we were through for the day. The "next time" came several years later. In one of the greatest leads of that era, Ricky flashed the entire *Green Arch* on his first try. Tobin and I followed.

Tobin would go on to solo the north face of the Matterhorn, the *Walker Spur*, and the *Shroud* on the Grandes Jorasses, would make the first alpine ascent of the *Harlin Direct* on the Eiger, the first ascent of the *Super Couloir* on the Dru, would repeat the hardest free climbs and big walls in Yosemite, and would sink his teeth into the Himalaya. He was, by most estimates, the world's foremost all-around climber during the late 1970s. But he wanted a life full of things that could never be, so he climbed as if time were too short for him, pumping all the disquietude, anxiety, and nervous waste of a normal year into each route.

I've traveled many miles since those early days at Tahquitz, have done my share of crazy things, and have seen humanity with all the bark on, primal and raw. But I've never since experienced the cosmic rush of watching Tobin, reaching for the promised land. He finally found it in 1980, attempting a solo winter ascent of Mount Alberta's north face. His death was a tragedy, of course. Yet I've often wondered if God could no longer bear the strain of watching Tobin lunging way out there on the sharp end of the rope, and finally just drew him into the fold.

Frankenstein

ROGER RUSHED into Camp 4 and over to my site. There'd been a climbing accident on the East Buttress of Middle Cathedral, two pitches below the summit, he said. A leader fall and a head injury. A helicopter was heading in to ferry Valley czars Jim Bridwell and Mark Klemens to the top of Middle to conduct a rescue. In case that plan didn't work, the Park Service needed another team to hike up to the summit, humping an enormous green backpack that lay at Roger's feet. If the Bridwell/Klemens team hadn't set down by the time we gained the top, I'd rap to the victim and . . . well, we'd flesh out the plan from there.

"You handle that?" Roger asked. He was a solid recreational climber but out of his league on a 1,600-foot face, was about 15 years older than me and a mentor who had skied 100 miles across Tioga Pass in winter, carted injured hikers out of the backcountry on his back, and serving as chief backcountry ranger for the park service, ran a government department with forty men. By coincidence, he was also my cousin. I didn't know what the hell I was doing—I was 18 and had only been in the Valley a few months— but if Roger thought I was worthy, I'd go with it.

"I'm in," I said.

"Meet me back here in 5," Roger said.

I dashed for Camp 4's rescue site, urgent to find someone who could help with the job. Luckily I found the Englishman

Ben Campbell-Kelly lounging around camp, recovering from an early ascent of the North American Wall (then one of the hardest big rock climbs on earth) with his countryman Bryan Wyvill, aka, The Blob. I explained the situation, and that I didn't know what I was doing and needed him along, and Ben said, "Let's go, man."

Roger, Ben, and I manhandled the pack into Roger's cruiser and a few minutes later he dropped us at the turnout below Middle Cathedral.

"Only got about 3 hours of daylight so you'll have to bust ass," said Roger. "You know where you're going?"

"Pretty much," I said.

I'd climbed the East Buttress the summer before, but it took all day and we hacked down the descent gulley at night. I didn't remember a thing about it.

I shouldered the pack and we trudged up through the pines toward the gully left of Middle. I couldn't have had a better man alongside me than Ben Campbell-Kelly, a proven veteran of these walls, solid as Solomon.

Shortly we entered a steep labyrinth of dead-end trails, teetering minarets, and low-angled choss corridors. We hadn't a clue about a proper path and never found one.

For 2 hours we flailed and cursed our way up that gully, sometimes hand-carrying the pack and shoving it through a pinch when we couldn't wiggle through with it on our backs. We could more easily have dragged a moped up that gulley than that pack. About halfway up we heard a copter circling above, and Ben and I wondered if we weren't killing ourselves for nothing.

When we finally broke out onto the shoulder beneath Middle's shapeless summit, Ben said he'd burned more gas and lost more hide grappling up that gully than he had climbing El Capitan. I shouldered the pig, and with Ben shoving from behind, we angled up grainy slabs toward the top. Only the crown of El Capitan glowed in light. We had maybe an hour before night fell like an iron gate.

A few minutes later we met a team who'd just topped out on the East Buttress. In their late 20s, both wore colorful, long-sleeved rugby shirts and thin, white navy pants, the formal costume of the 70s Yosemite climber. I wondered about these guys' lives, and their jobs that allowed them to have just fixed—for our convenience—two expensive new ropes above the injured climber, before dashing back to San Francisco for work and family. They'd fetch their ropes later, or never.

The two men said that gusting winds kept the copter from landing on the summit, scrubbing the Bridwell/Klemens rescue effort. I confirmed as much with Roger, over the walkie-talkie. We thanked the two San Fran climbers and moved over to the fixed lines. I clipped in and started down, battling not to get pulled over backward by the pack.

Ben shouldered the pig for the last rap and we touched down on a terraced recess by a big pine tree growing directly from the rock. The injured climber—I never learned his name—lay curled on a sloping ledge scarcely bigger than his body.

His partner, Peter Barton, sitting dejectedly on a shelf 10 feet below, had tied the victim taut to a cluster of anchors. Ben and I rigged a line off the victim's anchor and moved to a tapering ledge 10 feet lower. According to Peter, the victim had taken a tumbling fall and banged the back of his head. Though partially responsive at first, he hadn't moved in 2 or 3 hours.

I asked Ben what he knew about first aid and he said, "Nothing."

Since I was the son of a doctor, Ben reckoned I'd absorbed essential medical know-how by association, and suggested I climb up the rope to the victim and play medic.

The victim's breathing seemed smooth, though hurried. He mumbled now and then but couldn't answer any questions. On the back of his head the hair was raked off in one spot, but no blood or shocking dent. Whenever a life hangs in the balance the stakes suck you into a hyper-real space where you see and remember the gurgling sounds, the acrid smell of fear, the sharp cut of shadows on the wall—details you'd normally notice in passing all stand out in urgent detail. And yet how the victim looked, or even his age, I can't say. Had he looked at me, or said something instead of just lying inert, I might remember his eyes, or his face. But now it's all a blank.

I reported the victim's condition to Roger and he said to pack the guy into a sleeping bag—there was one inside the giant pack—and to keep his airway clear. It took all three of us to wheedle the victim into the bag. I felt useless, knowing this guy needed assistance we couldn't hope to provide. Roger said there wasn't much more to do, and to just settle in for the night. Back at park headquarters, Bridwell and two rescue rangers were devising a strategy for tomorrow. Pray the victim somehow holds on. Over and out.

Ben and I returned to the lower ledge and sat back. The slab dropped below for 20 or so feet, then the wall steepened and plunged out of sight. Peering off that perch, I hunkered down for my first bivouac on a rock wall.

We dug into the pack and found a headlamp, several gallons of water, a twelve-pack of lemonade mix, a wall rack, a lead rope, a great mass of pulleys and bewildering rescue tackle, a frightening 12-inch knife, two balaclavas, a second radio, several packs of batteries, a first-aid kit that folded out like an accordion, a shovel, a compass, two Ensolite pads, and a bunch of other stuff I can't remember—but not so much as a breadstick to eat.

"We're buggered," said Ben.

Thankfully we had a couple packs of smokes between us and we lit up, gazing into the gloom. Far below, the earth seemed to open up, then night crawled out and swallowed the wall and the world.

Ben, 30, had a rowdy head of red hair and an elegant sideburn-goatee constellation befitting the British academic he was in the public world. His calm, rational manner was a balm to my willies, which after an hour in pitch darkness were once more rearing up.

To divert myself I pried Ben about his many adventures on big walls in Norway, the Alps, and of course most recently the great El Capitan. His comments were so understated I came to believe that sitting there on that tiny ledge in my flimsy white navy pants and a T-shirt was no big deal after all. I admired myself for throwing in with the Yosemite hardmen and, around midnight, figured I was nearly one myself. Then it got very cold, and the victim started wailing in tongues. Peter asked what the hell we were going to do, and things went south from there.

BEN AND I took turns making sure the man didn't swallow his tongue or do something worse. The guy bit our fingers down to the wood, and sometimes his arms flailed and his legs churned inside the bag. We couldn't have been less helpful.

Around dawn, the victim quieted, and might have died for all we knew. The notion frightened me so I hand-walked up the slab and found him still alive, but apparently in a coma. We couldn't do a thing. I returned to the ledge and shimmied my legs into the big pack for warmth. I never knew a person could feel so wasted. Then Roger cut in over the radio. A copter was blading in from Livermore Air Force Base to attempt an "extraction." This was long before cliff rescue techniques had been standardized and neither Ben nor I knew what they were talking about. Roger explained.

Bridwell had reckoned that at our present location, the wall was sufficiently low-angled to allow a copter to hover some hundreds of feet above, and lower a litter down on a cable winch.

"That should be pretty good theater!" said Ben.

And we'd be seeing it momentarily, as the percussive thumping of copter blades started echoing up the Valley.

"Will you look at that bugger!" Ben yelled.

Whatever copter I had envisioned, it wasn't the monstrosity heaving to several hundred feet above. Big as a Greyhound bus, it looked like something out of Star Wars. Two enormous blades produced a pulsing thunder that rattled our bones and shot down a shaft of prop wash that swirled every pine needle and bit of turf into a choking tornado. I thrust my head into the big pack and when I pulled it back out, the surroundings looked as if they'd been scrubbed with a wire brush.

A soldier stepped from the open cargo bay door of the copter and lowered down on a cable, like a dummy on a string. He sat on a "Chaparral Leveler," a bullet-shaped cylinder the size of a fire hydrant with two fold-down metal flaps on the bottom. (Later someone told me they used to swoop the Leveler through "hot zones" during the Vietnam War and pluck out of the fire anyone who could mount the Leveler at speed.)

The giant Sikorsky "Hercules" stayed glued in the sky and the soldier slowly descended perhaps 175 feet until finally touching down on the slab a short ways below our ledge. Whoever piloted the ship was a deadeye who basically delivered the soldier to our laps. With his huge helmet and smoky visor, plus the dashing Air Force jumpsuit, the soldier looked like Flash Gordon.

The moment Flash stepped off the Chaparral Leveler he was unroped, 1,200 feet off the deck. His mountaineering boots ske-daddled on the slab as his hands pawed for a hold, and we knew right off Flash Gordon was no climber.

Ben quickly anchored off a loop of rope, handwalked down and clipped in Flash, who pulled up his smoky visor, exposing the face of a young boy, which he compensated for by screaming out his orders. The plan sounded basic and, surprisingly, went off without a hitch.

The copter lowered down a litter and we loaded up and lashed down the victim, who was winched straight into the hovering ship.

"OK," said Flash, staring at the ship still hanging directly overhead. "Who's going with me?"

"How's that?" Ben asked.

We'd figured Flash would ascend the fixed lines with Ben, Peter, and me.

"I'm going out on the Leveler," said Flash. "And it gets squirrelly with one man. I need another guy to balance the load."

"I'll go," I said without thinking.

"Good man," Ben replied.

He'd climb El Cap in a snowstorm but he wasn't daft enough to volunteer to get winched off a Yosemite wall on a guitar string. I wasn't courageous, I'd just opened up my mouth and blurted.

Just before sitting on the Leveler, Flash said not to worry and to simply hold on tight. We sat, face-to-face, on two metal flaps barely larger than my hand. This set us up like two guys bear-hugging with a flagpole between them. There were no straps or tie-ins at all.

Suddenly the cable came taut and my stomach fell into my boots as we were pulled off the wall and into midair. After 10 feet we started yawing side to side and the copter motored out away from the wall, initiating a harrowing pendulum. Lest we smack the face, the pilot swept even farther out into open space, away from the wall, which set us swinging in wild horizontal arcs. Only vaguely could I feel the winch pulling us up as we sliced through the air like trapeze artists hitched to the moon. I remember flashing on the saucy French tourist girl I'd met in the cafeteria, and how she'd probably have to spend the rest of her life without me now. The stuff that goes through your head in the thick of it . . . with nothing more to lose, I enjoyed the view as best I could.

About 15 feet from the cargo door, right when we stopped swinging, we began spinning, faster and faster. In 30 seconds I felt so dizzy I could barely hang on. Then they shut off the winch and we dropped a few horrible inches and wrenched to a stop. I glanced up and saw a flurry of airmen fiddling around the winch, which started back up with a lurch and then stopped again, with Flash and me dangling about waist-level with the open cargo bay door. Flash was nearest the ship, and one of the airmen reached down and yanked him on board. This instantly rocked the Leveler out of balance and I nearly fell off. For a moment the airmen, with blank looks on their faces, stared down at me dangling in space. Then Bridwell appeared from somewhere, grabbed a strut on the door, and reached down his hand. We locked arms; The Bird yanked and I shot off the flap and belly flopped into the bay. The Bird, who'd been spotting for the pilot, gave a thumbs up and the big ship banked and headed for El Cap Meadow.

Several medics huddled over the victim. His vital signs checked out and they figured his chances were good, which amazed and relieved me. (I later learned he did survive, following several operations to relieve pressure on his brain.) Several minutes later the big ship touched down. In a 50-yard radius the tall grass in Yosemite Meadow was pummeled flush as the pitch on a putting green. Bridwell and I jumped out and the ship thumped off for the trauma unit in Fresno.

Roger rushed up and started laughing and smacking me. I'd expected an official reception, or at any rate a swelling tourist mob. But it was barely seven in the morning and the three of us found ourselves alone in the middle of the meadow. In a few short minutes, everything went still and quiet, as if nothing had ever happened.

A few days later I drove back to Southern California to pick back up as a second year lit student at college. But with one foot still in the dirt, I felt like Frankenstein, fashioned from disparate halves. I grew up dreaming of tomahawks flashing and canoes gliding stealthily across lakes impossibly virgin and people climbing mountains for . . . I wasn't certain why. I never was, exactly, though to most of my profs and fellow students, whose aesthetics and technique I admired, climbing rocks, in literary jargon, was so much escapist trash. And at some level it probably was, but I'd return to that world for the next 30 years.

THE SUMMER after the rescue I fell in with Peter Barton, the partner of the victim on the Middle Cathedral rescue, and we teamed up for several big climbs, including the first ascent of *Stoner's Highway*, also on Middle. A year later, while ferrying loads up to the West Face of El Capitan, Peter lost his footing on a steep bit and died in a tumbling fall. A helicopter flew in from Livermore to recover Peter's body. Over the steep moraine below the West Face, the copter experienced mechanical problems and ditched in the boulders. The crew barely escaped when the ship burst into flames. His mother released Peter's ashes over Washington Column.

I haven't seen Ben since the rescue on Middle. I trust he's doing well.

Several years later, Roger went to the Grand Tetons and worked for the Park Service till he retired after 40 years of service.

Index

INDEX